BEYOND EXPIRATION

SURVIVING A CENTENARIAN PARENT

SETH VICARSON

QUARRY CREEK PRESS
ST. AUGUSTINE, FLORIDA

Copyright © 2024 by Seth Vicarson
All rights reserved. No part of this book may be reproduced or transmitted in any form or by any means, electronic or mechanical, including photocopying and recording, or by any information storage and retrieval system, without permission in writing from Quarry Creek Press, P.O. Box 840132, St. Augustine, FL 32080.

Thanks to Frances Keiser of Sagaponack Books & Design and to Beth Mansbridge of Mansbridge Editing & Transcription.

The material presented in this book is largely biographical. Out of respect for the privacy of individuals mentioned, I have chosen not to use actual names except my mother's nickname. Actual names of skilled nursing and assisted living facilities have also not been used.

The internet references and resources listed in this publication are current at the time of printing. They may be helpful, but the author cannot endorse or guarantee the efficacy of any particular reference or resource.

ISBN 978-1-7323501-3-7 (softcover)
ISBN 978-1-7323501-4-4 (hardcover)
ISBN 978-1-7323501-5-1 (e-book)

Library of Congress Catalog Card Number: 2024912443

Summary: A son's memoir of his mother's extreme longevity, eventual decline, and associated challenges. Experiences with healthcare and caregiving are explored.

FAM017000 Family & Relationships / Eldercare
BIO026000 Biography and Autobiography / Personal Memoirs
SOC013000 Social Science / Gerontology

Quarry Creek Press
St. Augustine, Florida

Printed and bound in the United States of America
First Edition

In memory of my beloved mother
and in gratitude for Thomas

"Life is not measured by the number of breaths you take, but by the moments that take your breath away."

—Maya Angelou

Contents

Introduction 1

Chapter 1 Meet My Mom 5

Chapter 2 Cracks Start to Appear 15

Chapter 3 Driving Miss Dot 37

Chapter 4 One Hundred Candles 46

Chapter 5 The Nightmare Continues 66

Chapter 6 A New Journey Begins 94

Chapter 7 A New Day Dawns 117

Chapter 8 2019 Bows to a New Year 142

Chapter 9 Breaks in the Clouds 161

Chapter 10 The Final Lifeline? 193

Chapter 11 I Wave the White Flag 225

"Final" Thoughts 241

References and Resources 245

About the Author 247

INTRODUCTION

The primary inspiration for this writing is my mother, who reached centenarian status and lived well beyond that milestone, defying life-expectancy norms. A member of the Greatest Generation, she was one of those rare individuals who "skated" through her 70s, 80s, and most of her 90s. Her last years and the travails associated with off-the-charts longevity are chronicled here in detail. Mom's journey through exceptionally advanced age was accompanied by forced change and unforeseen challenges that would have sunk the less hardy. As I traveled with her on the sometimes tumultuous voyage, it became apparent she was far stronger than me, her 1949-issue, baby-boomer son.

When I became Mom's primary overseer and eventual caregiver, the unrelenting nature of the task took me by surprise. I was unprepared. Emotional lows and physical exhaustion nearly toppled me when her care became more than I could handle. Yet, I found a way to survive. While rendering care, I experienced joy, depression, gratification, frustration, hope, desperation, guilt, forgiveness, and gratitude. I learned to accept my emotional swings as normal human responses, though saddling myself with guilt when I wanted it all to end. Ultimately, the end *did* come. I had few regrets, knowing I had done the best I could, even during those times when I had failed.

Both of my parents reached old age, which isn't out of the ordinary. Most children will face the same circumstance with at least one parent, usually both. Old age is an uncomfortable reality for many of us and assumes enhanced significance as we, too, grow older. This raises the question: When does old age occur and what are the ramifications? When I was around 5 or 6 years old, I remember asking Mom, "How old is Nana (her mother)?" I don't remember the answer, but had surmised Nana was *really* old because flabby skin hung on the underside of her upper arms. In fact, she was in her early 60s at the time.

When I was 12, my youthful mom reached her 43rd birthday. The number resonated in my prepubescent mind, and I perceived Mom had migrated into the "old-age sphere" because she advised me to not divulge her age to anyone in the neighborhood. Ever hear of hush money? Incidentally, Mom didn't give me as much as a penny. As an alternative, she gave me a stern warning. The incentive was sufficient for me to keep my mouth shut.

So, when *does* old age begin? Victor Hugo, a famous French writer who lived in the 1800s, took a stab at it. He said, "Forty is the old age of youth, fifty the youth of old age." Since he lived to be 83, I imagine his conclusion was reached after he had passed both milestones. This was a reasonable start for me to continue searching for the answer to my question.

As I entered my 20s and had a better grip on chronology as it relates to old age, I pegged the number at 55 to 60. My dad fell within this range. He was active, slim, and had no apparent physical maladies ... but his wrinkles were deepening. That's it! Wrinkles were the appropriate mile marker. But maybe not.

My assessment as to when old age begins has morphed as I've grown older, much like Victor Hugo's possibly did. It was evident the number was getting higher as my own birthdays continued to relentlessly flip like calendar pages, adding up at an ever-increasing pace.

When I was in my late 50s and had achieved wrinkles in the same places I remembered seeing on my dad's face, it was obvious a new assessment was warranted. Earlier estimates *had* to be way off, and I was a numbers guy. Never mind the subjective component. My long-standing old-age calculation of 55 to 60 was seriously underestimated. Twenty-first-century mathematics relating to old age demanded accuracy. Maybe semi-accuracy. Given this disclaimer and my admission that finding the number is elusive, I settled on 70. It's a convenient number that seemed appropriate and was still in the distance for me. And any number in the distance had to be closer to correctness than one in my rearview mirror.

Now that *I'm* 70-plus years old and armed with an abundant supply of wisdom, it's apparent the actual number—if there is one—isn't so important. I've concluded the number is variable, depending on who is asked and when they're asked. Some individuals may, in fact, seem old at 60, while some may be 90 or even older when the old-age crown becomes applicable.

No matter what the number is, many families aren't prepared for the realities of caring for aging parents. What happens when debilitation reaches the point when self-care is no longer an option? My work experience in Medicare-specific health insurance education included visiting skilled nursing and assisted living facilities. Touchpoints with these facilities proved instructive. Yet they were only a brief syllabus for the course that awaited me years later when I became Mom's "headmaster," in charge of her care.

At 65 years of age, my active, healthy, and slim dad retired from the insurance industry. He seemed poised to enjoy many years in retirement pursuing hobbies and traveling with Mom. The right boxes had been checked: Dad had always eaten wholesome, home-prepared foods, had never been overweight, and was a lifelong nonsmoker and nondrinker. His pharmacy cabinet was empty, thanks to flawless blood pressure, low cholesterol, and no heart or kidney problems. I had always felt if anyone should live to be a hundred, it was my dad. Sadly, it wasn't in the cards.

There were no apparent predisposing factors to suggest Dad would be slammed by relatively rare, late-onset chronic asthma when he was 66. It debilitated and diminished him to a shell of his former self. Dreams of an active and fulfilling retirement were dashed. Suddenly he became old, and at the age of 60, Mom was thrust into the role of caregiver. I didn't have a full appreciation of the extensive impacts it had on Mom until I became *her* caregiver. Dad's disease—and his obsession with it—dominated him for fifteen interminable years. He passed away at the age of 81, in 1992. Ironically, prostate cancer was the cause of death.

The end of fifty-one years of marriage didn't prescribe an end to Mom. Her "next steps" were summed up by the following statement she made at the funeral home: "I loved your dad with all my heart, and losing him is the hardest thing I've ever faced. Even so, I'm not crawling into that box with him. I'll grieve for him, but refuse to wallow in grief for the rest of my life." And she didn't. Mom was a month shy of her 75th birthday at the time and didn't consider herself old, and she wasn't. Several months later she began volunteering at the same hospital where Dad had died.

Mom wasn't one to sit for long and began traveling throughout the United States with three close friends, all widows. They called themselves "the wild and wacky widows," and Mom was the oldest, at least chronologically. She ended up outliving them all. Generally, they took two trips a year, and sharing costs four ways made the trips affordable. Being an excellent writer, Mom journaled and wrote extensively about their escapades across the country.

College football was another one of their passions. If the Florida Gators were playing in Gainesville, the widows were there in orange-and-blue attire to claim their prized, budget-friendly end zone seats.

Away games were a reason for them to party at home, and television provided upgraded seats on the fifty-yard line.

Unlike my dad, Mom was a poster child for "successful aging." She proved that advancing age can be a time of enjoyment, fulfillment, and service to others. Predictably, the laws of nature eventually caught up. Though her entry into what I consider "classic old age" occurred much later in life than what is considered ordinary, she didn't escape unscathed … and neither did I. Through the journey, I did some things right, made a few mistakes, and dealt with my own weaknesses. Being detail oriented, I journaled extensively. My mishmash of jottings spanning eight years coalesced into *Beyond Expiration: Surviving a Centenarian Parent*.

My hope is that readers will obtain a better understanding of evolving dynamics as parents age and what to expect when they can no longer care for themselves. *Beyond Expiration* is well-stocked with insights and should open a window of appreciation for anyone who needs care and those who provide it.

CHAPTER 1

MEET MY MOM

Though Mom was a registered nurse, she did not work in a formal setting after graduating from nursing school, except for two brief stints. She and Dad had jointly made the decision she would pursue the role of a traditional American housewife. This wasn't an uncommon arrangement during the post–World War II era. Thus her focus was lasered on my dad, my brother Max, who was almost six years older than me, and me, the model child.

Mom "minded the store" while Dad scooted off to work, clad in his gray or navy-blue suit. Mom was the meal planner and cook, dish washer (with my help), and house cleaner (sometimes with my help). As Nurse Mom, she dabbed Mercurochrome on our scrapes, kissed our bruises, and served as the kid shepherdess. The term was appropriate when we were growing up. Gender neutrality wasn't yet envisioned.

Widely known as Dot, Mom was imbued with a Southern accent and natural sweetness belying her innate toughness. She was multifaceted and capitalized on every minute life granted. Got church? Indeed, she did. Two Sunday services, another on Wednesday night, and choir practice on Thursday night were the capstones of her social calendar. She assumed the motto of the postal service: "Neither snow nor rain nor heat nor gloom of night stays these couriers from the swift completion of their appointed rounds." Mom *never* shirked any commitments, church or otherwise. Everyone knew her, even folks who didn't.

Mom's array of activities extended beyond her roles of wife, mother, and engaged church participant. She was a talented pianist, singer, artist, writer, and performed in skits.

Mom, at age 86, attired in a toilet-paper dress she made for a "fashion show."

Her training as a registered nurse was no secret in our understated, close-knit hamlet north of downtown Jacksonville. Her medical expertise was frequently tapped by neighborhood moms when their kids got sprains, sore throats, diarrhea, and other common ailments. Several older ladies in the neighborhood also relied on Mom's expertise when their physicians had prescribed vitamin B_{12} injections for "blood invigoration." Mom frequently administered the injections, though would *never* accept anything in exchange.

Occasionally, a knock on the door suggested cake, cookies, pie, or some other delectable offering of gratitude was waiting to be accepted. As a highly interested party, I excitedly peeked through the window to get a glimpse, hoping to see a plate covered in foil. I had seen this scenario play out numerous times and impatiently waited for my cue to lend a helping hand. Typically, Mom would open the door and earnestly assure the benefactor, "Oh, you *really* didn't need to do this." I thought, *Yes, you really did,* and gladly absconded with the treat, tongue hanging out.

When I entered kindergarten in 1954, for my first and most important infusion of formal education, Mom was offered the opportunity to work there. It was the inaugural year for the school and was sponsored by our church, which was a reasonable one-block walk from our house. It was a double win for the school: Mom served as the music teacher *and* the school nurse. This eight-to-noon job was also a win for Mom—in fact, a triple win. She was home when the kids were home, earned extra money for the family, and it was an opportunity for her to utilize her plethora of talents by working with children. And Mom loved kids. She remained a fixture at the kindergarten for twenty-two years.

Mom playing the piano in 1957.

Around the time Mom was in her 70s, most everyone addressed her as Miss Dot. She wasn't fond of it. The designation, *Miss,* was the source of mild irritation. This affectionate greeting was a mark of respect for older ladies, particularly in the South, which she understood. Yet, Mom perceived it as a reference to her age. After thinking about it, I couldn't recall Mom addressing any woman who was up in years as Miss.

"Don't Ever Put Me in a Nursing Home!"

I always remembered this exclamation from Mom and interpreted it as a directive for my future reference. She was still fairly young, in her 50s, when I first heard it. It was repeated often—too often. No doubt, her persistence and insistence were designed to enhance the likelihood of my compliance in the event nursing services should become a consideration. She expected her plea wouldn't fall on deaf ears.

Mom was personally familiar with the realities of health care and diligently visited relatives and friends who had been placed in nursing facilities. Occasionally, I accompanied her. These visits were eye-openers. I was dismayed to observe patients in wheelchairs lining narrow hallways, illuminated in harsh-white fluorescent light reflecting off polished vinyl floors. Forlorn expressions and hung faces seemed to reflect depression and hopelessness, perhaps abandonment. Whenever we passed by, a few lost souls would look up and stare, seldom uttering a word. Some returned our smiles. Most didn't.

I glanced into open doorways, frequently catching sight of someone bedridden and deserted. At least, passive company was provided by the muffled sounds coming from the hallway: conversation among the staff, sometimes unintelligible, or the rumble from medicine or food carts being pushed. Whether the resident was awake or asleep, mind-numbing television seemed to never be turned off.

Human interaction was brief and usually perfunctory for these all-but-erased remnants of their former selves. Sounds harsh, doesn't it? Unfortunately, it's a reality. Harried aides hastily delivered meals, dispensed medications, and provided bathroom and dressing assistance. There seemed to be no time for much else.

One of the aides told me that many residents seldom received any outside visitors. I wondered where their families were. Victims of heart disease, stroke, dementia, and accidents comprised the bulk of disabled residents, most of whom were enrolled in Medicaid. This government program pays medical and nursing facility costs for individuals who meet low-income thresholds.

I vowed to do all possible to defend Mom from having to face such a fate. She was a poster child for healthy living and her indefatigability never waned. In lockstep with Dad, she was a nonsmoker, nondrinker, ate healthy meals, and got ample exercise. Nonetheless, I knew the relentless march of time paused for no one. Mom was strong-willed, ran on high-octane fuel, and had an insatiable requirement for engagement.

I worried she would be subjected to a challenging adjustment if and when her throttles were pulled back.

Mom was one of those individuals who is sometimes called a successful ager. Her advancing age didn't seem to affect her ability to continue living life as usual. She was seldom ill—except for occasional colds—and continued to march forward, no matter what. Mom was much into utilizing medical services and kept up with annual and semiannual physician visits. She didn't hesitate to schedule in-between visits if she felt it necessary. If a test was suggested, she was in line to get it. Medical interventions didn't scare her off.

Alzheimer's Disease Steals a Friend

One of Mom's traveling companions and dearest friends, Peg, whom Mom had known for more than sixty years, was admitted to the memory care wing of a highly regarded nursing facility in Jacksonville. She was 80. At the time, Mom was 92. This former go-getter had been diagnosed with Alzheimer's disease over a year prior, although Mom had recognized telltale indicators well before the diagnosis. Peg, a stickler for punctuality, began arriving late for weekly card games at Mom's house. Peg attributed her lateness to various improbable traffic-related snafus. Excuses finally ran out. Her secret was unmasked when she got lost in our neighborhood and called Mom for directions. Concurrently, Peg's mastery in playing rummy began to deteriorate.

With family oversight, Peg continued to live successfully in her home as long as possible. When her forgetfulness escalated, she recognized the need to sell her house and car. Peg managed it all, bravely, while the neurons in her brain still permitted it. Her father had been a victim of the same disease, which gave her a heightened awareness of her own plight. In due time, Peg moved in with her son and daughter-in-law. As is frequently the case, her erratic behaviors and judgment lapses created an unsafe living arrangement. When Peg could no longer be left alone even briefly, her family was forced to surrender her care to full-time professionals in the memory care unit of a skilled nursing facility.

Frequently, Mom and I visited Peg and were delighted she called us by name, particularly during the initial months following her admission. Regrettably, time erased name recollection. She continued to recognize us for about two years and always greeted us with excitement. Peg was well-cared-for and remained upbeat and engaging—qualities consistent with her "social animal" personality. Peg's take-charge character was still intact. This was demonstrated by her quickness to provide direction to anyone who needed it, and some who didn't, such as the facility activity director. Peg eagerly participated in scheduled activities and was the self-appointed assistant director. And, she enjoyed her fellow comrades … most of the time.

One afternoon, we visited Peg in the activities / dining room where fifteen residents were seated around tables for an ice cream and cake social. A disagreement between Peg and Jewel, a tablemate, was in progress when we walked up. Peg hadn't eaten her piece of cake and noticed it was missing. She correctly suspected Jewel had taken it and asked her to return it. Jewel was indignant, and Peg didn't relent. A minute later, Jewel pulled a semblance of cake out of her pants pocket. It was thoroughly smashed inside a napkin, with greasy icing and cake bits oozing all over her hand. She slapped the mess on the table and scornfully demanded, "Eat the damn cake." Mom was about to tilt out of her chair, trying to conceal laughter.

The best was still waiting to be served, *by Peg*, when she declared, "They think *I'm* nuts, but Jewel is *really* cuckoo." Her innocent comment was as true as the morning dew. Similar exchanges among residents were commonplace and expeditiously managed by staff members acting as parents, telling the kids to behave. When an individual's unruliness became a nuisance, a stern lecture or even supervised expulsion to the resident's bedroom wasn't out of the ordinary.

Observing the variability in individual responses to dementia, regardless of the underlying cause, was astounding. In addition to cognitive dysfunction, personality manifestations ranged from belligerence to sweetness. Some victims were prone to chattiness, while others dwelled in silence. I surmised these characteristics were exaggerations of basic personality types. In some, as I later witnessed, an alternative personality emerged from the depths to assume control. Changes in personal appearance seemed to be a hallmark of disease progression as most individuals slipped into a predetermined, inexorable trajectory. Peg was no exception. Her impeccable dress and coiffured hair yielded to a careless presentation as she detached from her former self.

During one visit when Peg was edging toward the conclusion of her Alzheimer's journey, Mom shared two albums filled with photos. They were taken when Peg, Mom, and two other close friends had trekked together across the country. Peg's reaction was one of wonder: she stared at each glossy print, trying to figure out who and what was in front of her eyes. She slowly slid her fingers across photos that seemed to hold significance and occasionally pointed to an object such as her beloved automobile or her traveling companions. On one occasion, I asked Peg if she recognized who was in a particular photo. She answered yes. I clung to the hope a transient flicker of recollection had been liberated from imprisonment. This was unlikely. The same answer usually applied to any question.

Peg's engaging demeanor and conversant nature gradually ceded to a world of isolation and oblivion as she eventually ceased talking. She had no discernable cognitive ability and assumed a fetal position; it was suggestive that she had returned to the womb. Mercifully, Peg was released from her misery in 2015, at the age of 85, culminating a six-year battle. Her dad was 83 when he expired from the same disease.

Roomies

Peg had shared a semiprivate room and bath with Aileen, whose intellectual impairment was similar in degree to Peg's. At times, Aileen seemed to encounter a few rays of lucidity. Initially, both ladies could answer basic questions with reasonable accuracy before wandering into another universe with illogical jabber.

Their living quarters were standard: two twin beds with thin mattresses in need of replacement; two nondescript, scratched-up armoires; two well-used dressers; and two bedside tables topped with bolted-down institutional lamps. The atmosphere was depressing. A large locked window covered by venetian blinds provided visual access to the free world a few inches away. The ladies were allowed access from their room to the halls, nurses station, and adjacent community rooms. Exits to areas outside the memory care unit remained locked to minimize the chance of a resident wandering out and becoming lost or injured.

Aileen was around 80, well-presented, attractive, and a complementary match for Peg. She was engagingly warm, considerate, and gregarious. She frequently spoke of her three sons, calling each one by name and describing their career choices. She easily recalled her upbringing in a Queens, New York, Irish-Catholic family. Aileen expressed a strong dislike for the strict nuns who had been her teachers in school. She was a charmer who likely had experienced a rich, fulfilling life. Her photographs reflected an attractive family and elegant home. Some of her photos had migrated to Peg's half of the room while a snapshot of Peg's grandson was taped to Aileen's armoire door. Neither seemed bothered or even aware of the intermingling.

Peg's roommate surprised us with a resonant singing voice, which she joyfully shared with regularity. Her poise and breath control suggested formal training. On one occasion she began to cry while singing "My Bonnie Lies over the Ocean." When I inquired why she was upset, she couldn't remember. In the flip of a switch, the tears were replaced with a wide, toothy grin. The juxtaposition of relative mental sharpness to confusion was mysteriously fascinating, though heartbreaking.

Aileen lamented on several occasions she was no longer allowed to visit her sons in their homes. She said she couldn't behave. Almost jokingly, I asked why she didn't behave. She sheepishly responded, "I can't help it sometimes." Curious, I continued to probe about her misconduct. Much like a kid who had been scolded, she apologetically admitted she couldn't remember exactly what she had done, but believed she had been nasty. I couldn't imagine what this sweet, seemingly polite lady might have done. My enlightenment came a couple of weeks later when I was introduced to a completely unfiltered and unhinged Aileen.

Undoubtedly, Aileen's parents had been deceased for some time, although she didn't remember they were gone. In a schoolgirl's vernacular, she affectionately spoke of them as Mommy and Daddy, and expected to visit them soon. Peculiarly, Peg had referred to her own parents in a similar fashion and spoke of them in the present tense. She had no recollection of their deaths thirty years prior.

Loss of inhibitions was a constant among many in the memory care unit. Filters that normally throttle unacceptable behavior seemed to be parked in shutdown mode. A few individuals were emboldened toward rudeness, blurting unkind or inappropriate comments—some of which were painfully truthful. I overheard one resident advise a friend: "You have ugly hair." Unquestionably, the woman's hair was unkempt. The uninvited and hurtful remark was ironic, coming from someone whose own hair could have doubled as a squirrel's nest.

Aileen wasn't an exception to inhibition loss, although her deficit didn't predispose her to intentionally launch insults. Instead, her filtering mechanism short-circuited at the outlet regulating "naughty or nice." With Aileen, it spelled bawdiness.

One afternoon when Mom and I were visiting Peg and Aileen in their room, Aileen seized an opportunity to entertain her audience. She grabbed her sizeable breasts (she was clothed) and brandished them as if they were pistols while wildly laughing and blabbering, "Boing, boing, boing." After the mouth-dropping opening scene shocker had been unleashed, Aileen briefly retreated, transforming herself into a demure kitten. She purred, "Don't you want to see them? Your mommy won't mind … please ask her." With no chance for "Mommy" to respond, the wildcat returned in a flash, lunging at me with claws extended. She zeroed in on my crotch, and I yelled *"No!"* Aileen stopped in her tracks, appearing stunned.

Electrified, Peg shot up from her chair and commanded, "Stay away from my husband!" What a perfect line to stop an imminent attack, even though I wasn't the reincarnation of Peg's long-deceased spouse. I couldn't have scripted Peg's unexpected comment. It was thought-provoking that Peg's sense of propriety was sufficient to break through the maze of crossed wires her disease had so cruelly woven. Aileen's bawdy alter ego receded, allowing her domesticated persona to regain residence. Unharmed, I understood Peg and Aileen were the victims, not me. Within seconds, neither retained any memory of what had transpired. The entire "play" was perhaps a fifteen-second vignette I'll never forget. I surmise Aileen was an entertaining, free-spirited, and talented woman prior to her illness. I wish I had known her then.

It's important to understand that Alzheimer's disease is a progressive neurological disorder that causes drastic, irreversible mental deterioration before it kills. The ramifications are brutal.

A Parade of Loss

Mom began losing significant numbers of close friends and cousins who were near her age or younger. This exodus began when she was in her 70s. With the exception of two individuals, they were all gone by the time Mom was 90. As her contemporaries passed away, Mom "hung" with friends who were considerably younger, many 10 to 20 years her junior. Peg fell into this category. Mom had no problem keeping up with her much younger friends, and continued to enjoy extraordinary vitality and health for many years.

I watched Mom as she surpassed most everyone else in chronological age. Mom had three siblings, all younger, and she outlived them all by a long shot. Her brother died at the age of 82 and her two sisters both died at the age of 79. One of them, her sister Mandy, was one of the four "wild and wacky widows" who traveled together. Through it all, Mom remained focused on the future and took losses in stride. She once told me, "You can't dwell in the past." I think her attitude was a clue pointing to her ability to manage death as well as she did. Was her mindset inherent? I think it was. Some people seem to be born with a predisposition toward happiness and she was one of them.

CHAPTER 2

CRACKS START TO APPEAR

I didn't think Mom would get old, given her success at avoiding the fate for so long. This five-foot-tall, ninety-five-pound dynamo was a ball of effervescence and appeared much younger than her chronological years suggested. She had a pillow on her living room couch with the embroidered inscription: "Age is a number and mine is unlisted." Though unoriginal, it reflected her feelings. Mom didn't lie about her age, but didn't freely divulge it either. Her stance changed when it became irrefutable she was an anomaly for her age. This happened when she was 90, rendering her an instant celebrity. I didn't consider Mom to be "old" until she reached her late 90s. That's when old-age setbacks started to make themselves known.

For several weeks in the spring of 2015, Mom had been complaining about "something not being right" in her bowels. She didn't feel like eating and her bowel movements had been irregular. She was 97 years old. I suggested exercise, drinking extra water, and eating salads. This was "Dr. Seth's" prescription for enhanced digestion. "Nurse Mom" had a differing medical opinion and *insisted* her symptoms were indicative of an intestinal obstruction. I thought, *Yeah, sure.* Mom had always shared her symptoms, particularly those with the worst possible implications. Thankfully, her list of disorders had always been garden variety, and I dismissed her most recent self-diagnosis.

Mom's concerns escalated. They reached "pull-the-fire-alarm" status during the wee hours of Saturday, May 9, 2015, when sleeplessness and discomfort progressed into acute pain. She had mentioned on Friday afternoon she couldn't eat and her stomach was distended. Out of concern, I decided to spend the night at her house on the living room couch. At four in the morning, I was awakened by Mom's stirrings and could see light emanating from her bathroom. When I called out, she requested: "Seth, please come in here. I've been up all night and probably need to go to the hospital ... but not yet." She was sick and unquestionably in need of medical attention. Exercise, water, and salad remedies were no longer considerations.

Even though Mom was doubled over, she remained focused and in charge. She had taken a shower, was packing her suitcase, and had gathered insurance cards. Her extensive cosmetic arsenal had been assembled, which was all the proof I needed—Mom was in a pickle. Standard emergency procedures outlined in her personal handbook were followed to the letter. Pre-departure activity concluded at six in the morning when she pronounced herself ready for the fifteen-minute excursion to St. Vincent's Hospital.

I called my brother, Max, who lived minutes away. Mom dictated the following instruction: "Tell Max to meet us at the hospital. There's no need for him to come over here first, and tell him to eat his breakfast." I conveyed the message and called 911. Even though Max was almost 73 and I was 67, we were still her kids. Remarkably, Mom's steely nature and propensity to remain nonemotional during times of crisis remained defining traits. These traits were much in tune even after a night of sleeplessness and pain.

The paramedics were dispatched from the Jacksonville Fire and Rescue station several blocks away and arrived within five minutes. After checking Mom's vitals and giving her a brief once-over, they agreed with Mom's assessment: transport to the hospital was judicious. Before Mom crawled atop the stretcher, she scrutinized her hair one final time and wielded her ultimate weapon—the teasing comb. A few strands were out of place and she got them whipped into shape in a few seconds. A cloud of hairspray sealed the deal. No doubt, if surgery was needed, she wanted her hair to survive even if she didn't.

This would be Mom's second expedition, as a patient, to St. Vincent's. Her first was in 1943, when she gave birth to Max. As an aside, she was a current volunteer at the hospital. Twenty-two years of volunteer service had enabled her to make connections in the hospital. Plus, her volunteering netted two welcome amenities for Max and me: free parking and daily meal trays.

I was grateful that the ambulance's sometimes blaring, tranquility-piercing sirens stayed silent, and the neighborhood remained blissfully unaware of the commotion in the early dawn twilight. I followed the ambulance to the hospital and spotted Max waiting by the ER entrance door. After I parked, we walked into the hospital together. I asked, "Did you eat breakfast? Mama is going to ask you." He said he had. Right answer.

Not much was going on in the ER. With minimal waiting, Mom was attended by a pert and efficient physician who didn't appear old enough to be in the role. She suspected Mom's self-diagnosis of an obstruction might be correct. Tests were performed within the hour. Sure enough, an obstruction of some sort was evident.

"Mrs. Vicarson, we've identified a blockage in your small intestine. We're going to attempt nonsurgical methods first and it might resolve. If we're not successful, we'll consider surgery. If so, will you consent?"

Without hesitation Mom responded, "Why wouldn't I? I understand the risks, but don't want to leave this world with an exploded bowel."

Mom was transferred into a regular hospital room where the "clog-busting works" were administered for twenty-four hours. Disappointing to Mom, Max, and me, a "super enema" and associated pharmaceutical encouragements were ineffective in their attempts to blast through.

A nurse handed Mom several surgical authorization forms. True to character, there was no reluctance on her part to sign them. My upbeat countenance and words of encouragement were masks for the fear factor residing within me. I contemplated the worst as we waited for the gurney. *Can she withstand the anesthesia? What if she has a malignancy? Could surgery cause a heart attack?* Regardless, surgery was the only viable option.

Within a few minutes, the orderly arrived with the gurney. Max and I followed as Mom was spirited down the cavernous hallways leading to a cramped surgical elevator. *Oh, no!* I had experienced attacks of claustrophobia in *some* elevators and this one qualified. I took a Goliath-sized breath, held it, and stepped into the inescapable den. Unaware of surrounding conversation, I grasped the handrail and anxiously watched the last hints of hallway light disappear as the doors slammed shut. The elevator started its snail's-pace journey traversing the entirety of two floors. Or was it twenty-two? That's how it seemed. I could barely detect any movement, but a half ounce of reassurance was provided by the *clunk, clunk, clunk* confirming downward progress. I felt the telltale bounce signaling the elevator had reached its destination. Surely the doors would slide open without delay. These didn't. They were hopelessly sluggish. After being squeezed against the wall for an interminable amount of time (about thirty seconds), the walls started to close in. Mercy prevailed. The doors crept open, releasing us from the virtual tomb.

A short distance took us to the surgical suite where Max, Mom, and I were ushered into a cubicle a few feet outside the operating room. The usual flank of white curtains separating one cubicle from the next were all pulled back; we were the only Sunday morning clientele. I suppose the remaining populace was either hungover or in church. Within a minute or two, a surgical nurse, an anesthesiologist, and a surgeon popped into the room. They were calming and engaging while answering our questions. Mom's tolerance for anesthesia was my primary concern. After all, she was up in years. The anesthesiologist mentioned the risks, yet assured us Mom's excellent health indicated a much younger biological age than chronological. He didn't think her age posed a significant risk. The surgery was expected to last about an hour.

We found our way to the surgical waiting room where we were joined by Max's son, Kurt, and my partner, Thomas. We had engaged in mindless chitchat for perhaps forty-five minutes when Mom's surgeon stepped into the room. *Golly, that was fast. Had something gone wrong?* The news was encouraging. The surgeon explained Mom's blockage was a noncancerous stricture resembling scar tissue. He had removed a one-inch section of her small intestine. Mom was in recovery and no further treatment would be required. She breezed through the hospitalization and was released in two days.

Since Mom wasn't in a position to remain alone for extended periods, I stayed in her house while she recuperated. I was retired, and Mom lived fifteen minutes from Thomas and me. I could easily scamper home to shower, change clothes, and—since she didn't have the internet—catch up on emails.

Home Health Care 101

Prior to Mom's hospital discharge, the physician set the wheels in motion for her to receive intermittent home health care. Medicare approved twice-weekly in-home visits from a certified home health care nurse for a period of several weeks. This firsthand, personal introduction to home health care was a valuable educational experience and an integral contributor to Mom's recuperation. I was somewhat familiar with the service as a result of my former employment at a large health insurance company, but had never seen it in action.

From the visiting nurse's perspective, Mom was light duty. She didn't require physical therapy and remained ahead of the curve in her recovery. With each visit, the nurse evaluated the surgical incision and changed bandages. I watched as she uncoiled the stethoscope for the familiar eavesdrop on Mom's heart, lungs, and blood pressure. There was one additional tool extracted from the nurse's satchel—the oximeter. This painless device, resembling a Star Trek–inspired clothespin, measured the level of oxygen in Mom's blood without extracting a drop. They're commonly used and most of us have had one placed on a finger while in the doctor's office. The "jaws" were opened, positioned on the end of Mom's index finger, and closed. Within seconds, we had the report.

The findings were all encouraging. Mom's heart was beating, her lungs oxygenating, and she had sufficient blood pressure to maintain life. During one visit, the nurse asked Mom several questions to gauge her memory. I couldn't help but chuckle to myself, knowing Mom's memory was unwavering and better than mine. Her uncanny ability for accurate recall, whether yesterday or ninety years ago, was nailed tight.

Each home health visit lasted an hour or less. At the two-week mark, Mom was able to resume living independently, with occasional assistance from Max or me. My temporary status as a live-in caregiver ended—although intermittent visits from the home health care nurse continued for an additional two weeks. Mom had required minimal assistance from me. It had been a relatively easy gig. The confining nature of the two-week "mission" was my most pressing personal challenge. Incidentally, home health care is a Medicare-covered benefit, provided certain requirements are met. A more complete explanation of home health care may be found in the following publication: *https://www.medicare.gov/Pubs/pdf/10969-medicare-and-home-health-care.pdf.*

Four weeks following surgery, Mom was driving, singing in the senior adult church choir, and participating in a myriad of church activities. Shortly thereafter, she was back in her purple uniform as a volunteer in the cardiopulmonary rehab unit at St. Vincent's Hospital. Her faster-than-a-speeding-bullet rebound had me shaking my head in disbelief.

Compression Stockings Make Their Debut

I had seen them for as long as I could remember. They're usually white or tan, tightly clinging, and typically worn by the "infirm"—with apparent disregard for fashion efficacy. I never thought much about their function and figured they were a leg sock of some sort. They exuded old age, at least in my mind. I conjectured there wouldn't be a reason for me to become better acquainted. This proved to be an incorrect assumption.

Mom's ankles and feet had begun to swell periodically following her intestinal surgery. During an office visit with her physician, I was advised any one of several conditions could be responsible: too much salt, a failing heart, and/or failing kidneys. Mom's culprits were pinned to her heart and salt. She loved the salt shaker a bit too much. Her heart's output was no longer flowing like the Mississippi River, but consider this factoid: 97 years of near flawless operation equates to about 3.5 *billion* beats. This number is based on Mom's average heart rate of seventy beats per minute and my own mathematical wizardry, which was calculator enhanced.

Her medical circumstances weren't dire. A few adjustments to her medications and elevating her feet were starters. She was further advised to purchase compression stockings. These elastic wonders promised to diminish swelling even when Mom wasn't in a position to elevate her feet. I was sold. We departed the physician's office and proceeded to the medical supply store, expecting the visit to be of short duration. Buying a pair of calf-high elastic socks should be easy. We walked into the store to find a veritable universe of trappings, all promising salvation in the form of physical support and maximum comfort. Descriptions resembled the claims I'd seen in mattress commercials, minus the sleep component.

An entire wall, probably fifteen feet long and six feet high, loomed like a tsunami poised to crash on top of us. It didn't. The "tsunami" was crammed with boxes of compression stockings, all with secret identifiers. My head was spinning. We needed someone to help us navigate the maze. A skilled sales representative appeared as we were scouting an escape route. She informed us one size doesn't fit all and finding the right fit requires several measurements. This was only part of the formula for success. Stockings were numbered according to compression level (tightness)—the higher the number, the tighter the fit. Mom's physician had specified a midrange number of fifteen to twenty. Various colors were shown, some less obvious in appearance than their counterparts. A few were opaque while others were sheer. To further complicate the selection process, knee-high, waist-high, or thigh-high models were awaiting adoption. Toe style—open or closed—was a detail requiring consideration.

The white ones were summarily disqualified; they were too recognizable. Mom's sartorial considerations would never have permitted such a transgression in glaring spandex for public display. I didn't blame her. Mom specified a sedate, medium-tan stocking. It had to be sheer, knee-high, and open-toe. We were making progress, until being advised the desired stockings in Mom's size and prescribed compression level were not in stock—except for a pair in white. Her "Not on my legs" reaction was swift and sure. Instead, a tan, *closed-toe* reasonable facsimile tumbled off the shelf. Easy enough. All Mom had to do was take the stockings out of the box when she got home and put them on. I had a pair of tight-fitting calf-high socks and surmised Mom's stockings would work much the same way. We were done and I was ready to scoot out.

Not so fast. The sales rep suggested it would be worth our time to allow her to demonstrate proper application. I must have thrown a we're-in-a-hurry countenance. She swiftly informed me: "There's a specific method to this. You need to watch me put them on your mom." We sat down.

The sales rep unfurled the stockings. They were exactly as described—compressed. Undoubtedly, the rep had selected the wrong size, and I asked, "Don't we need larger ones?" With a chuckle, the rep told me no. In a flash the sales rep put her hand in one of the stockings and inverted it. The capacity of the stocking to s-t-r-e-t-c-h demanded inclusion as a scientific marvel. With deftness, she pulled it up on Mom's leg and smoothed it out. The rep took it off, planted it in my hand, and, with a smile, directed me to "give it a try." So I made one, two, three attempts … all three strikeouts. I couldn't get them all the way up Mom's legs without wrinkles and creases, which sabotaged their intended support and comfort. Mom tried it and *she* struck out. The tan monsters were one heck of a challenge, and the rep put them back on Mom's legs. Frustrated, Mom plunked down fifteen bucks for the pair. The sales rep offered a hearty dose of encouragement as we trotted out. Her parting words were "It takes practice, don't give up. You'll *soon* get the hang of it." At least Mom was able to get them off at home before going to bed. We had been advised the compression stockings weren't to be worn at night.

Soon didn't arrive until I watched a number of videos on YouTube, all affirming "easy as pie" techniques promising success. After multiple trials with many errors, I got better at it, but still struggled. Much to my dismay, mastery wasn't in the cards for Mom. Numb hands, insufficient hand strength, and impaired flexibility doomed her. This new dynamic added an additional complication to Mom's life; she needed daily assistance to get the stockings on. A trek to her house each morning was an unavoidable and disruptive chore. Help was on the way! Max agreed to attend my training school and, following graduation, he was pressed into service on alternating days.

Additional aid came in the form of a thirty-five-dollar device called a donner. It's a simple metal contraption worthy of being on display in a museum of contemporary art. The donner simplified stocking application. Don't ask me to explain how this gadget works, yet it does. Don't assume the donner made stocking application effortless—it didn't. Even so, it was a welcome improvement to the previous method occasionally resulting in the "agony of defeat." For unknown reasons, the swelling in Mom's feet and ankles abated and many days she didn't need to wear the stockings.

Medical Alert Button Saga

Mom called one evening to report she had fallen in the garage earlier in the day. She had tripped while running to answer the kitchen phone and fell against the car's front bumper before ricocheting to the concrete floor. After collecting herself, she was able to get up and walk around. Besides being sore and bruised, she was okay. Mom had been lucky, and I considered the incident a warning. She had recently celebrated her 98th birthday.

Mom's disclosure prompted me to procure two medical alert devices. One was a neck pendant and the other resembled a wristwatch. A simple push of the quarter-sized alert button on either device automatically dialed an emergency operator who could talk to Mom, summon help if needed, and notify me. It was an ideal solution offering security and peace of mind. Additionally, I called Mom nightly between nine thirty and ten o'clock. We had agreed *she* would call *me* if she hadn't heard from me by ten.

The safety net was riddled with holes. At times, Mom didn't hear the phone ring when I called. In most instances, the TV was turned up to eardrum-shattering levels, or she was taking a shower and couldn't answer. In either case, the phone would default to voice mail, which she didn't regularly check. Occasionally, Mom inadvertently dislodged her phone from the cradle, disabling it. If I called while it was disabled, the result was a busy signal. Thus, having her call if she hadn't heard from me by ten would cool my heartburn.

Mom was a talker and had an abundance of friends. It wasn't unusual for her to be gabbing on the phone for extended periods. Since she didn't have call waiting, I frequently encountered a busy signal. This, or an unanswered phone, suggested four possibilities: Mom was talking, or the phone was off line and she forgot to call me, or she didn't hear the phone ringing, or she was sprawled out on the floor—bleeding and unconscious. I usually assumed the last one.

Busy signals occurred often enough to require instituting some work-arounds. The first was to call Mom's cell phone. This was usually pointless since she kept it in her purse and couldn't hear it ring. Or she hadn't charged it for days and the cell was dead. If contact hadn't been made by ten thirty, the second course of action was to call the phone company and have them check for conversation on Mom's line. If conversation was detected, I didn't worry. If not, I drove fifteen minutes to her house in a near panic mode. This happened too often.

The medical alert devices and monitoring cost $400 per year, which I considered a smart investment. She gave me cause to reconsider the expense. Weekly, either Max or I spent one day with Mom to take her to lunch and assist her with shopping. I couldn't help but notice she was seldom wearing either alert button when I visited. When questioned, she responded, "Since you were coming over, I didn't put it on." Several days prior, Max had been told the same thing when he asked Mom about the whereabouts of the medical alert devices.

With well-founded suspicions, I conducted an unannounced reconnaissance to Mom's house one afternoon. It was brutally hot. Much to my dismay, she was sweeping the driveway with a worn-out, nearly useless broom. Her face was red from heat, and I banished her to the safety of the great air-conditioned indoors while I finished sweeping. Within a few minutes, my face was as red as Mom's had been, although mine was partly from anger. Besides Mom's risking heatstroke to remove harmless oak tree litter, a medical alert device was nowhere to be seen. There was an explanation: she wasn't wearing one. Though the driveway had been blown off several days earlier, Mom wouldn't allow the "blemishes" to wait for the yard guy's return. Nothing out of place was permissible, and Mom's overboard fastidiousness drove me nuts. There's no debate the segment of her DNA controlling neatness didn't survive the spin that fashioned my genetic assortment. Dad was neat-as-a-pin as well. Maybe they had adopted me.

Once inside the house, I spoke to Mom about her two blatant transgressions: subjecting herself to possible heatstroke and not wearing an alert button. She explained it would be several days before the yard guy would be back and by then the driveway would be an *absolute mess*. Her definition of *absolute mess* didn't correspond with the debris dotting her driveway. Still, Mom couldn't leave it alone. It would be a cinch for me to blow the leaves when visiting Mom during the week. So, I did. It took two or three minutes.

Mom effortlessly deflected the second offense. She simply "forgot" to wear the alert button. Again. In an act of contrition, she hung it around her neck before I left. Her gesture of compliance made it hard to remain agitated, though I wasn't a believer. On the way home I called Max and suggested he pop in on Mom for an unannounced compliance check within the next few days.

I received a call from Max several days later: "Seth, I just got back from Mom's house and she wasn't wearing either device. The pendant was lying on the kitchen counter and she couldn't recall where the wrist thing was. I found it in the bathroom."

"Max, what did you say to her?"

"I reminded her of the necessity to wear it and hung the pendant around her neck. She told me she had forgotten to put it on and insisted she had worn it earlier in the day. Perhaps she had."

Mom's memory was unfailing, and I suspected her "forgetting" was by design, even if subconsciously. My first inclination was to call her and express my disapproval. My cooler head prevailed and I decided to wait. Our evening phone call would be a better time to bring up the topic. I called at nine thirty and didn't get a busy signal—a welcome sign from the cosmos. It took forever for Mom to answer, which wasn't unusual. Initially, I didn't bring up the alert button topic, hoping she would confess her sin at some point during the conversation. She didn't, so I broached the subject.

"Mama, are you wearing your alert button?"

"I *did* have it on and took it off *before* I got into the shower."

"It's waterproof for that very reason. What would you do if you fell in the shower and couldn't get out?"

"Seth, I'm careful in the shower and I always have the portable phone nearby."

"Mama, you *can't* assume that. What if the portable is dead? Why take a chance when it's avoidable? Please wear one of the alert buttons."

Mom had irritated me, and the situation caused us to have words—a rare occurrence. Nothing I proposed made an impression. It seemed evident she wasn't going to make a concerted effort to wear either device. She offered several excuses: "I forget to put it on." "It's too heavy around my neck." "The wrist button is hard to get on." "I can always get to a phone if I need help." Predictably, the "snake" eventually bit her.

The Cane

The ravages of 98 years of living were evidenced by the spreading cracks in Mom's armor. Her balance was under assault. She teetered at times as if inebriated, but refused to use a cane. There's a story. Shortly after Mom's fall in the garage, her physician advised her to start using a cane. The aforementioned medical supply store was an emporium of all sorts, and I remembered a large collection of canes on an aisle near the compression stockings. I hauled Mom over and we perused an impressive selection.

We considered various shapes, colors, and styles. The selection process was effortless when compared to compression stockings. Mom settled on a model imprinted with brightly colored florals and butterflies. On her next visit to the physician, I watched her proudly present the cane to him, seeking and gaining his approval. When we returned home, Mom propped the cane against the kitchen wall—where it remained enshrined as an ornament. She seldom used it. When reminded the cane's primary function was to provide personal stability rather than be admired for its decorative attributes, she snapped, "I don't need it. I'm not feeble." I feared Mom would end up eating her words.

Her statement was the equivalent of "hot water" being poured on my head, and I seethed. I had gone out of my way to get the "had to have" cane and couldn't unravel her careless approach to not using it. In a scolding tone, I retorted, "You're prone to fall without warning and a cane might prevent it. I can't force you to use the cane, so consider the risks." I felt disrespected. It was clear Mom was struggling; she couldn't accept "being old."

Mom fell several times at home, with minor consequences. Without exception, she called to advise me she had fallen ... but wasn't hurt *much*. I made several trips to her house when the "wasn't hurt much" description was unconvincing. When asked if she had been using the cane, her response never varied: "It doesn't help. I always fall backwards." And she usually *did* fall backwards, but a physical therapist had previously pointed out that using a cane would force her body to tilt *forward*. Mom's stubborn refusal to comply with a reasonable safety precaution placed her at increased risk for a disastrous fall. She kept me exasperated.

The elephant in the room was stomping around yet ignored by our fiercely independent mother. She was rapidly approaching the crossroads where hard decisions would have to be made. Max and I were aware she couldn't live alone in her house indefinitely. This was an unsettling realization. Three factors added leavening to the mix: Thomas and I were contemplating moving to St. Augustine, Max and Lois (his wife) were considering a move, and Mom's neighborhood was in decline. Nonetheless, Mom remained resistant. She wasn't interested in moving anywhere. Period. We continued to tiptoe through the tulips in an effort to keep the bee in the hive for the time being. *Where's the valium?*

We understood Mom's predicament, which is an all-too-common consequence of aging. She wasn't willing to cede her independence and couldn't handle the thought of leaving her house. This was compounded by the stinging probability she might be forced to detach from her church, her oasis. The church had been an integral part of her life for seventy-plus years. It all boiled down to an undeniable reality: the water was inching up to Mom's neck, but she stubbornly refused a life raft.

Mom at 98, Seth at 68.   *Mom's cane.*

Hindsight

Hindsight is twenty-twenty, and I realize we should have strongly encouraged Mom to move into an independent living apartment when she was in her mid-90s. I had made the suggestion at the time and toured what I thought was a perfect location, but was met with a brick wall. There's no question that Max and I didn't want to upset Mom's applecart, but it would have been in her best interest *and ours* to have done it. Independent living communities are designed for seniors who don't require assistance yet are looking to scuttle the hassles of home maintenance. Tired of cooking every meal? Residents in these communities have the option to enjoy prepared meals with fellow residents in a dining room. Additionally, independent living communities are an anchor for activities that promote socialization.

Most individuals who enter independent living do so at ages much younger that what would have been appropriate for Mom, particularly when it's their choice. When it's not their choice, it's a different ballgame.

The cost of independent living varies widely, depending on the type and size of housing chosen, amenities offered, and the level of luxuriousness the community provides. Some independent living apartment communities are subsidized by government agencies, making them affordable to low-income individuals. I've had the opportunity to visit several and found them adequate, with few frills. The following website might prove helpful if looking for low-income, subsidized housing opportunities: *https://www.hud.gov/topics/ information_for_senior_citizens.*

Other information may be found by searching *subsidized senior housing* on the internet.

Moving an aging parent is traumatic, particularly if against their will, and leaving them in their home as long as possible is desirable. "Aging in place" is a term used to describe this strategy. It's the ideal arrangement and, based on my interaction with seniors, most prefer to take this approach. I hope to do the same when it's my turn. Mom was an example of aging in place until we were forced to make other arrangements. I checked into the cost of obtaining daily sitter service for Mom when she was no longer able to remain in her home alone. I was quoted $20–$25 per hour. Get your calculator out. The following websites pertaining to aging in place are informative:

https://www.nia.nih.gov/health/aging-place-growing-older-home and
https://www.ruralhealthinfo.org/toolkits/aging/1/overview.

Continuing care retirement communities are an A-to-Z type of arrangement which encompasses independent living, assisted living, and skilled nursing facilities—all under the same umbrella. An individual requiring no care can enter the community as an independent living resident. When care needs increase, the resident can transition to assisted living (moderate care needs), and later to skilled nursing (significant care needs) without leaving the campus. These communities tend to be costly and are unaffordable for many, including our family. If interested in exploring this type of care, the following resources might prove helpful: *https://www.seniorliving.org/continuing-care-retirement-communities/#cost* and *https://health.usnews.com/senior-care/caregiving/articles/continuing-care-retirement-communities.*

I'll discuss assisted living and skilled nursing facility care later in this book.

Mom Receives a Harsh Wake-up Call

For a number of years, Thomas and I had owned a second home in St. Augustine, forty miles south of Jacksonville. At last, the planets aligned and we permanently relocated in December 2015. I was wary of being an hour away from Mom. Fortunately, Max lived less than ten minutes from her and could respond if she got into trouble or had a pressing need. I routinely made twice-weekly trips to Jacksonville to check on Mom, take her to appointments, and help her with shopping. There were instances when Max and Lois left town for a week or so. When this occurred, I brought Mom to St. Augustine to stay with Thomas and me.

It was May 9, 2016, exactly one year to the day since Mom's prior hospital admission for the bowel obstruction. The phone rang a few minutes before seven in the morning. It was Max, calling from Mom's house. She had telephoned him with concerning news: she had fallen and was hurt. She had hopped out of bed around six o'clock to go to the bathroom, ignoring her cane. Mom crashed into the corner of her desk before tumbling to the shocking-pink, well-padded shag carpet. My thanks to Pepto Bismol for providing Mom with the color inspiration. I'm sure Proctor & Gamble would be gratified to discover their product had been useful for a purpose unrelated to treating gastric distress.

Mom had transformed herself into a real-life "I've fallen and I can't get up" pretzel as depicted in print ads and television commercials. I was reluctant, yet dared to raise the obvious question to Max: "Was Mom

wearing the medical alert button?" She wasn't, but had gotten lucky …
this time. Her fall was close enough to the desk where she could reach
up to the portable phone and knock it to the floor. That's how she was
able to summon Max.

He gingerly helped Mom extricate herself from the pink sea that
had cushioned her fall and likely prevented a broken hip. With his
assistance, she was able to hobble to the bathroom. The maneuvering
resulted in intense pain across her rib cage and "Nurse Mom" diagnosed
herself with a "rib involvement." She didn't want Max to call 911,
emphasizing, "I don't want to go to the hospital. They can't do anything
much for a cracked rib and time will eventually take care of it." He
called 911. Jacksonville Fire and Rescue arrived while Max and I were
conversing, and Mom was treated to her second annual ambulance ride
to St. Vincent's.

Hurriedly, I put myself together, threw some overnight items
into a suitcase, and began the forty-mile trudge up to Jacksonville's St.
Vincent's Hospital. It was a typical Monday morning rush hour on I-95;
creeping traffic and frequent lane changing was the rule. Drivers (myself
included) futilely attempted to jockey into better position by changing
lanes on the crammed track. I wasn't panicky, yet was aware my driving
suggested an underlying nervousness. The morning radio newscast was
negligibly effective in supplanting my preoccupation. My thoughts
about Mom's injuries and possible repercussions were in the driver's seat,
even though I did the steering. An hour and ten minutes after leaving
St. Augustine, I entered the familiar hubbub of the emergency room and
was directed to Mom's cubicle.

I noticed Mom's impeccable hair. It was proof she had followed
her second guideline for emergencies. Calling Max had been her first.
The self-diagnosis proved to be partially correct … times three. X-rays
indicated she had fractured three ribs on her left side. Though bad
enough, we were relieved to hear the structural wreckage was confined
to her ribs. Notwithstanding, her pain level was *off* the charts, which
was duly noted *on* the charts. She was admitted into the hospital. Mom
maintained her usual unemotional demeanor, saying nothing about the
fall. Of course, I had a few questions that needed answers.

"Mama, why did you fall?"

"Seth, I don't know. I remember getting up and maybe I tripped. I
honestly don't know what happened."

"Had you been dizzy?"

"No. I remember standing up and falling hard against the desk."

I wondered if her cane might have prevented the fall, but didn't bring it up. I had expressed my opinion on the topic previously.

Her lack of detail was concerning, yet I was mindful that falls were common among older adults for various reasons. I trusted the team of medical professionals to evaluate Mom and formulate an effective treatment plan.

During Mom's hospital stay, the uphill mending process began. Despite painful injuries, she was required to participate in twice-daily physical and occupational therapy sessions. To explain, physical therapy (PT) focuses on improving an individual's range of motion and balance, increasing strength, and reducing pain. Examples include stretching, calisthenics, light weight lifting, and mild aerobic exercises involving movement such as walking or going up and down stairs. Throw in a few hot packs, cold packs, electrical stimulation, and massage. Voila, you have PT 101 in a nutshell. Mom's precarious situation disallowed some of the aforementioned procedures. Her therapy included standing, sitting, walking with assistance, and twice-daily breathing treatments to prevent pneumonia.

Occupational therapy (OT) provides support to individuals who are challenged by routine daily tasks. Think of actions normally accomplished without much thought or effort. They're called activities of daily living (ADLs). If you're able to feed yourself, bathe yourself, dress yourself, comb your hair, brush your teeth, and poop and pee without creating a hazmat site, you probably don't need occupational therapy. If a disabling injury or illness has rendered these types of activities difficult or not possible, OT might be of benefit.

Mom was one step ahead of the game. Her rib fractures were on the left side and she was right-handed. Even so, this accommodation was dwarfed by twin nemeses: extreme difficulty getting in and out of the bed, and sleeplessness. Finding a lasting "sweet spot" proved elusive; unrelenting discomfort subverted her quest for sleep. Equal opportunity was given to lying flat, being propped up, lying in the fetal position, and "sanctuary" in the recliner. Multiple pillows placed at various strategic outposts littered the hospital bed to cushion Mom from herself. Alas, there was no field of dreams. Even worse, the logistics of getting Mom in and out of bed without unleashing the "charge of the light brigade" across her rib cage was daunting. The certified nurse assistants (CNAs) were well-trained and exercised extreme caution as they handled Mom with utmost gentleness; her fragility demanded nothing less. Even so, her grimaces and occasional screams were hair-raising.

As painful as bed embarkation and disembarkation were, Mom wasn't allowed to remain parked there during the day for extended periods. For stabilization and support for walking, she was loaned a human-propelled vehicle for use while hospitalized—a used walker with low miles. This piece of "senior-appropriate" equipment was received with a profound lack of enthusiasm. The therapist who delivered it prevailed. Mom was given instruction, passed the "operator's test," and was required to "drive it" with close supervision from the therapist. The walker represented tangible proof that life had changed. This was hard for Mom to accept. Undeterred, she was doggedly determined to meet the challenge with the idea the walker wasn't necessary. She viewed it as a temporary pain in the neck instead of a much-needed aid.

Sitting long hours with Mom in the hospital was taxing. I probably didn't need to be there as much as I was. It was hard to break away. The weight of my confinement with Mom was lightened by Max and Lois, who brought lunch and provided relief any time I needed a few hours away. To avoid a tiresome commute each day, I set up camp in Mom's house, where I spent the nights.

Mom remained hospitalized for three days, and a protracted recuperation was promised. New challenges resembled thunderstorms on the horizon. Now what? Mom's dismissal from the protective care of hospital professionals represented the beginning of an eye-opening pilgrimage in caregiving. Unquestionably, she couldn't be left alone, and hiring private duty, 24/7 sitters wasn't feasible—cost was prohibitive. We were advised Mom would require assistance and ongoing therapy for about six weeks in a home setting. The gravity of the six-week sentence reverberated. Staying in her house would be a major complication for me, the designated caregiver.

With Max on board, though with reservations, Thomas and I made the decision to bring Mom to our house in St. Augustine. She was hesitant. She didn't want to be away from her home, friends, and her doctors. I understood, yet felt Mom was being unreasonable. After all, if I was willing to be her caregiver, it should be according to my terms. It took a smidgeon of convincing, but Mom came around. She would be receiving in-home therapy in familiar, nonthreatening surroundings, and I wouldn't be pinned down in her house. Confident, I assumed it would be a manageable assignment that could be handled without much fanfare. After all, I was a veteran with two weeks of experience from my tour of duty the year before.

In retrospect, taking Mom in at this point was ill-advised. She should have been placed in a skilled nursing (rehab) facility for her initial period of recuperation. Mom had begged us to not place her in rehab, and I convinced myself I could handle the task. I didn't have a clue of what I had stepped into.

I Won't Pay with Cash Again

Since Mom's first walker was on loan for her to use while hospitalized, she needed to obtain her own means of transit in order to remain mobile without posing a security threat to herself. I was advised Medicare would approve payment for a new walker, provided a physician prescribed it. This is normally a straightforward process. It wasn't. The prescription was faxed to the supplier, and they verbally confirmed Medicare had approved payment. All I had to do was pick up the walker and remit a sixteen-dollar copay. When I arrived, the clerk couldn't locate any record of payment from Medicare. Yet the walker had been pulled from inventory, with my name on it. An unpaid invoice was attached and I was charged the full amount—eighty dollars. It was almost closing time. Mom needed the walker, and I was in a hurry. Stupidly, I paid the specified amount in cash. The clerk detached the invoice from the walker, wrote something on it, and placed it in my hand. I gave it a dismissive glance and bolted out the door with the walker. Mom was scheduled to be released from the hospital the next day, and getting the walker beforehand was my primary concern. Once the supplier's bookkeeping caught up with Medicare paperwork, I expected to receive a refund.

The situation progressed from irritating to ludicrous. A few weeks later I received a notice from Medicare showing they had paid for the walker. Hooray, I'll be getting a refund! I continued to read the notice and saw where a sixteen-dollar copay was due the supplier, which was reimbursable by secondary insurance. At this point, the copay was a relatively immaterial technicality. I pulled the invoice, which was in a sock drawer (my filing system is unorthodox), and read it. The invoice didn't indicate I had paid as much as a penny. The clerk had scribbled, "Picked up by customer." That was it. I should have taken a moment to peruse it before dashing out the supplier's door.

I called the supplier and they verified receiving payment from Medicare. When I requested a refund for my initial cash payment, they stated there was no record of it. And, to add a second layer to the cake, the individual who handled the transaction was on long-term disability leave. Dumbfounded, I asked why they would have allowed me to skip out the door without paying for the walker. I was informed, "Mr. Vicarson, Medicare had paid for it, except for the copay." Strangely, the supplier didn't bill me for the sixteen-dollar copay, which according to their records, was due. I didn't offer it; they had initially been given eighty dollars.

While my tale of woe was politely received, it lacked sufficient credibility to warrant a refund. I had nothing to support my position and wrote it off as a lesson learned. Even worse, I concluded the individual who received my cash payment had deposited it in her purse. This chapter had a footnote.

Nearly a year later I received an improbable yet apologetic phone call from the supplier; they were processing a refund. I was astounded. Accidentally, an auditor found the receipt showing my eighty-dollar payment—it had been posted to someone else's account. Somehow, the receipt had been parked with unrelated papers in the abyss of a miscellaneous file. My vindication exceeded the financial restitution in importance, although I gladly accepted the money. My reimbursement was sixty-four dollars. They subtracted the sixteen-dollar copay, which secondary insurance reimbursed. Easy arithmetic, though a complicated process.

The moral of the story is twofold. I shouldn't have jumped to the conclusion of eighty dollars being pocketed, even though circumstantial evidence suggested guilt. Second, it pays to review receipts when received.

Reality Hits

It didn't take long for the nuts and bolts of caregiving to prove my initial assumptions false. "Prior service experience" had been grossly overrated. My caregiving role a year prior had been a walk in the park by comparison. The first three weeks caring for Mom were a killer. I was her 24/7 bodyguard, butler, pharmacist, nurse, secretary, cook, clothes washer, and dish washer. I seldom left her side except when she was sitting or sleeping. My days—and nights—were exhausting. I felt and looked rung-out on some days. Envisioning the endpoint of her recuperation kept me focused on better days ahead.

Medicare provided in-home therapy visits three times weekly, and they were invaluable aids to Mom's rehabilitation. The therapists exhibited patience and a genuine interest in Mom while she chiseled at the mountain, one chip at a time. Her progress was ploddingly slow yet measurable.

I slept on our living room couch, a few short steps from Mom's bedroom, where even the slightest creaks awakened me. Sleep was transient. My fear of her falling in the middle of the night thwarted my ability to find a dream-filled interval. Mom usually got up twice during the night to go to the bathroom, and I suspected she might attempt it without calling me. She *did* try it once, but couldn't find a way to wiggle or slide out of bed without help. During the attempt, her squirming and grunting awakened me.

"Mama, what's going on? Do you need to get up?"

"Yes, but I didn't want to bother you."

Her concern for my lack of sleep exceeded her own well-being, and I reminded her the consequences of another fall could be disastrous.

Each bathroom trip, whether at night or during the day, was a ten-minute misadventure Hollywood writers could have scripted. It took a few minutes of gentle pulling and controlled turning, in slow movements, to get Mom out of the bed. The slightest miscalculation thrust her into outer space—and *any* move seemed to be the wrong one. I remember seeing Mom, steely and resolute, cry three times in my life. Getting her out of the bed when pain from broken ribs overwhelmed her was one of those occasions. There was no "yellow brick road" to be found.

Once she was up, I tightly held her right upper arm as we walked eleven short steps to the toilet. Walking was the easy part. Before she could sit, I helped Mom slip her pajamas down. On one instance, she told me, "Seth, don't you dare look at my sagging rear." And I didn't. Through it all, she still flashed her ever-ready, keen sense of humor. Methodically and with precise intent, Mom bent her knees and began the delicate task of lowering herself. She grasped the windowsill with one hand while I stabilized the opposite side by gripping her upper arm with both hands. "Seth ... hold it a second and let me catch my breath. I can barely stand this." A few moments later she squarely docked on the waiting seat, and I walked out of the room.

After an inordinate wait, I received the all-clear message: "Seth, I'm done. You can come in." Hallelujah, mission accomplished! Almost. I had to get her back into the bed, which required the same arduous process we had endured a few moments before—in reverse. Whoever coined the phrase, "Getting there is half the fun," hadn't taken this trip.

Prior to my self-appointment as Mom's caregiver, I had been accustomed to receiving eight or nine hours of sleep each night. That got blown to the wind. Significant sleep loss became an unexpected and unavoidable nemesis. I was the pilot *and* flight attendant assigned to Mom's nightly roundtrip, "red-eye flights" to the bathroom. Every morning I was exhausted *before* crawling out of the bed. Lost sleep remained lost since my genetics weren't programmed for afternoon napping.

Bathing was a logistical challenge, though less formidable than the dreaded bed. I installed grab bars in the shower, covered the floor with a nonskid pad, and positioned a shower chair within range of the showerhead. Thanks to the occupational therapy provided by therapists, Mom was able to shower and dry herself. This in itself was a major victory. Dressing and undressing were chores for Mom. I extended a helping hand when needed, which was most of the time. With a bit of logistical forethought, we managed to avoid embarrassing situations in the process.

At about the three-week mark, Mom's pain level began to diminish. She needed no assistance going to the bathroom, with dressing, or getting in and out of chairs. The bed was stubbornly less forgiving. Mom still required hands-on assistance, yet was able to sleep without wincing at every move. Her accelerating response to physical therapy was inspiring, particularly for someone 98 years old. Mom's unwavering determination didn't go unnoticed as I watched her transition toward self-care; she was relying less on me and more on the walker. The distinct clanks of this four-legged conveyance announced Mom's increasing cadence as hesitant shuffles transitioned to confident steps.

Mom's sprouting self-reliance was evidenced by her expressed intentions to return home soon. As her progress gained traction, I continued to prepare her meals, wash, dry, and fold her clothes, and dispense her medications. It was a full-time, though thankfully, temporary job. By the end of the fourth week, Mom felt she was ready to return home. There was no argument from me. The physical therapist concurred and arranged for the remaining two weeks of in-home therapy to continue in Jacksonville. I moved Mom back to her North Jacksonville house during the third week of June 2016.

Again, as was the case exactly one year before, Mom's return to health was quicker than expected. She was less self-sufficient than she had been, yet still seemed capable of living alone with occasional support provided by Max and me. How much longer Mom could live in her house was a prevailing question my brother and I couldn't dismiss.

Four weeks of down-in-the-trenches involvement in caregiving had been enough to provide me with a key takeaway: I had become emotionally and physically frayed in a relatively short time ... and I wasn't bucking for an encore. The experience had "wised me up" to the complexities of caregiving and the all-encompassing nature of the commitment. Caring for Mom had gobbled up my time, and the strain on my overall well-being was a wake-up call. I had underestimated the task and overestimated my resilience.

Mom's recuperation with us included bright spots. Thomas frequently sat with Mom during the four-week ordeal, giving me one- or two-hour breaks. These "mini vacations" were lifesavers, paving the way for me to attend a church service, run errands, or go to the gym. The importance of being able to step away cannot be underestimated. I found that any diversion was helpful. Thomas' acts of mercy were a direct contributor to the maintenance of my mental stability and overall physical well-being. He was and is a saint.

An Epiphany for Mom?

Mom had harbored an underlying disapproval of the relationship Thomas and I had been blessed to share for over thirty years. Her feelings had never been overtly displayed and, through the years, she had consistently been cordial toward Thomas. Unfailingly, Mom had included him when she hosted family gatherings. The "unspeakable" subject was one not to be brought up by Mom or by me. It was plainly an uncomfortable topic for Mom, and it wasn't in my nature to force a discussion. So I didn't. Many times, "airing out the laundry" does more harm than good. Life has taught me that.

Actions, when borne from the heart, can be change agents *to* the heart. Thomas' extension of his love and care for Mom allowed her to see him through enlightened eyes. I think it changed her perspective. Mom seemed to come to an acceptance of Thomas, and our relationship, which had previously eluded her. On a subsequent occasion, she told Thomas she loved him. What a milestone.

The time Mom and Thomas spent together during her stay with us gave them the opportunity to forge an unlikely bond. Good can be borne from bad and this facet of Mom's recuperation proved it. This was personally gratifying and brought me immeasurable joy.

CHAPTER 3

DRIVING MISS DOT

Mom successfully navigated her car with relative ease and proficiency until she was 99. While her driving was mostly limited to points of interest in the neighborhood, she occasionally drove outside the immediate area. The most distant was an eight-mile drive north on I-95 to drop off or pick up friends at the airport or shop at the adjacent River City Marketplace. This is a major shopping and dining haven for anyone living in Jacksonville's northern reaches. However, Mom's increasing balance challenges put a stop to her shopping excursions unless Max or I was with her.

Intentionally, Mom kept a full plate ... no dust collected on her shoes. She had volunteered at St. Vincent's Hospital for twenty-three years, relinquishing her purple vest a few months shy of her 99th birthday. Teetering balance, neck troubles, and a diagnosis of early-stage macular degeneration in one eye forced Mom's hand. Since her driving route to the hospital included a five-mile stretch on I-95 south and a flirt with the I-10 interchange, the deal was sealed. Her driving on I-95 in both directions ceased. So we thought. I later discovered, by Mom's forced admission, her occasional trips to the shopping area near the airport hadn't stopped. This is a story unto itself and will be afforded special attention in a few pages.

Unlike the character in *Driving Miss Daisy*, Mom didn't need a driver when her years suggested otherwise. It might seem ill-advised for Max and me to have allowed her to continue driving as long as we did, but Mom's physiological age and capabilities belied chronology. We occasionally rode with her to assess her driving skills. Our verdict was unanimous: Mom was competent behind the wheel.

Mom was five-foot, one-inch tall—as reported by her—at the apex of her vertical development. Her height became a challenge in driving when osteoporosis began whittling her down. She was around 80 when it became bothersome. Instead of having an unobstructed view *over* the steering wheel, she was almost to the point of peering *through* it. Her peripheral sightlines were becoming impaired. Mom recognized it was less than an ideal situation and improvised a corrective strategy. Undeterred, she inserted a three-inch-high pillow in a pillowcase which coordinated with the car seat color and commissioned it for use in her car. Her worthy seat accompaniment provided the necessary elevation she had sought and continued in the role for years to come. Mom had grumbled about being short waisted (relatively long legs and a short torso) for as long as I can remember. Fortuitously, this condition allowed her feet to reach the gas and brake pedals even with the seat-elevation enhancement.

Mom's height continued to diminish as the years advanced. When she was 90 and topped out at four foot, eleven inches in height, a second pillow adjustment in her car became necessary. This time around, there was less concern for aesthetics. A one-inch-high, brown corduroy cushion Dad had used for back support in his desk chair was reassigned to the car. Once again, Mom was elevated to a loftier perch where she could play in the traffic without fear of running into a nearby vehicle. This arrangement successfully served Mom as she continued to defy the norms. When she was in her mid-90s, we were made aware of motor vehicle challenges unrelated to her height.

A memorable chapter involving Mom and her 1998 Buick LeSabre occurred *in* the garage. I think the commotion occurred in 2012, when Mom was 94. She forgot to open the garage door and clobbered it while attempting to back out. In the bat of an eyelash, the door was fashioned into a bent, dislodged, and inoperable piece of steel. Poor Max. My unsuspecting brother got the call from Mom, requesting his assistance. She explained something was wrong with the garage door; she couldn't get it to open. When he inquired about the particulars, she suggested he should come over and see for himself. Mom expected he could disengage the car from the entanglement and fix the door. Given my uselessness in dealing with anything mechanical, I was off the hook, thankful my talents required less fuss and muss than what's necessary to resurrect a bashed garage door.

Max did not disappoint Mom. The garage door was no match for my over-the-top capable brother, whose many-hours-long labor resulted in it being returned to full operation … twice. Mom inflicted a second, less lethal dose of disfigurement to the garage door in an encore performance about a year later. Mom's garage doors didn't have a stellar relationship with vehicular incursions even prior to her assaults. Her three-years-younger sister ran into a previous door twenty years before. She was creeping up the driveway and hit the gas instead of the brake. The outcome needs no further explanation. State Farm replaced it.

Mom called me one afternoon to advise she had been involved in an incident at the Pollo Tropical, a fast-food Cuban place. The establishment was eight miles from her house, near the Jacksonville airport, and she had trekked up I-95 to get there. But wait a minute. She had supposedly stopped driving on the interstate when she resigned from the hospital volunteer gig the month before. Mom sounded okay, but that didn't keep my heart from skipping a few beats. I visualized she had been knocked down in the parking lot and her purse stolen.

She had a penchant for "spinning a yarn," which is great for storytelling but dispensable when reporting an incident possibly involving personal or vehicular injury. As she dove deeper into a lengthy monologue, I lost patience and asked her to get to the bottom line. Characteristically, she retorted, "You need to hear all the details to understand exactly what happened, so hold your horses." I held them—and my tongue.

The bottom line was shared after Mom completed her recitation of immaterial details. She hadn't been robbed. While waiting in the drive-thru for her roast pork with yellow rice and black beans, she fell asleep. While slumbering, her foot fell off the brake and the LeSabre rolled into the back of a Chevy Malibu. Curiously, the jolt didn't wake her up. She was awakened by a gentleman knocking on her window. Startled, Mom assumed he was trying to break into the car. Eventually, he persuaded her to crack the window. When he asked Mom if she was all right, she declared nothing was amiss and inquired why he was asking. He warily broke the news about the mishap, suspecting this "little old lady" might require special handling. Mom was stunned and couldn't believe she had come close to knocking his car into Georgia. There was no damage to either vehicle. Mom assured the driver of the car receiving her "hello" she simply had fallen asleep. They both drove off, uninjured, with wafts of Havana permeating their vehicles.

Since she and the car had survived without a scratch, I avoided having to fight forty-five miles of traffic each way to check her out. It was troubling that she had fallen soundly asleep in her car. I recalled Mom had recently mentioned she was falling asleep at odd times during the day. She conjectured narcolepsy (a sleep disorder) might be the culprit. Unconvinced, I attributed her dozing off to night-owl habits. Mom had a habit of staying up late, getting up early, and wasn't one to nap. A year later, we found out something else was going on. It wasn't narcolepsy.

Following "the Cuban caper," Max and I prevailed upon Mom to cease driving on I-95 in either direction. She had reached the same conclusion. We began driving her anywhere she needed to go, other than places within a few blocks of her house. This left Mom with four destinations where she was allowed to drive: the hair salon, her church, a neighborhood grocery, and the home of a close friend. She could negotiate all with relative ease and caution … until she proved me wrong.

Caught

It was my week to tackle Mom's shopping at Walmart. She wouldn't be with me, which was becoming the rule rather than the exception. I dreaded having to battle the hordes of humanity, all of whom condensed on *my* aisles. It was a characteristically oppressive and breezeless summer morning with layers of humidity suspended in lifeless air, clinging to anything it touched. It seemed inhumane to leave the habitable confines of my climate-controlled Subaru for the unavoidable transfer across the simmering asphalt desert. Not wanting to be a heatstroke victim, I forged ahead until reaching the gush of cooled and dehumidified air flowing from the gates of the "celestial city." I didn't mind running this errand for Mom (okay, I grumbled to myself), since the stifling heat and crammed store were potential traps for a 99-year-old woman.

It was an effort to focus on my shopping task while ambling through the store. I was preoccupied with something else involving Mom. Prior to the shopping excursion, I had dropped by her house to retrieve and review her lengthy shopping list. Max and Lois were out of town for a few days, and Mom was in a rush to leave so that she could retrieve their mail before attending an event at her church. Before dashing from Mom's house, I opened the garage door. Her recent history with it suggested the added precaution was prudent.

I plopped into my car, which was parked behind Mom's LeSabre, and watched her settle atop her carefully constructed front-seat nest. Predictable preliminaries commenced as I watched her finagle the rearview mirror down and sideways, lean toward it, and inspect and pick the front and sides of her hair—again. It had been no more than a few minutes since she had completed the morning ritual of reconstructing her coif with surgical accuracy in front of her full-length bedroom mirror. What the heck did she miss? It was a never-ending source of befuddlement. I decided her hair arranging deserved a name: *floosing*. Mom was *floosing* her hair. Sounds similar to *flossing*, except it's not a dental procedure.

At last, she returned the mirror to its appropriate-for-driving position and the taillights illuminated. I expeditiously exited the driveway before being pushed out by Mom. Moments after I left the house, a rumble of thunder snagged my attention. A second clap greeted me a couple of minutes later as I turned north off Tallulah Avenue onto Main Street. This is a lightly traveled four-lane thoroughfare a few blocks from Mom's house. After I drove less than a mile on Main, sheets of water about two hundred feet in front of me descended from the sky without warning. Within a few seconds, a torrent of rain blinded me, instantly turning the dry pavement into a lake. I had slowed to about fifteen miles per hour when a beige flash zoomed past me in the left lane as we crossed the Trout River Bridge. Whatever it was forded a sizeable puddle that generated a tidal wave. My windshield was immersed and the baptism left me looking for a life raft.

A few seconds later I was able to identify the offender. It was Miss Dot—my mother! I watched in disbelief: She steered the LeSabre to the right lane only a few feet in front of me and weaved between the yellow stripes that delineated the lane's barely visible boundaries. I feared her car would hydroplane, jump the right curb at the base of the bridge, and end up in the alligator-occupied marsh. It didn't. Her final maneuver on Main Street was a sudden swerve back into the left lane to make a left turn. She nearly missed it.

I was riled and followed Mom a quarter mile to Max and Lois' house. Their neighborhood had dodged the deluge.

Mom was surprised to see me walking up to her car, which she had parked in the driveway. She asked, "What are you doing here?"

My response had an edge as I asserted, "Mama, don't you realize you were all over Main Street and driving too fast?"

She answered, "Seth, if I had been advised it was going to rain, I would've stayed home. I have more sense than you think. Before I had a chance to slow down, the rain was coming down so hard I couldn't see the lines. I almost missed my left turn ... and for your information, I wasn't exceeding the speed limit."

Her statements were true, painfully so. Her vision was apparently not as sharp as we thought—maybe she needed new glasses. She should've seen the impending rainstorm and slowed down in advance. This wasn't the case. The posted speed limit surely didn't apply to such hazardous road conditions. Relief that Mom—and I—had survived in one piece cooled my irritation and shifted me to a lower internal gear.

Mom Folds, Game Over

A few weeks after Mom's near calamity on Main Street, she began fretting about her driver's license renewal. It would coincide with her 100th birthday in a few months. She had misgivings about being able to pass the vision test. This was attributable to her sight in one eye being slightly compromised by early-stage macular degeneration. Her overall ability to drive in fair weather wasn't in question, particularly in the few square blocks constituting her world. In spite of this, time wasn't on her side. A halt to her driving days was coming soon. Until then, she was "certified" to drive *in favorable weather* to her aforementioned neighborhood hangouts, and nowhere else.

Mom added a third pillow to the car seat's ascending tower of power. She appeared to be sitting on an uneven stack of nonconforming pancakes. Her latest seat fix created a logistical complication that had been lurking on the horizon: her leg length was no longer sufficient to account for the jacked-up seat height. The pedals were barely within reach of Mom's foot. She tipped us off to the rising dilemma when she asked if there was some sort of pedal attachment to make them taller. I wasn't aware of any such accessory and, even if there was, we weren't going there.

This latest development, coupled with Mom's slowly declining eyesight, spurred us to begin conversations with her to permanently apply the car's brakes. We wanted it to be her decision, but expected our once freewheeling, self-sufficient mother to put up a fight. She didn't. She surprised us by making the decision before being coerced. Mom stopped driving in July 2017, six months prior to her 100th birthday. This was a major lifestyle change for her, Max, and me. We began to chauffeur Mom to multiple destinations except her church; her friends graciously took care of that detail.

When Mom stopped driving, she chose to keep her cherished LeSabre safely tucked into the garage and her car keys stored in her black purse ... just in case. We respected the psychological component and didn't force her to sell the car. It represented security and had provided twenty years of dependable transportation.

Mom never inserted the keys into the ignition again. Max maintained the car until the following year, when car insurance costs nudged Mom to let it go.

Rearview Mirror Perspective

"Don't criticize a man until you've walked a mile in his moccasins." This Native American proverb gained significance when Max and I allowed Mom to drive as long as we did. Possibly, our friends questioned Mom being behind the steering wheel as long as she was. Admittedly, there were times when I had made similar judgments about "old" drivers. Mom changed my perspective.

I recalled times when impatience had commandeered my higher self while driving. Being trapped behind a vehicle poking along at thirty where the posted speed limit was forty-five drove me bananas. When the opportunity finally presented itself and I was able to pass the perceived obstacle, I couldn't resist peeking into the trudging car to get a view. It wasn't unusual to see an elderly, slumped-down driver tightly grasping the steering wheel with both hands, holding on for dear life. One thought would temper my pause from patience: someone's mom, dad, or both were the occupants, and my impatience was exchanged for empathy. Nowadays, the poking driver is likely to be someone distracted by a cell phone ... and empathy isn't the emotion that comes to mind.

Determining the right time to extract a cake from the oven is primarily a function of adhering to the recipe. Unfortunately, there isn't a straightforward recipe for determining if and when a parent's car keys should be taken. It's not always a unanimous verdict if Mom or Dad is on the jury. And one of them usually is. When driving privileges are revoked, it's a new world filled with challenges for the parents *and the kids*. We had been fortunate. Mom's finely honed adaptation skills, coupled with adequate support from family and friends, enabled her to continue enjoying a meaningful life without crippling interruption when she stopped driving.

What happens when there's limited or no outside support? Or family members are a thousand miles away? This all-too-often occurrence repeats itself with predictable regularity, leaving elder Americans to fend for themselves. It's a dilemma packed with ethical as well as logistical implications. Answers are sometimes elusive.

A Twist to Mom's Macular Degeneration

It was a Saturday morning when Mom awakened to a troubling change in her vision. It was the same eye previously diagnosed with dry-form macular degeneration. Mom was spending the weekend with Thomas and me, and she mentioned her vision had become partially shaded by an irregularly shaped curtain that had been dropped. On Monday morning, I drove her to the retinologist's office in Jacksonville. The news was unsettling. Mom's previously slow-moving, dry-form macular degeneration had transitioned to the wet form; a blood vessel in her eye was leaking fluid, distorting her vision. This form of the disease inflicts damage at a rapid pace, but there's reason for optimism. If caught early, the disease is treatable, and Medicare covers the majority of costs.

Mom was administered a grisly sounding yet tolerable eye injection to arrest the leak. There's a downside: injections aren't a one-and-done type of treatment. They must be continued on a periodic basis or leaks can rapidly progress, causing irreversible damage. Mom initially needed an injection each month. When her condition stabilized, injections were reduced to every eight weeks. Occasionally, the frequency of her injections was modified when deemed necessary by the physician.

She responded favorably to treatments. The "curtain" that had obscured her vision gradually dissipated and her sight returned to acceptable acuity. Soon thereafter, a routine eye exam revealed wet-form macular degeneration in the other eye. This came as a surprise; Mom hadn't noticed any visual changes. We were off to the races again, with a second schedule of injections. Since each eye was on a different timetable, injections weren't scheduled on the same day. The logistics of getting Mom to the doctor's office was a chore consuming most of the day. It necessitated a drive from St. Augustine to North Jacksonville to get Mom, followed by a backtrack to South Jacksonville for the appointment. Once Mom was released from her appointment, the same trip in reverse awaited. It was an exercise that burned 120 miles roundtrip, frequently in heavy traffic.

I grew to dread the appointments, which frequently were complicated by long wait times in the doctor's waiting room. On one occasion the doctor had been called out on an emergency, and we sat in his office four hours. Most visits were one and a half to two hours long.

A disruptive medical obligation had been introduced into Mom's life—and ours. Max and I shared the responsibility of taking Mom to the appointments. We strived to mitigate the unpleasantness surrounding eye injections with something enjoyable. How about fried shrimp? This was one of Mom's favorites, and we made a point to incorporate whatever Mom wanted into the day's agenda. The injections greatly slowed the progression of the disease, and Mom's central vision remained intact. Our efforts to preserve Mom's vision were repaid many times over.

Chapter 4

One Hundred Candles

Mom loved a party, and her 100th birthday screamed for a celebration. She was outgoing, engaging, and had multiple contact points with individuals from all walks of life. Her church, volunteering, and the neighborhood where she had lived since 1948 were major incubators of friendships. Consequently, many of her friends lobbied for a birthday party. The event had been proposed well before the let's-have-a-party bombardment began.

Party planning wasn't in my bag of tricks; however, Mom's church threw a lifeline Max and I thankfully accepted. The fellowship hall was suggested and we secured it ten months prior to the January 2018 event. Ample parking and easy access made it the perfect location. Additionally, the church had outstanding in-house food service and preparation; we were overjoyed to let them do it all. Of course, Max and I covered the costs. What about decorations? Mom's Sunday school teacher and church friends saw me as a deer in the headlights and suggested that I let them do it. No arm-twisting was necessary.

We decided a Saturday date would be ideal even though Mom's actual birthday fell on a Sunday. We desired a time when most people could attend and concluded early- to mid-afternoon should be ideal. So the hour was set, and Mom's gala would be billed as a drop-in from two o'clock to four. Selecting an appropriate mid-afternoon menu was a significant detail that required hammering out. Even though it wasn't a lunchtime affair, we wanted food options to be delightful and substantial enough to prevent anyone from being hungry.

I was asked: "How many people do you wish to invite?" Coming up with a number was a guess and we didn't want to slight anyone. Mom was truly beloved. Depending on the number of invitees, we concluded attendance would range from seventy-five to a hundred, perhaps a few more if weather conditions were favorable. January in Northeast Florida could be sunny and eighty or downright blustery and cold—a wild card for sure.

To avoid mailing invitations to Mom's church friends, we opted to have RSVP invitation cards printed and distributed at the church six weeks prior to the event. We mailed fifty to individuals who weren't part of the church crowd. Within three weeks, the number of people who had confirmed to attend was more than 300. The number swelled to 400 by the following week. We were flabbergasted. The church fellowship hall could easily accommodate a crowd much larger, so space wasn't a worry. The food service director requested a final estimate one week in advance and the number was 460. We wanted to provide sufficient food quantity to serve all guests, yet didn't want baskets of leftovers either. I wondered how many of the 460 would show up. It was a juggling act.

Sunny and Sixty

After months of planning, the appointed Saturday arrived. I was anxious and excited, expecting the event to wow Mom. It was a cold morning, yet had warmed to sixty degrees by the 2:00 p.m. start time. The chill was tempered by unobstructed sun and windless conditions— graciously benign.

I had expected Mom might need some nudging toward timeliness. Not so. Her hair was ready for presentation with all quadrants handcrafted and frozen in attentive obedience. As was usually the case, Mom was a study in impeccability. She had chosen to wear a black, half-sleeved blouse adorned with silver flecks, a silver scarf, and black dress slacks. It all played perfectly with her mostly silver hair, still thick with natural black highlights. She was our queen for a day!

Mom, ready for her 100th birthday party.

We zipped into the church parking lot forty-five minutes early, eager to see the transformed fellowship hall. Outside the front wall of the building, we were greeted by a hard-to-miss, three-foot-high, twelve-foot-long *HAPPY 100TH, DOT* sign. Max's son and daughter-in-law had procured it, thinking it would make a splash from a distance. It did. An even bigger splash awaited inside.

As we walked through the spacious fellowship hall lobby, our eyes were guided to a red mirage in the distance. Red-clothed tables with ample seating were positioned well behind the food tables, also cloaked in red. Multicolored balloons throughout the room wafted in invisible currents created by air escaping from ceiling vents. An eight-foot table, topped by a multitiered display of fruit, was a work of culinary artistry. Varying cuts and shapes of watermelons, cantaloupes, and pineapples cascaded to the tabletop. Additional food tables were equally eye-popping with an abundance of savory eats. The decorations created instant drama and were perfectly designed for a festive air.

Throngs of friends, young and old, flowed into the hall to join the burgeoning crowd. Mom was seated in the front of the room, where she could greet well-wishers as they entered. Many stories were shared and Mom was showered with affection. Tummies were full and leftovers sparse. Mom's jubilee had been flawlessly planned and orchestrated; it was a success by any metric … the most important being Mom. The event was a sensational birthday present for Mom and one of the best investments in her joy we could have made. It was one heck of a celebration. The final tally of partygoers was 500.

It's May … Run for Cover

I'm not one to lend credence to jinxes, but May's approach and its past association with significant medical events for Mom left me pondering the subject. I hadn't received any specific forebodings from the tea leaves lying in the bottom of my kettle. However, it was impossible to ignore that anything could happen at any time, especially for someone 100 years old. Mom's past dalliances with cataclysms during the fifth month of the year weighed on my mind. My quickened respiration eased when the calendar page advanced to June. May 2018 had shown a much kinder face than its previous iterations. In fact, Mom's health was stable and she continued to demonstrate an unusual capability to live at home alone, with assistance from her church friends, Max, and me.

The summer sun continued to shine graciously on Mom as the ensuing months pointed favorably toward fall—my favorite season. In unerring predictability, September dawned hot and steamy—conditions that weren't and still aren't agreeable with my physiological programming. One might think a Florida native with seven decades of exposure should have immunity to these meteorological elements not fit for human habitation. Perhaps my maternal grandmother's Canadian heritage was passed to me in the form of a preference for cooler climes. Nonetheless, seven months out of the year were glorious and this was enough incentive to remain living in Florida. During the hot months when self-imposed hibernation was generally the rule, I sought an occasional breather in a locale offering the promise of a livable external environment. My liberation was at hand!

I had completed packing for a long-planned trip to Germany and France, where four friends would join me. A twelve-day excursion awaited, including a seven-day cruise plying three renowned bodies of water—the Rhine, Moselle, and Main Rivers. I was scheduled to depart on Monday morning, September 17, 2018, for Nuremberg, Germany. All travel-related boxes had been checked. Euros—enough for busses, taxis, and trains in Europe—were safely concealed in a money belt. I had checked, rechecked, and rechecked again to make sure my passport was on top of my suitcase. No doubt this obsessive monitoring was due to disturbing dreams of checking in for an international trip and discovering I had forgotten my passport. This horror had never occurred. Although, in 1983 I had the misfortune of forgetting to pack underwear for a trip to Breckenridge, Colorado. Buying underwear was an easy fix. Passports ... not so.

At five thirty on Friday afternoon of September 14, my world unexpectedly became a Tilt-A-Whirl. Moments before, I had rolled into my driveway following a day-trip to Gainesville where I had attended a meeting at the University of Florida. Before my hungry, deflated body had a chance to exit the car, my cell phone rang. I could see Max's name displayed on the screen. I had expected his call and deduced it was relating to my trip. It wasn't. I was rocked with distressing news that Mom had fallen at home and sustained undetermined injuries. An ambulance was on the way, and Max was at her side. He said Mom was in staggering pain yet totally lucid. Anxiety gripped me as I considered, *Could this be it?* The *it* being the beginning of the end.

With adrenaline pumping, I ran inside the house, slung together two poorly constructed PB&J sandwiches, and gathered a few clothes and toiletry articles. I was back in the driver's seat in ten minutes. At least I would have something in my stomach for what would likely be a long night with no food access except for the rubbish-filled contents of hospital vending machines.

It was rush hour for the poor souls caught in the southbound highway frenzy and my compass was pointing north; I didn't have to fight for open spaces on I-95—a sizeable favor. I could feel my heart beating harder and faster than usual as I whizzed up the highway, smugly noting the unbroken cavalcade of humanity in crawling cars, pickups, RVs, and semis escaping south from Jacksonville. I judiciously freed the first sandwich from the plastic baggie and hungrily chomped down. With each bite, an ooze of jelly and peanut butter escaped the bread's safety, onto my fingers, which I had no choice but to lick. The sticky goo had also collected on the bread's crusted edges, requiring additional licking in an attempt to contain the spillage. In my haste to leave the house, I had failed to include a "glob blotter." I would have paid five bucks for a paper towel (full size) at that moment. Though messy, my dining experience while traveling up I-95 was a culinary delight. Maybe that's an overstatement. In any case, the plastic baggie housing the sandwiches found a second life trapping *some* of the mess.

As I mindlessly navigated my northward progression, I reflected on Mom's 100th birthday celebration a scant few months earlier. I was grateful we had capitalized on the rare opportunity to commemorate it, wondering if this latest incident would circumvent the need for 101 candles. Thanks to a steady tailwind, light traffic, and no "governmental" interruptions, I reached St. Vincent's Hospital—Mom's home away from home—in less than an hour. The hospital had become a familiar destination, a far cry from Nuremburg. I suspected my feet wouldn't be touching German soil any time in the foreseeable future.

After briefly seeking refuge in the men's room to wash the slime off my hands, I easily found my way to Mom's compartment in the ER. Max was standing at her side while the same caring physician who had attended to her in May 2015 checked her vitals while waiting for the orderly to take her for X-rays. The translucent oxygen tubes slithering across the bed into Mom's nostrils flashed me back to 1978, when Dad was first hospitalized with asthma and struggling to breathe. The passage of forty years hadn't softened the memory.

The physician suspected fractured ribs and a back injury, an assessment corroborated by Mom, the always on-duty nurse. Mom's heartbeat was erratic and her blood pressure topped 200, possibly attributable to pain and worry associated with the unknown component which serious injury poses. It was one of those rare times when Mom was visibly alarmed.

Mom was communicative and able to recount the event resulting in her collision with the unforgivingly hard floor. She had been sitting on a stool at her kitchen counter when she apparently fell asleep and tumbled sideways to the floor. The impact awakened her to breath-grabbing chest and back pain. Incapacitated, she was unable to get up. Somehow, over the course of two hours, she managed to scoot, on her back, in tiny increments to the dining room where she could reach a portable phone and call Max. I didn't ask why she hadn't pressed her medical alert button. The answer was glaring … she wasn't wearing it. I made no comment, though quietly seethed; it was water under the bridge and the bridge was failing.

We had attributed Mom's increasing spells of falling asleep during the daytime hours to a trifecta of old age, boredom, and a habit of routinely staying up late. We were wrong. As it turned out, she hadn't drifted to sleep when she fell from the stool or when she plowed into the Chevy Malibu at the Pollo Tropical drive-thru. Frighteningly, she had passed out from diminished blood flow to the brain, caused by a slow heartbeat.

For years, Mom had been aware she had a condition called bradycardia, a slower than normal heartbeat. No known problems had been encountered until this most recent event. Mom's heart rate was a scanty sixteen beats per minute when the paramedics reached her. Sixteen beats a minute are barely enough to keep a person alive. There wasn't any question why she had been "falling asleep."

The X-rays showed Mom had five fractured ribs, all on her right side, and a compression fracture in her spine. The lung wasn't punctured. That would have been catastrophic. Medications to boost her heart rate were marginally successful, raising it to the low thirties—enough to keep her engine charged, but well below the target of sixty beats per minute. Her blood pressure came down to a manageable level and she was stable.

It was necessary for Mom to be admitted as an in-patient. Except there was no room available. We were advised she might be stuck in the "holding pen" all night. So we waited in the cramped, uncomfortable, and sometimes noisy space while watching the monitors that confirmed her status of being alive. Two rigid, white plastic chairs—probably manufactured with school cafeterias in mind—complemented the sterile, high-tech cubicle motif.

We waited until midnight, when Max and I agreed one of us should go home and get some sleep. So I took flight and crashed on the couch at Mom's house. Max called at seven o'clock that morning to report Mom had been transferred at two thirty to an intensive care room close to the nurses station. He left shortly thereafter. I wondered how a room became available in the middle of the night unless the previous occupant had "gone to glory." Hopefully, this wasn't the case.

I hauled myself back to the hospital, arriving in time to meet the cardiologist who had been called in. Mom knew the guy, which was no surprise; she knew everybody. He was affable, 40-something, and tall enough to be a basketball player. The doctor was reassuring when advising Mom she needed a pacemaker. He mentioned he had recently successfully implanted a pacemaker in a man 103 years old. Mom was three years younger. With no hesitation she authorized the procedure and confidently said, "Schedule it, I'm aware of the risks." I had no idea what to expect, yet believed Mom could withstand the operation. After all, she was invincible.

I had no choice but to cancel my trip, grateful Mom's accident occurred *before* I had arrived in Europe. Getting back from Germany or France on an emergency basis would have required me to find my way to an unfamiliar airport in an unfamiliar country, alone. A king's ransom would likely have been exacted for a last-minute flight home; it would have been a royal predicament. I was deeply disappointed. A long-anticipated European excursion had evaporated, condensing into an odyssey not relating to planes, trains, or ships.

The Loon Lands

Without incident, the cardiologist installed a pacemaker in Mom's upper-left chest area the following morning while Max and I waited. The incision was about two inches long, with the outline of the device clearly visible beneath the skin. It performed perfectly and Mom's heart rate responded in kind. What a relief. She had two side effects from the anesthesia, both common: nausea and fuzzy-headedness.

Mom's pain level from the fractures continued to be intense, which made the pacemaker worriment fade in comparison. I expected she would become increasingly lucid as the day progressed, but the opposite occurred. By late afternoon, Mom began hallucinating. Evidently, her cerebral wiring had been short-circuited by a cocktail of drugs—all legal. Of all things, her "trip" centered on an arachnid invasion. The incursion was announced by Mom when she exclaimed, "Giant spiders are on the ceiling. Seth, get them out of here!" She was frantic and loud enough to elicit the concern of a nurse who came running into the room. I was unable to convince Mom there was nothing on the ceiling except white paint. She settled down when I told her I would spray the spiders with a can of Raid. The nurse explained that postsurgical hallucinations weren't unusual and were attributable to a combination of anesthesia and pain medications. Prior to the pacemaker surgery, Mom had expressed a fear of getting "loony" as a side effect to the drugs she knew would be administered. She nailed it.

Her hallucinations and general state of agitation prompted me to spend the night on a cot in her hospital room. I had never seen her in an unhinged mental state. She was almost to the point of being out of control. I feared she would attempt to get out of the bed … and she tried. At two or three o'clock I was awakened from a light sleep by grunts and moans from Mom; she was stuck in a contorted position in the bed, with her feet poked through the bed rails. I hailed a nurse via the assistance button on the TV remote. We were able to finagle Mom back into her fenced compound. Mom needed to urinate, hence her attempt to slip out of the bed. She didn't have the presence of mind to call for a bedpan.

I was up most of the night since Mom's agenda didn't include much sleep. Interruptions were frequent as marauding spiders invaded Mom's perceptions. Bedpan calls and beeps from the medical gadgetry in the room disturbed the peace with impunity throughout the night. Twice an hour, Mom's blood pressure was automatically taken by the ever-present cuff on her arm. Without fail, I rolled out of the cot to see how high or low the reading was, making sure the pacemaker was working. It was.

Dawn broke and Mom's hallucinations waned. A rough night ceded to morning brightness as filtered sunlight crept through the cracked blinds. It was an encouraging omen and she returned to lucidity. There was one aspect of her recovery that didn't compute: though now lucid, she continued to insist the room *had been* infested with spiders during the night. Her mind was fixed and I couldn't change it.

Mom's morning lineup of activities hadn't been divulged, although a visit from the cardiologist was expected. I referred to him as Dr. Wonderful since Mom referred to him as "simply wonderful." Earlier than I expected, Dr. W. bounded into the room to examine Mom. He was pleased with her heart's response to the pacemaker and her ability to answer his questions intelligently. Overall, she was responding favorably despite her internal scaffolding being in shambles. Dr. W. detected no cardiac anomalies and cleared Mom to begin rehab after breakfast. He mentioned Mom might be released from the hospital the next day, based on notes from the attending hospital physician. Neither Max, Mom, nor I had seen him. I reacted with astonishment and asked, "What? Isn't it way too soon?" Dr. W. countered that from a cardio perspective there was no reason to keep her. Anything outside of heart-related concerns was the hospital physician's call. It wasn't what I wanted to hear.

Dr. Rubion, Mom's hospital physician, sauntered in a few minutes later and introduced himself. He was perfunctory in his approach and displayed no warmth. He informed us Mom would be transferred from the intensive care unit to a private room later in the day. She received, at most, a sixty-second "examination" from him. He exuded an air of disinterest and didn't utter a word pertaining to Mom's possible release the next day. When I attempted to question him about the timing of Mom's discharge, dismissively he walked toward the open door while stating, "There's no reason to keep her for more than another day." I followed him out the door while expressing my concern about Mom's hallucinogenic episodes, a detail he apparently had missed. The brief pause in his forward progress and the blank look communicated indifference. He shrugged and resumed walking. In a matter-of-fact tone, he bellowed, "Be prepared." I contemplated, *Be prepared for what? Am I a Girl Scout?* I stood frozen, watching him fade into the corridor's background.

Mom was in considerably worse shape than she had been sixteen months prior, when she was hospitalized for three days with three fractured ribs—and nothing else. She was now beginning her third day of hospitalization and could barely move due to *five* fractured ribs *and* a spinal fracture. Releasing her the next day was befuddling.

Breakfast arrived not long after Dr. Rubion had fled to his sanctum. Mom was partially propped up on her left side at an angle in the bed, with three pillows for support—not conducive for eating. She was helpless and unable to reposition herself, and I was ill-equipped to handle her. I considered the logistics of getting Mom straightened and fully propped up in bed without killing her in the process. I hit the call button. Two nurse assistants promptly answered and positioned themselves on either side of the bed. After lowering the head of the bed to a flat position, they firmly held a loose sheet that had previously been placed under Mom. With synchronized precision they cautiously pulled Mom straight back. The head of the bed was raised, allowing Mom to bend at the waist instead of the middle of her spine. She was set for success. Let's eat!

Mom was able to use her right hand for light duty. She could feed herself! This was a gift when considering the fractures resided on the same side. Mom picked at her breakfast consisting of eggs (she detested eggs), grits (she loved them if floating in butter), toast, orange juice, and coffee. She took a few bites of toast and stirred the grits, eventually eating about a third of the mush before pushing it aside. She wouldn't consume anything else other than the coffee. Mom's palate was far from eclectic and she had numerous dislikes. The rejected eggs and juice were waiting for a certain death in the hospital dump, which concerned me. I had no choice but to rescue them; they found a warm home in my stomach.

Breathing exercises constituted Mom's first form of physical therapy. They began an hour after breakfast. Maureen, a fresh-faced therapist, entered the room with a smile and an upbeat attitude. She was tiny, probably in her late 20s, and hauled a jumbo duffel bag containing a myriad of "toys." She pulled out a lightweight, handheld plastic device called a spirometer. Mom and I were intimately familiar with it. Dad had used one twice a day for fifteen years. Now it was Mom's turn.

Maureen's size and demeanor belied her true persona. She was a taskmaster, exactly what Mom needed. Dutifully, Mom slowly inhaled and exhaled through the spirometer's accordion tube while being coached. Two things were evident: Mom was proficient in its use, and her lung capacity needed improvement. Maureen emphasized Mom would need to be vigilant with the exercises following her release from the hospital. Maureen's words, *release from the hospital*, reinforced my chills of what might be coming next.

Whew. Therapy was over for the day ... Mom thought. Not the case. Lung sprints were the tip of the iceberg. The real games were about to commence. While Maureen was packing up her bag of surprises, another therapist came in. His name was Tony. He was a cordial yet stoic type of guy, 30ish, and built like a ninja warrior. His mission, which surely would be accomplished, was to get Mom out of the bed. I thought, *Oh God, help us.* He had an even larger duffel bag than Maureen's. It was filled with belts, bungee cords, hooks, and unidentifiable gear suggesting torture in a dungeon. I wondered what might be inflicted on Mom.

The spinal and rib fractures should heal in a few weeks. The associated pain, sometimes agony, was scarier than the fractures. I held my breath while Tony lowered the overall bed height and eased Mom to the edge, where she was able to firmly plant both feet on the floor. I watched as if I were a student. He placed a canvas belt, several inches wide, around Mom's hips where he could safely hold and keep her steady. He faced Mom, remaining close. He directed her to gradually shift her weight to her feet while he held the front of the stabilizing belt. Haltingly, she stood up. Tony directed Mom to take slow steps across the room while he continued to face her, keeping the belt taut. They turned around and came back to the bed, where Tony stepped aside, allowing Mom to rotate and ease down onto the mattress. Tony had Mom repeat the exercise a second time and they were done. Even though hampered by considerable pain, Mom had performed the assigned tasks. It was far from a walk in the park, yet it represented a significant emotional lift. It was the first time Mom's feet had been firmly planted on the floor since her tumble. The steps she valiantly took were giant leaps, even though they were accomplished in distrustful shuffles.

Her most pressing obstacles were ahead, with the toilet—synonymous to Mount Midoriyama—yet to be conquered. The mount would remain unscalable until she could stoop securely. For the time being, the bedpan would remain a stainless-steel proxy. Mom held this piece of medical equipment in limited esteem. In her mind, it represented personal diminishment.

Lois relieved me in the midmorning. I vamoosed to Mom's house to shower and sleep, and returned around three o'clock to set Lois free. I remained at the hospital until Max reported for the night shift. I hoped it would be a peaceful night for Mom and Max. The night before hadn't been. Two dinner trays, one for Mom and one for me, were brought in at five o'clock. A comfort-food-lover's delight didn't remain on the tray for long; I devoured the assortment of pork chops, mashed potatoes, broccoli, salad, and a slice of apple pie. It was a feast for the famished. There was an added bonus. Mom displayed an appetite and ate a fair portion of her dinner. Things were trending up.

The beguiling early evening placidity was pierced by a sudden and unexpected breach when Mom excitedly pointed to the foot of her bed and hollered, "Seth, get them out of here!"

I had no idea what she was referring to and asked, "What are you talking about?"

She continued to holler: "Get those kids. Hospital regulations don't allow them to run amuck in the halls and I don't want them in my room."

I tried to diffuse her agitation, urgently insisting, "Mom, there aren't any kids in here."

She was adamant. "They *are* in here. You need to have your eyes checked. Can't you see them? Where are their parents? Go report them now!"

No amount of pleading or attempts to dissuade her made a dent. I was concerned she would try to get out of the bed in an effort to round up the imagined intruders.

The curtain had been raised on a world-class hallucinogenic onslaught that coincided with gathering late-day shadows. The unthrottled kids running in and out of the room were stagehands for the spiders, waiting for their performance cue. Once given, they returned en masse as goliaths for a second act. Holy cannoli, did Mom take a trip! She was farther "off the grid" than she had been with the previous evening's assault. Such bizarre extracurricular activities weren't supposed to be on the agenda, and I wondered what precipitated such discombobulation in Mom's brain. After all, her thinking had been without incident the entire day. Her psychedelic reprise was downright scary.

Early evening and nighttime plunges into altered mental states are common among individuals suffering from dementia. There's a term for it: *sundowning*. The term is appropriate since many disconnected behaviors associated with dementia coincide with the setting sun. Gratefully, Mom didn't have dementia, but was exhibiting behaviors as if she did. The on-duty nurse expected Mom would eventually return to her "full, upright, and locked position." I wasn't sure. The nurse attempted to assuage my concerns by saying, "Your mother will eventually get over this. It might be another day, a week, or possibly more." *Possibly more?* That gave me the shivers.

Typical for Max, he arrived right on time, in fact, a few minutes early. It was around seven thirty. I regretted having to alert him Mom had gone "nuts" again and a sleepless night might be on tap. The slumber party wasn't for me, at least for the time being, and I scampered home to St. Augustine. Complete disengagement in the form of real sleep awaited. There were no spiders, medical devices, or kids to awaken me.

My night was blissful. As feared, Max's was far from it. He called the following morning to report Mom had misbehaved. It had been another rambunctious night. He got no sleep. Zero. He told me she had drifted off for brief periods, but pain kept waking her up. Confused, Mom resumed her private war with proliferating spiders and unharnessed kids. Mom's delusional state created a treatment problem. Effective painkillers and sleeping pills were now off-limits; they could trigger an added dimension to Mom's expanding psychedelic experience. The only option to even suggest pain relief was ibuprofen, which was the equivalent of attempting to kill a dragon with a pea shooter.

Max and I had agreed to take turns spending the night with Mom, while Lois offered to sit with her for several hours during the day. We couldn't keep up our private-duty nursing for long and hoped

Mom would turn the corner—before we collapsed. I didn't think any worsening in her situation could occur, but it did. Another "circus" was lurking, waiting for the ringmaster to arrive. I clocked in for my dreaded round, not wanting to be there, feeling guilty for a less than stellar attitude. At least a befitting hospital meal bolstered me prior to the commencement of activities in the center ring.

The evening and night were abysmal. Right on schedule, beginning at seven thirty, Mom assumed residence in the "outer limits" once again with the return of her familiar castmates, which still consisted of rampaging kids and spiders. However, Mom dropped a significant clue that the tentacles of her delirium had crept into deeper crevices when she asked, "Whose house are we in? What are we doing here? Why am I not in my house?" "Crazy as a bat" was an appropriate characterization of her mental state, and I had no choice but to let the bat fly. It was a long night ….

To enhance the dynamic, Mom flooded herself and the bedsheets, necessitating a linen change during the early hours. What sparse stillness the night had offered was sabotaged, resulting in Mom being unavoidably jostled while two attendants did what was needed to keep her dry. Mom howled, "Stop it, stop it! This is hurting me." Even in her delusionary state, she was horrified to have urinated in the bed, and apologized profusely. Her dignity suffered a double body blow when she was placed in an adult diaper. It was heartbreaking to see my beloved mom in such desperate straits.

An Unexpected Visitor

The night had raised the misery index to a new level and, on cue, its horrors moderated before sunrise. If anything, Mom's overall condition seemed worse even though her heart was performing at sixty beats per minute as programmed by the pacemaker. Whiffs of breakfast wafting around the room nabbed my attention, but not Mom's. The bedwetting incident and lingering embarrassment were forefront in her thoughts. She was still feeling humiliated. As a secondary worry, she asked where the spiders and wild kids had gone. Instead of appealing truthfully to Mom's sporadic lucidity, I asserted the spiders had been exterminated and the kids were with their parents. It was the winning ticket. Previous attempts to convince her the invaders were imagined resulted in a pointless argument. We weren't going there again.

Where was Dr. Rubion? We wondered where he had been since my initial meeting with him. His absence was countered by the nursing staff who had shown genuine attentive concern. Since his cryptic statement a couple of days prior, advising me to be prepared, he hadn't given an ounce of guidance to any of us. We needed to be made aware of projected timelines.

A few soft taps on the door announced an early morning visitor prior to breakfast. Magdalena, a hospital social worker, came into the room. A floor nurse had suggested the visit. I welcomed any consultation and desperately needed a guide to steer us through whatever was coming next. It was disturbingly evident that Mom needed significant and continuing professional care. Magdalena suggested Mom's next step should be admission into a skilled nursing facility. In a split second, the comment hit Mom's "Pentium processor" and, with an air of certainty, she chimed, "You mean a nursing home. I don't want that. I want to stay here or go to Seth's house."

Mom's words echoed between my ears, bouncing back and forth for a few seconds while I sensed a rush of blood to my face. Magdalena empathetically pointed out that Medicare wouldn't pay for additional days in the hospital. Her next sentence needed no further explanation. "Mrs. Vicarson, the level of care you will need cannot be effectively provided by your son. You need to be in professional hands."

It was a harsh dose of reality for Mom. She became stone silent. The advice of the social worker was inarguable, and Mom's worst fears were going to be realized. My mind was going in a dozen different directions.

Magdalena had been a godsend and I was breathing easier. This was merely a pause. My breathing quickened again when she nonchalantly dropped a bombshell, leaving my mouth gaping: "Seth, please take my business card. Call me with your family's decision at your earliest possible convenience. Your Mom's discharge is expected sometime early this afternoon."

It was 8:00 a.m. In disbelief, I stuttered, "Today?"

She reiterated, "Yes, today. Weren't you or someone else in your family advised of this yesterday? Your hospital physician was supposed to have advised you."

I tried to conceal my ire, but the flushing in my neck was probable evidence my internal thermostat was about to blow. Magdalena was surprised to hear no one in our family had seen or heard from Dr. Rubion at any point during the preceding day ... and one of us had been there the entire day and night.

At a minimum, I had assumed Mom's release would be another day out. Her mental deterioration and fragile physical condition suggested it, and we hadn't been advised to the contrary. Magdalena's dumbfounding newsflash had me swirling. I felt backed against the wall, even panicky. I didn't know what to do or how to do it. There were too many loose ends to be identified and too few hours to manage them.

Magdalena easily read my bourgeoning exasperation and took a few minutes to provide some overdue direction. It was a relief to hear the process for Mom to enter a skilled nursing facility would be coordinated by the hospital. I surmised Dr. Rubion had authorized it even though he hadn't communicated this to Max or me. Magdalena would set the wheels in motion for Mom to be transferred to a qualified facility when I informed her which facility we had selected.

Time was of the essence. I called Max and we concluded a St. Augustine location was essential since I would be Mom's point person. Thomas and I were living there and, in a few days, Max and Lois would be moving to a new home which was halfway between Jacksonville and St. Augustine.

Both Thomas and I made a few calls, obtained intel from trusted friends, and narrowed the search. Two facilities made the cut and each had space available. Thomas disrupted his work schedule to visit them prior to noon. While he was conducting site visits, I scurried to Mom's house to gather additional clothes and supplies for her stay in the St. Augustine facility. A two- or three-week rehabilitation was expected. After rehab, all bets were off. I dreaded the possibility that her care might land in my lap again.

Thomas reported back before noon. The two facilities were equally clean and similar in size and appearance. Since Mom's primary focus was physical therapy, we defaulted to the facility holding a slight edge in that category—Forest Meadows. The location was a fifteen-minute drive from our house, which eliminated the commuting hassle to and from Jacksonville. What a bonus! The decision was communicated to Magdalena around noon, and I signed the authorization papers for Mom's transfer shortly thereafter. Magdalena couldn't tell me what time Mom would be discharged, but stated it could be any time. It became apparent that *any time* in "hospital speak" didn't necessarily mean what was implied.

The waiting game began, and Mom was none too thrilled about her impending transfer. She was upset with Max and me for "agreeing to have her put into one of those places." Her comment angered me; despite this, I kept my cool. I had been living on pins and needles since May 2015 and accepted that pent-up anger and resentment were part of it. Mom's latest incident, even though not preventable, reinforced my emotions. The hours passed and we sat, ready yet pensive. One o'clock, two o'clock, three o'clock … and not a word. Mom's hour-long rehab session in the hospital began at 3:00 p.m. This seemed strange, if in fact her discharge could be at any moment. I quizzed one of the nurses about the holdup and was advised the paperwork from Dr. Rubion hadn't been received. I could feel the smoke coming out of my ears and sarcastically responded, "It figures." I immediately regretted the statement and apologized to the nurse.

A few minutes before five o'clock, the phantom of the hospital opera—Dr. Rubion—appeared in Mom's room. I first considered he might be an apparition. The notion was dashed when he announced, "We're keeping your mother another night. I'm not satisfied she's ready to leave, but she will be tomorrow." This curious, startling statement buzzed through my barely functioning brain. I wondered when the decision to keep her had been made and why we hadn't been advised earlier. Surely, this wasn't a last-minute decision. I concluded the doctor had failed to check off Mom's name on the "passenger manifest" in a timely manner and the ship had sailed. Perhaps I was right. Perhaps not. I believed Mom's condition was such that she *should* be kept, regardless of the reason.

Unlike our previous interaction, the doctor was cordial and willing to answer questions. It was a moot point; few questions remained. They had been answered previously by the nurses and Magdalena.

I was startled at this latest soap opera twist, yet relieved Mom wouldn't be subjected to an evening transfer to St. Augustine. Max and Lois had made plans to continue packing for their move, thinking Mom would be in Forest Meadows and no one would need to stay with her. To my relief, he and Lois were able to switch gears, affording Max another opportunity to bunk in Mom's room of horrors for the night. Not in the mood to drive to St. Augustine, I crash-landed at Mom's house.

Gosh, did I ever sleep. Not like a log, since I'm not sure how a log sleeps, if it does at all. But I *can* relate to our beloved pug Bella who doesn't merely sleep; she passes out. Similarly, I collapsed into the caressing, overstuffed cushions of Mom's cut-velvet, 1970-era couch, which I considered the most comfortable in the world. (It was the last time I spent the night in my childhood home.)

I hadn't been advised when Mom would be released, but expected it would be late morning. Why I assumed this is anyone's guess; there was no foundation for it. I walked into her room early enough to see Max finishing the breakfast items of no interest to Mom. One glance at Max and I didn't have to ask. But I did. "Max, how was the night?" He told me it had been another theatrical extravaganza with multiple encores. I shook my head while gazing at the floor, wondering if and when the terrors might end.

Dr. Wonderful, the cardiologist, had checked on Mom before I got there and told Max the pacemaker incision was healing well and her vitals were excellent. He was encouraging and predicted her hallucinations would eventually resolve. I wanted to believe it, but sheltered doubts. Even though I dreaded Mom's departure from the hospital, this was offset by no longer having to commute to Jacksonville.

Max left, and I waited with Mom while we watched *Let's Make a Deal*, followed by *The Price Is Right*. Dr. Rubion came in to advise us Mom's release would occur after lunch. And we waited. At three o'clock, we were informed Mom would be leaving within an hour. This was my nod to grab her personal items and clear out. The skilled nursing facility was waiting for Mom's proof of insurance, power of attorney, and my signature on an abundance of documents authorizing a constellation of permissions. I darted to my Subaru and motored to St. Augustine before rush hour began in earnest. There was ample time to sign documents, meet staff members, and ferry Mom's belongings to her room.

After a five-day, $110,952 hospitalization which Medicare substantially whittled down and paid (other than a $1,340 deductible that Mom's Medicare supplement covered), Mom was discharged on September 19, 2018. I felt it was premature, yet received assurances she was ready for the next stop on her journey toward recovery. St. Vincent's had provided exemplary care, and our leaving the cocoon of protection was disconcerting. Mom's apprehension seemed to consume her. My own misgivings had to remain hidden. I was the head cheerleader.

At four thirty, Mom was safely delivered by a medical transportation service to Forest Meadows, situated in a pastoral, wooded area of town. Not surprising, the building was plain yet spotless, surely an attribute "Nurse Mom" would favorably note. The rehab unit was spacious, seemed appropriately equipped, and was well-staffed; my initial impression was favorable.

When Mom arrived, I made sure she saw me when the attendant swung open the back double doors of the transporter. An exuberant reception wasn't on Mom's agenda. She took advantage of the opportunity to express her displeasure of being "put into a nursing home." Since Mom had been riddled by confusion and was wracked by pain and fear, I tried to discount the remark. Nonetheless, her true feelings were troublesome and reinforced the guilt I had served upon myself. I attempted to smooth Mom's ruffled feathers by assuring her that rehab wasn't a permanent arrangement. I insisted: "You're here to get well and will be out of here in two or three weeks. Mama, you can handle this." I hoped the reassurance might stimulate a ray of positivity.

Mitigated Guilt

I'd never anticipated Mom, the human equivalent of the Energizer Bunny, would land in such a state of despair. Her contemporaries had suffered one of two fates: they required nursing care at much younger ages or died with little preamble. I had presumed Mom, particularly at her age, would fall into the "little preamble" category. This notion had been disproved and I shuddered at future implications. Surely I was prepared to steer Mom through skilled nursing. My career role prior to retirement gave me an invaluable opportunity to participate in numerous initiatives with senior facilities throughout the state. In some circles, I had been regarded as an "expert." A drastic adjustment to that falsehood was waiting to knock me into a new reality.

I loved Mom profoundly, always had. Surprising to some, she could occasionally be difficult, which belied her easygoing, composed, and considerate nature. Mom was fretful and a first-degree worrier. These traits were well-masked by her never-failing sense of humor, always on tap and disarming. A friend of Mom's shared a story pertaining to a hard-to-miss rosebud tattoo that blossomed on a young woman's upper-left breast. I was told the friend whispered into Mom's ear, "Doesn't leave much to the imagination." Mom couldn't let such a golden moment pass, and added, "Give her some time. It will turn into a long-stem rose."

As a registered nurse, Mom was objective in dealing with medical situations, with one exception—herself. It was heart-ripping to survey the inescapable quagmire swamping her. Yet when I conducted a rewind of events going back several years, it was evident Mom had exhibited a pattern of nonchalance and disregard for opportunities that would have enhanced her well-being. There was a laundry list: Mom's failure to wear the medical alert button won first place. Her penchant for noncompliance was no secret. Her refusal to use a cane or walker merited second place. Her refusal to drink water, as prescribed by her physician to combat frequent urinary tract infections, was third. Sweeping her driveway in ninety-five-degree heat received a dishonorable mention.

Mom had been responsible for stoking the fires, and her rebuffs to move to a safe, affordable, independent living community was another contributor to her predicament. Had she been less cavalier and open to alternatives, some of her miscues might have been avoided. When I allowed myself to appraise Mom's situation—at thirty thousand feet—I felt less guilty. Still, my emotional swings saddled me. One moment I could be angry and resentful and the next might find me depressed. I didn't consider professional counseling, but realized after the fact that I should have sought it.

My advice to anyone caught in the crosshairs of caregiving is to consider support groups and to possibly engage in the services of a counselor. Many services are available online. Check your private insurance or Medicare for coverage details and out-of-pocket costs. The references below may be of assistance:

https://www.medicare.gov/Pubs/pdf/10184-Medicare-and-Your-Mental-Health-Benefits.pdf,

https://www.aarp.org/caregiving/life-balance/, and
https://www.aarp.org/caregiving/local/info-2017/lgbt-resources.html.

Life is filled with *mights* and *what ifs*. This begs the question: At what point should a child force a parent to move? Maybe I'll figure it out prior to the time I reach a hundred. Mom had supplied some clues as a starting point.

CHAPTER 5

THE NIGHTMARE CONTINUES

With no downtime, Mom's stretcher was rolled from the transporter to her semiprivate asylum where she was cautiously shifted into the bed closest to the window. The oxygen generator was fired up and its maze of tubing created an instant bond between Mom and the machine. She looked around, tentative, agitated, and confused. Her attention was grabbed by unfamiliar surroundings, compounded by the inescapable misery created by multiple fractures.

The space was strangely familiar, similar to the room Mom's friend, Peg, had occupied some years prior in the memory care facility in Jacksonville. The bed next to Mom's was vacant, which proved to be a gift, or perhaps not. The room was bright, airy, attractive, and functional. Walls were ornamented by a flat-screen television, a picture depicting a beach scene, and a rectangular corkboard mounted next to the window. The room had one chair, handsome but uncomfortable. I took it as a suggestion to keep visits short. The upscale fabric and polished wood arms brightened the room, but lounging was clearly not part of design considerations.

On cue, a cute-as-a-button and bubbly activity director, Bambi, swooped in to extend a brief welcome, go over a packet of information, and ask a few questions. The glazed look in Mom's eyes communicated disinterest. I waited for Bambi to offer an Otis Spunkmeyer Chocolate Chunk Cookie or perhaps a bottle of Geritol. That wasn't in the cards, though either would have been an attention-getter. After she ducked out, I transformed myself into a megaphone and delivered an abridged account of facility features and available activities to Mom. I made sure the TV remote / call button was within easy reach and showed her how to operate it. I planned to go home for the night after she had eaten.

A meal tray was delivered not long after Mom had digested my rendition of the official welcome speech.

She moved the colorful assortment on the dinner plate around with her fork and exclaimed, "This food is awful! I can't eat this … what is it?"

In an upbeat voice, I introduced the meal selection: "Mama, your plate has delicious roast beef, creamy mashed potatoes, and soft-cooked green beans on it. These are things you like. I'll cut the roast into bites you can handle."

It was an exercise in futility. Mom barely touched anything on her plate and pushed it aside. I interpreted it to be a sign of protest. Hunger strike! Certainly, the overriding determinants of her dissatisfaction were threefold: she missed her home, was miserable, and had been thrust against her will into an environment she considered hostile—all of which I understood.

I scurried to the bathroom to set up Mom's toiletry articles, check supplies, and splash some water on my face. The off-white everything— walls, tiles, towels, and headlight-equaling fluorescents—accentuated my own "oldness" while I stood in front of the mirror, transfixed. The reflection was unforgiving. I looked haggard. It was impossible to dodge previously undiscovered wrinkles and blotches 69 years of living had forged. Bags and sags draping my bloodshot eyes completed the story. I wanted to run for a facelift. It had been a grueling day and I looked forward to meeting Thomas at a local Italian spot for dinner.

My hopes for "world peace" were dashed when Mom's voice abruptly sliced through the bathroom walls with the command: "Seth, get them out of here … tell them to go." I took a deep breath. Mom had again tripped into the sphere of altered reality, earlier than usual. I alerted the on-duty licensed practical nurse (LPN) to Mom's departure from "solid-state" and expressed a concern she might try to get out of the bed. It wasn't equipped with bedrails. Much to my astonishment, she advised me that bedrails weren't allowed in nursing facilities—they were considered a hazard. I didn't believe it, yet a quick search on my smarter-than-me phone substantiated it.

Mom's room was an uncomfortable distance from the nurses station, another reason for my uneasiness. Additionally, the facility staff seemed to be spread thin and might not be equipped to provide the level of watchfulness Mom might need. It was apparent she shouldn't be left alone, considering her faltering sanity. There was no telling what she might attempt during the night.

I expressed my concerns to the LPN, and she agreed Mom's mental state posed an increased risk for falling from the bed. Restraining Mom was an option neither the LPN nor I wanted. Undoubtedly it would add to Mom's misery, but might be necessary. In an effort to reduce the possibility of restraints, I asked for and received permission to stay with Mom for the night. My hopes to enjoy some quality time off the clock and dinner with Thomas evaporated. As a consolation prize, he brought me a hamburger. I scarfed it down while pretending it was a filet mignon.

Nesting in a Skilled Nursing Facility

Have you wondered what it might be like to live in a skilled nursing facility? I surely hadn't, but was about to be given a once-in-a-lifetime immersion. Mom feasted on a banquet of apparitions while her mind transmigrated in and out of the ozone layer. It had been four days since surgery and the beat still dragged on. I gave up trying to convince Mom her projections weren't real—I was too spent to deal with it. Slumped in the decoratively appealing yet inhospitable chair, I roused the TV from its slumber with a robotic punch of the remote button and was rewarded with instant distraction. But, that awful chair ... it was its own jailor, a thornlike reminder of what promised to be an interminable night.

With my own back infirmities to contend with, I couldn't buy an ounce of comfort. So I slid from the chair and ambled to the closet assigned to the unoccupied half of the room. Hoping for a rummaging bonanza, the fruits of my plunder were limited to a pillow and blanket. I returned to my chair with a semblance of upholstery materials and loosely molded them into the chair. It provided some cush for my tush. Shortly after I had resettled into my refurbished residence, Mom chirped, "Seth, I need to pee. The girl needs to come in here." How Mom could have the presence of mind to make a rational request while waging battle against nonexistent adversaries was baffling. A stroke of luck graced us when I caught a glimpse through the partially open door of a CNA (certified nurse assistant) passing by. I ran into the hall and requested her assistance. She responded: "I'll be back in a minute or two." Ten minutes later she came into the room, pulled the privacy curtain, and worked with Mom to place the bedpan into its appropriate position. The mission was accomplished with less fuss and muss than I had expected.

Beep-Beep-Beep

During the evening, Mom's confusion was heightened by unfamiliar surroundings. At times she became frantic, especially when hallucinations were in control. My presence had a calming effect and possibly kept her from injuring herself. Mom dozed off for brief intervals. When not sleeping, she was in pain, agitated, and confused. It was a repetitive cycle with no remedy. Each minute's tick was slowly followed by the next; the hours seem to freeze in time. My tuckered-out body parts affirmed the blanket and pillow fix wasn't designed for all-night duty. I frequently stood up and propped against the wall, in a daze. The TV had a hypnotic effect on Mom, seemingly providing a temporary shield against her perceived assailants.

Mom's flight to the wild side continued unabated into the advancing night hours, when I reached the bottom of my barrel of patience. During one of her skirmishes with enemy elements, exasperation overcame me and I yelled, "Mama, there aren't any spiders or kids in here. It's midnight and I need to get some sleep. Please zip it or I'm going to leave, and they'll have to restrain you." I walked out and wandered to the end of the hall which was flanked on both sides by a stretch of unoccupied rooms. Thomas stayed up late each night, and I called him from a vacant room. I vented for five minutes. It helped. When I returned, Mom had retreated to a rare dwelling place of quiet repose. (She wasn't dead.) I turned off the TV and left a dim light behind her bed illuminated. The vacant bed next to Mom didn't remain unoccupied. I gathered the blanket and pillow and moved to greener pastures.

I eased onto the sheetless, rubber-surfaced hospital bed next to Mom's, steeping like a tea bag. Submerged in deep contemplation, I was infused with various degrees of being pissed off. I envisioned an alternative universe, wishing for a bed securely tucked away on a river cruise floating somewhere in Germany. What an idyllic setting, a fantasy that almost was.

My nighttime daydream was upended before midnight by disconcerting bursts of shrill, closely timed beeps coming from down the hall. They were reminiscent of a fire alarm, but less ear-shattering. Still, the racket was raucous enough to wake anything sleeping within fifty feet of the source, including Mom. *Beep-beep-beep-beep!* The incessant nuisance signaled someone's distress. One minute, two minutes, three minutes passed. After five minutes, my mounting impatience drove me to crawl from the bed and peer into the hall for a quick assessment. I could see a flashing light above the door to the room next to Mom's and heard a clear call coming from inside: "Somebody, please help me. I have to go to the bathroom." I proceeded to the nurses station down the hall. No one was there, and I waited.

Several minutes later, a CNA came running down the hall and, after seeing me, assumed there was trouble with Mom. I steered her to Mom's next-door neighbor. The CNA was previously aware of the need, thanks to some sort of electronic secretary. She killed the untiring alarm while explaining that a staff associate had required her assistance with another patient. Mom's next-door neighbor received the necessary attention, and peace returned to the valley.

I surrendered to the confines of my confiscated mattress, but there was no rest for the weary. Mom started to unravel … again. I ignored it and she eventually calmed down. I earned, at most, three hours of sleep (with one eye open). Any spells of quietude were arrested by Mom's frequent moans and mumblings. There were two bedpan calls: 1:00 a.m. and another around 4:00 a.m. It wasn't my desire to wake the entire populace by utilizing the call button, which invoked the clamorous alarm. After considering options, I ambled to the nurses station both times to request assistance and received it. This wouldn't be the case later on.

With the unerring predictability of a Swiss train, Mom became clearheaded again with daybreak's arrival. Concurrently, I got another taste of skilled-nursing-facility frustration at 7:30 a.m., fourteen hours into the game. Mom's bladder was in full-speed-ahead mode, thanks to the diuretic pills she had been taking to reduce swelling in her legs and feet. This go-around, I asked Mom to press the call button—I wanted to measure response time. The world was already up and the beeps would be less bothersome than during sleeping hours. Mom's alarm cried for fifteen unanswered minutes. She wasn't alone. Additional alarms up and down the hall were singing, creating a not-so-melodious chorus. Undaunted, I retrieved the bedpan and, with Mom's guidance, positioned it. Mom didn't let the opportunity pass without a jab: "Now you see why I don't want to be here." I sure as heck didn't want to be there either.

When Mom's breakfast tray was delivered by a CNA, I asked why alarms had remained unanswered for such a lengthy amount of time. I was astounded to learn that bathroom calls were second fiddle to meal trays. Otherwise, meals would get cold. I thought about it and understood the rationale. Even so, the ratio of CNAs to patients wasn't in the patients' favor, particularly during mealtimes. Unfaltering alarms and waiting were included with the price of admission.

With a modicum of elation, we experienced a noteworthy victory at breakfast: Mom ate most of her grits, a piece of buttered toast, and drank a glass of orange juice. Exasperated and out of steam, I beelined home where I luxuriated in a ten-minute shower followed by a first-class breakfast—a bowl of oatmeal and a plate of scrambled eggs (the kind enhanced with vitamin D and omega–3 heart-healthy fatty acids). I considered throwing myself a pity party, but was too pooped to attend. I slept through it for two hours.

I returned to "the camp" after lunch, hoping to find Mom in reasonably upbeat spirits, and she was. She was adjusting to her new surroundings, though complained about the "lousy chicken concoction" served for lunch. I couldn't judge the merit of Mom's assessment and discounted her description.

Noticing Mom's supplemental oxygen flow had been scaled back, I asked her about it. The "head nurse," so described by Mom, had informed her the flow needed to be reduced. I had no idea who the "head nurse" was, yet expected our paths would soon cross. Another positive development: the swelling in Mom's feet and legs had noticeably subsided. This, coupled with Mom's reduced need for oxygen, were positive smoke signals—the pacemaker was breathing new life into my battered mother.

There was an additional reason to be encouraged: A therapist had visited Mom earlier and conducted an hour-long evaluation. Mom would be receiving in-room therapy visits beginning the same afternoon.

Hell Week

Mom required close watching, and the overworked staff members couldn't provide the level of oversight she needed. Accordingly, being retired and of questionable mind, I was self-conscripted into Mom's "care brigade." I felt it necessary to spend as much time as possible with her until she was mentally stable. Surely, the clouds would part and the sun would break through at any moment ... but that didn't happen.

My sentence, though self-imposed, would include a string of tedious nights plus an excess of day shifts. And on the seventh day, I intended on resting. After all, God set the example.

I sought to mitigate the challenging undertaking of balancing my own well-being and sanity against Mom's. Obviously, Mom's needs were more immediate. I wanted to dodge the responsibility but couldn't. Even so, remaining captive on a 24/7 basis was plainly impossible. So I carved out time for myself during periods when Mom was lucid and could safely remain unattended.

It was advisable for me to monitor Mom when her meals were delivered, to encourage her to eat. With this in mind, I awarded myself two "vacations" each day: one in the morning from about eight o'clock to ten thirty, and an early evening respite from around six to eight. This restorative personal time was burned before I realized it and, occasionally, it was necessary for me to stretch it a bit. Twenty-five to thirty minutes of each "parole" was appropriated for transit time to and from the house. The remaining time was utilized for napping, taking showers, eating, catching up on mail, ferreting through Mom's bills and my bills, scheduling and canceling appointments, shopping for essentials, and attempting to squeeze in a few minutes for exercise.

I was grateful that Thomas usually had dinner ready. He was also my trusted counselor when I was scouting high buildings for a possible jump. Occasionally, I purchased a meal at the facility when Thomas had to work late. The food wasn't fantastic, yet was generally passable and gave me a yardstick to measure Mom's negative fare reviews, which I learned were jaded. Admittedly, there were a few meals that shouldn't have been released from the kitchen.

Mom's physical therapy sessions were scheduled twice daily: midmorning and midafternoon. I made a point to meet each therapist and observe Mom's response to their rehabilitative techniques. Mom's first full rehab session began with breathing and balance exercises, followed by sitting, standing, and walking short distances. The therapy methods and protocols were similar to those I had observed in the hospital. Mom was pushed to attainable limits and she fully cooperated. On the second day, the afternoon therapist disconnected the oxygen—it was no longer needed. Mom's heart was leading the charge with life-sustaining regularity.

At this juncture, Mom's familiar and formidable adversary was pain. Intense bouts were readily communicated by guttural gasps, particularly upon standing and sitting. Tackling these two basic building blocks of mobility and self-reliance proved ambitious, as Mom's back injury refused to go unnoticed. With assistance, ever-persevering Mom managed to stand. Once on her feet, she pushed through the next task—walking—while relying on her walker for stability and balance control, with the therapist within inches of Mom.

Mom's romp with disaster was considerably worse than in May 2016 when she had three rib fractures. Consequently, her rehab was intensified. I couldn't help but project what might lie ahead. I worried about Mom's expected release in a couple of weeks, maybe three, fearing her care might once again fall in my lap. I secretly hoped her stay in the skilled nursing facility might be extended, even though Mom wanted to be shown the exit at the earliest possible moment.

She continued to insist she would be returning to her home in Jacksonville. I applauded each of her halting steps marching toward recovery, yet was careful to not offer false hope. The likelihood of Mom living alone in her home again was nil. She would require sitter assistance, which was unaffordable on a long haul, and Max and I would be too far away to easily check on her. I spoke to one of the physical therapists about Mom's lofty expectations and they agreed to help her recalibrate them.

Since Mom couldn't easily sit down or stand up, the toilet remained an off-limits sculpture. Its position as an inelegant art object would have to remain for the time being. The therapists advised me the "sculpture" would be returned to its intended use as specified by the inventor when Mom's strength returned.

In the meantime, my sometimes off-center musings allowed for my own inventiveness to surface. The thought crossed my mind that with a spot of sanitation, the toilet could be repurposed for foot washing. It made perfect sense. I visualized pouring an appropriate quantity of a fragrant, therapeutic agent into the bowl. It had to be a blue liquid. Picture the fascinating visual effect of the blue "syrup" slithering through the calm clear water, effortlessly swirling to the bottom of the bowl, filtering throughout the porcelain lake. This in itself might invite a moment of meditation. Foot refreshment could be accomplished by an initial soaking, followed by sloshing them around in the bowl. Flushing a time or two should deliver an instant rinse, all accomplished while seated on a stool.

If nothing else, my whimsical improvisation was a reflection of my need to retreat to a mindless, seldom-tapped locale. Surely, Mom hadn't encountered any problems with her recent traipses into far-out sectors. As a salute to her, I conjectured it was reasonable for me to float in the clouds for a few minutes.

Mom's compromised balance and overall frailty were complicated by another debilitation—dowager's hump, also called kyphosis. Never heard of it? Don't feel rained on. It's an upper spinal disfigurement and in Mom's case was the result of osteoporosis (bone loss). For Mom, the condition caused a severe hunchback. She was unable to hold her head up, forcing her to look down when walking. Consequently, her visual perspective was restricted, further compounding the balance dilemma.

It was saddening to watch Mom struggle while she grappled with becoming one of those "bent-over ladies." The tiresome condition caused her to be uncomfortable and created embarrassment. However, there was another side to the story. Mom had a prior opportunity to slow down the progression of her postural deformity. When she was 98, she was aware of her head beginning to tilt forward. Her physician ordered a round of twice-weekly in-home physical therapy treatments for six weeks. I drove to Mom's house to observe one of the therapy sessions. The exercises were straightforward and not difficult. Balance and muscle strengthening in her upper back and neck were the primary targets.

The therapist was crystal clear in explaining the exercise regimen was a daily requirement. "Mrs. Vicarson, I'll be here two days a week. You'll need to continue doing the exercises on your own the other five days. Do you understand?"

Without hesitation Mom answered, "Oh yes."

Mom's compliance was hit-or-miss. I called Mom daily, sometimes twice, to check on her progress. The following phone conversation typifies Mom's approach to the outlined program of self-therapy:

"Hey, Mama, have you had a good day?"

"Yes. I've felt okay, but haven't done much of anything. I intended to go through some old papers, but didn't."

"Did you do your neck exercises?"

"Seth, you don't have to remind me. I haven't had time to do them yet, but will."

"It's five o'clock, Mama. Why haven't you had time? When are you going to do them?"

"I'll do them when I get to it."

"You told me you forgot to do them yesterday. So, will you at least *try* to do them today before you get settled in for the night? The therapist will be with you tomorrow and she's going to ask."

"Yes, Seth, I know. I'll do them later."

I surmised she wasn't going to follow through, and she didn't. *Later* didn't come until the therapist arrived for the session the following day. Not surprisingly, Mom scuttled the exercises after the six-week course came to an end. To my annoyance, she commented that the physical therapy hadn't helped. Of course not! She hadn't done the exercises.

Since Mom was in the custody of Forest Meadows, she couldn't hide from twice-daily therapy sessions. Given her current state of affairs, neck therapy wasn't a consideration even though her deformity was increasingly pronounced.

As the days—and nights—dragged on, I struggled to keep my head above water. Max and Lois had been confronted with a litany of unforeseen setbacks relating to their in-progress move, chaining them to their property. Thomas helped me when he could, but a demanding, full-time law practice kept him pinned down. Two cousins who lived in St. Augustine gave me a few hours of relief on several occasions, which were a godsend. These gestures, though insignificant in their eyes, were significant in mine.

I made an effort to befriend facility employees, all of whom I genuinely liked, with perhaps the exception of one CNA who openly paraded a sour demeanor. While anyone's lack of enthusiasm for slinging meal trays, changing urine-saturated sheets, and cleaning rear ends is understandable, certain personality types are better suited for this undervalued work than others.

The LPN (licensed practical nurse) assigned to Mom was a no-nonsense, efficient professional named Vivian. She was in her 50s and originally from New York. After all, this *is* Florida, which *everybody* recognizes is a satellite location for the Empire State. I grew to respect Vivian's expertise and dedication. I *did* question her assessment of a medical development ten days into Mom's recuperation. This will be explored later.

Mom was frequently seen by Hope, a registered nurse (RN), and also by Marie, a nurse practitioner (NP). Think of an NP as a super nurse with a master's degree (or higher) in nursing, with the authority to write prescriptions, order tests, and render diagnoses. Both women were caring, infused with warmth, and consummate professionals. Marie was the individual Mom had initially dubbed the "head nurse."

The physician associated with the facility wasn't the warm, fuzzy type. He visited Mom perhaps once a week, expending three or four minutes per visit. He listened to her heart and lungs, and took a quick peek at her ankles while projecting a hurried, disinterested attitude. I surmised his role at the skilled nursing facility wasn't his primary consideration. Whether or not his routine services were truly necessary couldn't be answered by me. Observably, Marie provided frequent visits and a higher level of care. She displayed genuine concern for Mom and her care was dispensed with a dose of reassurance.

Got Cranberry Juice?

It was discouraging to see no improvement in Mom during her first few days in rehab, despite concerted physical therapy efforts. She was losing weight and her overall mental condition seemed to be worsening. On schedule, hallucinations commenced each evening when the outside light began its daily ebb. Some were accompanied by her attempts to exit the bed, which I thwarted. Mom's escapes into insanity continued off and on until three or so in the morning. That's when *my* "sleep time" began, lasting until 7:00 a.m., when the facility came to life.

A new adversary—daytime confusion—introduced itself to Mom on day four at Forest Meadows. Something was off. Mom ate little of anything and drank no liquids unless coerced. This wasn't a new development, but had become increasingly problematic. Mom's disdain for drinking liquids, including the flavored varieties, was well-documented. There were two exceptions to her eating aversion—desserts and fruit juices. In other words, sugar. No prodding was required. At least a few empty calories could be counted on to fuel Mom's sputtering cylinders.

I assumed the role of mealtime sheriff in Mom's room, usually on duty to coach and push her to eat. Occasionally she was on her own during lunch, when responsibilities called me from the post. There simply wasn't enough time in the day to do it all. Understandably, the frenzied CNAs weren't deputized for this type of time-consuming duty, and Mom might take a full hour to finish a meal—assuming she ate it.

Mom had been fever-free throughout the entire tribulation. This changed when she began running a low-grade temperature, coinciding with the onset of her daytime confusion. Vivian, the LPN, suspected a urinary tract infection (UTI). This was nothing new. Mom's refusal to drink enough fluids to keep her "waterworks" performing optimally was legendary. When challenged, she wasn't hesitant to point out she had forgotten to drink it, or that drinking water made her go to the bathroom too frequently. This last one says it all. Undeniably, numerous UTIs had been part of Mom's medical landscape for years and, according to my mental notes, she was overdue. This time, it came with a twist.

Vivian pulled me aside and told me she had put in a call for Marie to come over. As a warning, Vivian said, "I'm fairly sure she'll need to catheterize your mom in order to get a urine sample. It's an unpleasant procedure, but I haven't been successful using ordinary means." I dreaded it for Mom and anticipated her reaction would be less than favorable. I was wrong. She didn't complain and braved the five-minute procedure while I imagined how much it must have hurt.

Got water? Sorry, Mom. The answer is yes. The CNA brought water several times during the afternoon and evening and required Mom to drink it. There was an additional option for Mom to enjoy—cranberry juice. If Mom had a UTI, this simple prophylaxis might hold the infectious critters at bay until they could be microscopically identified and a targeted antibiotic started.

Ejection

The night following Mom's catheter procedure was a jam-packed mess. A roommate surely wouldn't have appreciated the turbulence. I was grateful the extra bed next to Mom had remained unassigned. Mom's UTI-agitated bladder, unaccustomed to an influx of fluids, begged for mercy. Accordingly, Mom had frequent urges to urinate. All … night … long. I had become a pro with the bedpan and found it more efficient to tend to Mom's needs than round up a CNA.

One unexpected, positive development occurred that night— Mom's hallucinations got sidelined. This was offset by a worsening level of general confusion. Throughout the night she had no idea where she was and questioned why we were "in a hotel." With insistence, she pleaded, "Seth, take me home. I want to go home in the morning." Her moans, mostly from pain, continued to keep me in alert mode. There was no telling what might be next.

Morning came and I was frazzled. Breakfast was delivered around seven thirty. In a daze, I watched Mom twirl her fork through the eggs and grits while protesting, "I can't eat this mess. I hate eggs and the grits need butter and salt. There's no extra on the tray." I hustled both condiments from the dining room and added them in quantities sufficient to bring life to the defenseless grits, per Mom's request. Mom's taste buds wouldn't be the only thing to take notice of the added salt. Her blood pressure would surely "taste" it as well. I figured, *What the heck*. A check later in the morning revealed an acceptable blood pressure.

Mom ate the grits and a piece of bacon while downing a glass of tangy-sweet cranberry juice. When I was satisfied no further progress was forthcoming, I departed for Shangri-la—my own bed. As I was leaving, Mom asked, "What time are we checking out?" I replied, "Not yet," and kept walking. This exit strategy had worked for Dr. Rubion at St. Vincent's Hospital and it worked for me.

I slept through Mom's lunch and returned late in the afternoon, feeling less of a zombie. I hated to see she had been placed in a diaper. No explanation was necessary. I presumed she'd unconsciously lost bladder control or couldn't get bedpan assistance fast enough. In the meantime, the test results had come back and, as suspected, Mom had a significant UTI. Oral antibiotics were prescribed for seven days and the first pill had been dispensed during lunch.

Mom's looniness during the afternoon made me wonder if a serious brain disorder was in progress. I asked Vivian if the physician should be called, and she assured me Mom's confusion was coming from the UTI. It's baffling that Mom's bladder could somehow affect her brain to the degree it did. Mom hadn't exhibited confusion with prior UTIs, but this installment was exacerbated by a host of complicating factors that perhaps predisposed her to the "added attraction."

Staying with Mom night after night was a lesson in patience, endurance, and appreciation for the staff who worked in the nursing facility. The education exceeded anything I could have obtained in a classroom. Of course, I wasn't there to receive a certification, but considered awarding myself a sheepskin before *I* needed to be admitted. I continued to persevere, hoping Mom would turn a corner. Until then, I intended to do whatever was necessary to safeguard her. There was no telling what she might attempt as long as the "out-to-lunch" warning was affixed to her forehead. At some point, someone would occupy "my" bed and, selfishly, I hoped it would happen at the earliest possible moment. Mom's care had all but taken me down and I was over it. A roommate would, in effect, be a default guardian. Great for me, not for the roommate. Although, Mom might be a guardian for the roommate as well.

With dread, I watched the elongating shadows cast by the trees outside Mom's room. The shadows had become messengers, signaling another skirmish was possibly at hand with spiders, out-of-control kids, and—heaven forbid—new combatants in formation for the next attack. What a way to cap the day … but please, not prior to mealtime.

I could hear the squeaking wheels of the dinner cart coming down the hall. Tantalizing whiffs suggested a beef dish was on the way while we waited for the trays to enter the room. Mom prejudged the meal and proclaimed, "It won't be good." This was before her fork had a chance to spear what was being served. I had ordered a tray for myself and it was delivered with Mom's. She remained nonplussed. Once she observed me inhaling the gravy-swamped Salisbury steak and mashed potato sidekick, she decided to explore further. The suggestion registered and she dug in with a degree of gusto. On a "gusto scale" of one to ten, she clocked in at six. I witnessed a miracle of sorts when she declared the dinner to be pleasing.

Darkness fell upon the earth and I beheld yet another miracle. The expected evening hallucinogenic offensive hadn't yet materialized: a curious lull. Though Mom's confusion hadn't abated, she wasn't embroiled in imaginary hostilities. At least not yet. I waited … and anticipated. Maybe bombs bursting in air would be next? The assault never happened. Mom's cerebral circuit breakers held firm and blocked the advance.

Since Mom was in a diaper, it was necessary for her bathroom calls to be handled by a staff member. Changing a diaper was *waaaay* too personal in nature for me to do. Around one thirty in the morning, Mom "needed to go," and I walked to the nurses station to round up a CNA. She was filling out paperwork and responded within a couple of minutes. I hadn't considered their jobs required the completion of substantial paperwork.

At four in the morning, I was stirred from light sleep by conversation in the room. An LPN I hadn't met and the CNA who had provided assistance at one thirty were performing a routine check on Mom. One asked Mom if she needed to use the bedpan. She did. I inquired if something was wrong. In a raised voice, the LPN roared, "Sir, you need to get back to your room. You're not supposed to be in here. Who are you?" Unbelievably, she was not aware of my frequent presence in the room. I explained who I was and why I was there, only to be lectured that facility rules prohibited overnight visitors.

I was dumbfounded to hear of *the rule*, and that it had taken someone seven days to uncover the infraction. But wait a minute ... I was Mom's caregiver, not a visitor. Wisely, I deduced this defense wouldn't be well-received and didn't offer a rebuttal. I silently rested my case on the blue rubberized mattress supporting me. The "bouncer LPN" exercised leniency and didn't lead me out by the ear. I was allowed to remain an "illegal" occupant for the remainder of my "shift." Except for the unpleasantry, my night had been substantially better than the one before.

Later in the afternoon, I spoke with Vivian about the terse lecture the startled LPN had given me. Vivian verified the four-in-the-morning FYI was correct. She stated the rules had been bent because Mom's overall condition had been precarious. Needless to say, I didn't check in to the "hotel" for overnight accommodations again. One ejection was sufficient. Fortuitously, the pause in Mom's hallucinations was no fluke—they never returned. I believe the timing was providential.

As hoped, the antibiotic performed admirably. Mom's confusion evaporated by the third day and, by the fourth, her urine was painlessly flowing. Not to be shortchanged, she took the full seven-day antibiotic regimen per FDA guidelines.

Back on Track ... for a While

I was ecstatic to be released from overnight duty at Forest Meadows. Nonetheless, my days remained consumed with Mom's care. Her decades-long pleadings to never be placed in a nursing facility haunted me. Mom's fear wasn't the "garden variety"; it was a deep-seated phobia. In her view, people in nursing facilities were "throwaways," frequently forgotten and left to die alone. I believed her shadowed perspective contained some truth. She had seen a lot. Through the years, Mom had observed helpless living skeletons who were the victims of strokes, dementia, and undisclosed ravages usually associated with old age. These types of afflictions forced them into nursing facilities for long-term stays when there were no alternatives.

Mom's angst was related to her prior observations from visits to nursing facilities and had little to do with Forest Meadows. Certainly, there have been well-documented instances of intentional abuse and unacceptable conditions in some nursing facilities, but I believe these are outliers. I wanted Mom to feel secure and have confidence in Forest Meadows as a place for rehabilitation. My goal was to demonstrate she hadn't been forgotten. I continued to be present each day from about eight in the morning till six in the evening, with a two- or three-hour break during lunchtime.

At the same time her UTI faded, Mom began to make chartable progress. She took sustained walks in the hall with the therapist closely guiding her movements. Mom regained the ability to sit in a chair and stand up. This was monumental! The way was paved for her to claim victory over another antagonist—the toilet. It had been a lofty goal, yet one Mom ardently pursued. "Potty training school" was scheduled in another day or two. I began to breathe with increasing sighs of relief as we approached the two-week mark.

Mom required ongoing bolstering to counter her frequent mentions of how awful "the place" was. It wasn't, and negative comments irritated me to no end. Her challenged physical condition was the true source of the *awful* designation, not the facility. Occasionally, I brought lunch or dinner to Mom from an outside source. She seemed to appreciate intermissions from the humdrum house offerings even though her appetite was close to nonexistent. Considering her overall condition, she probably wouldn't have eaten haute cuisine even if it had been served on fine china.

C What?

As the UTI found its place in the annals of Mom's medical history, a replacement was waiting to assume front and center attention. Mom had been plagued with mild constipation concurrent with her stays at St. Vincent's and Forest Meadows. This wasn't a major concern and was attributed to the aftereffects of anesthesia, physical inactivity, antibiotics, and drinking insufficient amounts of water—Mom's favorite nonobservance. The relative quietude of her slumbering intestines came to an abrupt end on day twelve at Forest Meadows. They became electrified while I was enjoying the last of an afternoon lunch break at home. When I returned, I didn't have to be told she had become a natural disaster site. The odoriferousness of the occasion precluded the need for a formal introduction. Vivian was in the room. She asked me to leave for about a half hour while she and the CNA got Mom—and her surroundings— cleared of hazmat and decontaminated. I gladly accepted the invitation and fled to the nearby visitors' lounge where I found sanctuary. Twenty minutes later, Vivian sounded the all-clear signal and gave an account of the afternoon excitement.

Good news came first. Mom's UTI was clearing and the diaper had been replaced by a less offensive piece of protective equipment. Mom was overjoyed. Briefly. Regrettably, the timing proved to be premature. The most recent breach, which was far worse than the urinary spills had been, wasn't contained. I couldn't fault anyone for a lack of clairvoyance. Vivian said she had obtained authorization to dispense two loperamide pills (generic Imodium) for diarrhea control, and promised me Mom would be closely watched. I thanked her and took a moment to ask a question that, unintentionally, struck a dissonant chord.

Mom's explosive diarrhea raised a red flag, and I asked Vivian if Mom might have contracted *C. diff* (*Clostridium difficile*). It's a nasty, sometimes hard-to-control intestinal infection. My comment didn't land in receptive territory. Vivian became defensive, bordering on gruff, when she advised me *C. diff* was unlikely. She insisted Mom's poop didn't have the characteristic smell or color and the episode wasn't severe enough to suggest it. She emphatically stressed that strict sanitation protocols had been followed "to the letter." Her bristled reaction rendered me speechless. Vivian had interpreted my questioning to be an inference that Forest Meadows was at fault for Mom's condition. I profusely apologized and expressed appreciation for the care Mom had been given.

Though I was confident Mom's diarrhea wasn't the result of improper sanitation, the pings on my internal radar had been activated by two prior introductions. First, my personal and professional visits to nursing facilities had provided a general familiarity and respect for *C. diff*. Second, a friend my age had nearly died a year prior from *C. diff* while a patient in a Jacksonville hospital. Her illness piqued my curiosity and I pursued a deeper dive into the subject at the time. I learned the disease was highly contagious and targets the vulnerable in nursing facilities, assisted living facilities, and hospitals. Curiously, many exposed people don't get sick; however, there's an overriding determinant that greatly increases risk among those in compromised health—antibiotic use. Mom certainly qualified. Her recent use of antibiotics wasn't limited to the UTI. She had taken a generous allotment following the pacemaker implant.

I returned to the room and found Mom upset, despondent, and feeling as if someone had punched her in the gut. She made a comment that brought tears to my eyes: "I don't understand why all of this is happening to me. I never thought I would end up in such an awful predicament." I didn't know what to say. Evidently, Mom thought that when her time came, she would simply go to sleep and not wake up. And to be honest, I had thought the same thing.

Mom was swaddled in diapers again. She stated, in a matter-of-fact tone, "I've never experienced diarrhea this severe. It came on before I knew it and I couldn't stop it. I thought I was going to pass out from intense cramping." Much to Mom's revulsion, by the time she called for assistance, which she promptly received, it was too late. She lost all bowel control before the bedpan could be employed. Mom needed assistance several additional times during the day, one of which required another diaper change. Mom had eaten no lunch, had no desire to eat dinner, and the "potty training" session was scuttled.

The next day, Mom was improved; her episodes were controllable and less frequent. The diarrhea extravaganza resolved on the third day, but remained a pesky, off-and-on problem for the rest of her recuperation at Forest Meadows. It was concerning that her less than robust appetite continued to degrade. She complained of nagging abdominal discomfort for days following the initial diarrhea episode. It seemed to be the new normal, and antidiarrheal pills assumed staple status in Mom's pharmaceutical assortment.

Two days after Mom had recovered from the acute phase of her intestinal upheaval, she was escorted by the physical therapist to the "dance." *The* day had arrived. A portable toilet with handles on each side for gripping had been placed over the "real" toilet. It was a worthy throne, waiting for Mom to take her seat as reigning queen. I watched … and prayed for a successful practice run. Mom steered the walker into the bathroom with navigational assistance provided by the therapist. She slowly turned around and edged down in a single, well-controlled descent while holding on to the side handles. Her capability to sit and stand on her own was a milestone. "It was a beautiful day in the neighborhood," and I expected Mom would be participating in a live performance any day.

The following morning, Mom informed me: "I was in a lot of pain last night and got no sleep. I hurt all over. My ribs, my legs, my back, and even my ankles ached something terrible." How could they not? She was a beat-up lady. I asked her why she hadn't requested a Celebrex pain reliever; it was available and had worked well in the past. Her response was memorable.

"I'm not taking that. There's a stroke risk associated with it."

I had to counter, and responded, "Yes, if you take high doses for an extended period, there's a slight risk. The amount you've been prescribed hardly puts you in a risky category."

Her mind was fixed on the pill's tiny risk and not the relief it offered. She wouldn't take it. Mom had tried every nerve in my body, and I wondered, *Why am I continuing to beat myself up trying to care for her?* Of course, the reason was obvious: I loved my mother and her care was a personal commitment.

"I'm Itching"

October 7, 2018, was day seventeen in the facility. Or was it day eighteen? Counting on my fingers has a few drawbacks. Regardless, a new aggravation introduced itself to Mom's growing list of maladies. My phone rang at nine o'clock that night. It was Mom and she was beside herself.

"Seth, I need you to come over here. My hands and arms are itching and I've about scratched them to death."

"Mama, you have lotion on the bed stand. Have you used it?"

"No, I can't reach it. I can't lean over due to my cracked ribs."

"Have you called the nurses station down the hall?"

"No, I didn't want to push the button and wake everybody up with the blasted beeping."

"You need to push the button, Mama, and ask someone to help you."

"I hate to bother anyone."

"Mama, there's no need for me to come down there. An assistant can easily help you."

"I'll try it, but it will probably take them forever to get in here."

"It might not. Please call them."

About ten minutes later, Mom called back to advise me the CNA had applied the lotion.

The next morning, I walked into Mom's room while she was picking at her breakfast. I had hoped to hear she had slept well. She hadn't. The lotion had provided no lasting relief and the maddening itch kept her up until four in the morning, when it spontaneously stopped. Mom hadn't been in scratch mode since. I mentioned Mom's itching disorder to Vivian, and she suggested a Benadryl pill might work if the itching recurred. Similar to a tortuous dream, the itching returned with a vengeance later in the evening. Mom asked for a Benadryl, but there was a problem. It couldn't be dispensed—there was no order for it on her chart. To make matters worse, no one was on site to authorize it. Almost in tears, Mom called me. I was taken aback to learn they couldn't give her this commonly taken over-the-counter medication. In fact, Mom had taken it many times in the past and gave it to me when I was a kid.

Another miserable night was assuredly in store for Mom unless I attempted an end run. We had the generic equivalent to Benadryl in the kitchen pantry. Thomas had recently obtained it for Bella, who was temporarily given two pills a day per the vet's suggestion. If you're surmising what happened next, you're correct. With Bella's medication in hand, I hightailed it to the facility before the close of visiting hours. Mom was scratching as if she had fleas. No doubt, I had the right medication. Her hands and arms were alarmingly red from being clawed and they glistened with a film of overly applied lotion. I popped one of Bella's pills into Mom's mouth and stayed with her for thirty minutes to make sure it didn't kill her. The itching stopped. Kudos to Bella's (and Mom's) veterinarian.

The next day, the nurse practitioner added Benadryl to Mom's chart. To Mom's discouragement, the itching became a recurrent problem. The cause was not identified, so I decided to give her an appropriate diagnosis: GOK's disease (God Only Knows). I learned about this diagnosis from Mom in the 1960s.

Grace, an Unexpected Gift

Mom had enjoyed a private room for over two weeks, until an 85-year-old lady named Grace claimed the vacant bed. She was recovering from recent gall bladder surgery and had been admitted into Forest Meadows for rehab. The timing was opportune and Grace was a godsend. She was conversational yet not overly so, courteous, mentally sharp, and physically strong. She wasn't a typical 85-year-old, but what's typical? I expected her stay would be brief since she didn't appear to need extensive rehab.

Prior to Grace's arrival, eating and physical therapy were Mom's primary activities. Television and crossword puzzles rounded out the day. Mom was highly evolved socially, a true social animal whose personal history was immersed in involvement and interaction. It perplexed Bambi (the activity director), and me, that Mom, who was an artist and loved crafts, had been disinterested. She wouldn't participate in planned games and craft projects in the recreation/dining room.

Additionally, Mom was unwilling to eat in the dining room where she could meet residents who were in similar situations. I couldn't figure it out.

Grace preferred to remain in the room during mealtime and didn't participate in group activities—an ideal pairing for Mom. Keeping a watchful eye on Mom, Grace wasn't reluctant to press the assistance button when she or Mom needed help. Also, Grace was an excellent conversationalist, which dovetailed beautifully with Mom's gift of gab. I noticed a positive change in Mom after Grace moved in.

Third Down, Seventy-Five Yards to Go

Mom's progress during her third week was gathering a few puffs of steam. She wasn't running the hundred-yard dash, yet could amble ten yards and back with the walker without grimacing. Glimmers of light were sometimes apparent, although the end of the tunnel wasn't in view. Routine tasks were still an ordeal for Mom. She couldn't get dressed without assistance. Putting on *any* article of clothing from undergarments to a blouse was a task. Shoes were another foe. Her most comfortable and supportive pair—lace-ups—were hard to negotiate. Mom couldn't bend over to the degree necessary to slip them on or tie the laces. It was encouraging to note headway was being made. The physical therapists diligently worked with Mom to employ work-arounds to overcome her dressing challenges.

If this ordeal were a football game, Mom's cleats still had untold yardage to traverse and she was getting close to being out of downs. Medicare had authorized Mom to receive three weeks of rehab at Forest Meadows, which initially seemed to be an ample allotment. Now, with less than one week remaining, I feared there would be insufficient time on the game clock for her to reach the goal line. If it became necessary for Mom to stay in Forest Meadows after Medicare benefits ceased, a substantial out-of-pocket cost to her—around $300 per day—would result. And this was the base rate I was quoted. Nervously, I watched two hourglasses: one representing Medicare benefits with sand falling at a quick pace, and the second glass representing Mom's progress, flowing at a slower pace.

Her progress assessments, required by Medicare, were periodically completed by the therapists. If their documentation showed Mom was responding favorably to treatment and additional therapy was deemed medically necessary, Medicare might recharge the first hourglass with additional sand. This would give Mom extra rehabilitation time in Forest Meadows. As much as I wished to exert a bit of influence (I had none), it was out of my control. In the meantime, I anxiously kept tabs on Mom's trajectory and stood by.

Mom continued to be plagued with frequent out-of-the-blue episodes of diarrhea, nausea, and abdominal pain. Spells were symptomatically treated with loperamide (antidiarrheal) pills. The bouts were less severe than what she had experienced during the first salvo, but her appetite remained poor and she ate next to nothing. Her stamina had taken a hit and her response to physical therapy did as well. Mom insisted "something was going on" and expressed concern that the cause of her gastric distress hadn't been identified. Mom was astute and her medical hunches were usually correct or close to it.

As I observed daily sunrises and sunsets heralding each day's arrival and passage, I couldn't ignore the sand in Medicare's hourglass continuing to flow without restriction. I became frantic when two days remained. It was evident the amount of therapy and skilled nursing Mom needed couldn't be accomplished in such a short window. She had enjoyed a few days of encouraging progress toward the end of the week, but a bout of diarrhea halted the momentum. It was disruptive enough that therapy sessions had to be canceled. Mom was an equal impediment; she continued to press for her release at the earliest possible second. Her urging was counterproductive and kept me in a state of exasperation. Unfortunately for us, Grace had been discharged and her absence exacerbated Mom's restlessness. We hated to lose Grace's company, yet were pleased her recuperation had been rapid.

When weighing alternatives to Mom's impending loss of Medicare benefits, Max and I reached the conclusion that our best option—if Medicare didn't authorize additional time at Forest Meadows—was for her to remain there until she was stable enough to leave. I felt we would have no choice but to pay the stratospheric daily charges, which I expected would be for a relatively short time. And truthfully, my concerns weren't confined to Mom's well-being; they included Thomas and me as well. I was emotionally and physically frayed and not prepared for our significantly compromised mother to come live with us—at least not yet. But ... is anyone *ever* ready for such a commitment? I had a sick feeling in my stomach and feared what might be in store for us when Mom left Forest Meadows.

Resignation

I wasn't one to remain glued to a butt-busting aluminum bench in the final minutes of a football game when last rites for my team were all but pronounced. Forty points for the opposing team and less than twenty for mine, with five minutes remaining, was sufficient encouragement for me to leave. I was out of the stadium ahead of the impending mass exodus of revelers turned wailers, some submerged in mindless inebriation.

Mom wasn't anywhere near the need for last rites or a last drink, which she would *never* have allowed near her lips for *any* reason. Nonetheless, circumstantial evidence strongly suggested her Medicare-paid engagement with Forest Meadows was reaching a conclusion. Surely, the axe was going to fall when the referees emerged from their huddle. I expected them to present us with a Skilled Nursing Facility Advance Beneficiary Notice. In some circles, it's called a Notice of Medicare Non-Coverage. In either case they spell the same thing—you stay, you pay.

I should have patiently remained in my seat and been less willing to throw in the towel. As the game clock was counting down toward its last tick, an unexpected Hail Mary pass hit its mark. The Skilled Nursing Facility Advance Beneficiary Notice was intercepted before time ran out. Gratefully, Medicare's benevolence was extended for an additional week. I was singing hallelujahs while Mom sang "Abide with Me" in resignation. With an additional seven days added to the Medicare hourglass, my relief was palpable, even at the cost of Mom's disappointment. Max and I never told Mom we had considered extending her stay at Forest Meadows in the event Medicare benefits ceased.

The additional week at Forest Meadows turned out to be pivotal. Mom's progress quickened as the therapists continued their quest for meaningful results. Of utmost importance, the toilet regained its status as "a haven of refuge." Mom's endurance and confidence trended upward and this was reflected in her improving frame of mind. The week afforded a bonus: the extreme pain associated with her fractures subsided. The bend had been rounded and flickers of light were dancing at the tunnel's end. If only the pesky bug—whatever it was—would stop dancing around in Mom's intestines.

As the seven-day extension at Forest Meadows approached its termination, I was advised "the notice" would be forthcoming. It was planted in my hands two days prior to Mom's discharge. Concurrently, Forest Meadows had requested and received approval from Medicare for home health care to commence (based on the physician's order). Mom would be receiving continuing therapy at home on an intermittent basis for a few weeks. She was ecstatic to learn the month-long "imprisonment"—her word for the ordeal—had a definite end date. I was reasonably comfortable Mom had recuperated sufficiently for me to care for her at home without killing myself in the process. Nonetheless, I dreaded it.

Max and I Have a Difference of Opinion

Max and I had seldom disagreed about Mom's care, but this was an instance when we did. He strongly maintained Thomas and I shouldn't saddle ourselves with Mom's care and thought she should be placed in a nursing facility. We agreed to disagree and didn't argue about it. Max was upfront. He stated he didn't have the skills, capabilities, or temperament to be a caregiver and reiterated he wasn't in a position to take Mom in. This wasn't earth-shattering news. I had always been aware that he and I were made from different clay. He excelled in areas I didn't and vice versa. There was no misunderstanding; Mom's day-to-day care would squarely rest on my shoulders, with Thomas' support. This isn't to imply Max wasn't willing to help out. He or Lois sat with Mom on many occasions. Max was a loving brother and our communication lines were always open.

Based on my conversations with friends who've been forced to thread the parental caregiving needle, disagreement among siblings isn't out of the ordinary. In fact, I think it's more the rule than the exception. Caregiving seems to default to the child who lives closest to the parent, but upon occasion the parent has to move when the willing child lives in another city or state. It's seldom straightforward and the ride might be bumpy.

Two Forest Meadows Residents I'll Never Forget

Gladys stole my heart; she was the occupant in the room directly across the hall from Mom. In her mid- to late-70s, Gladys was attractive, well-dressed and groomed, slight in build, and sweet as honey. She had a companion: a stuffed toy fox, which was always at her side. Gladys was usually seated in her wheelchair in the hall, close to her room, petting the auburn-colored fox while cradling it as if it were an infant. Frequently, I made a point to stop and chat. Each time I saw Gladys, she introduced me to her beloved fox and invited me to pet it. I admired it, probably overly so. It was my way to validate the importance of her significant other.

On one occasion, Gladys asked me to wait a minute. She did a one-eighty and wheeled inside her room to retrieve something special. A few moments later she returned, beaming, and handed me a piece of brightly colored artwork she had crafted in the activity room. The piece of paper, taken from a coloring book, contained simple animal shapes Gladys had filled in with colored pencils. I gushed over her talent, and she rewarded me with a broad smile. Perhaps she realized a sense of self-worth, even if momentary. When I left, her memory of my visit left as well.

Gladys seemed hungry, not for food but for something outside her grasp—a sound mind. Even though brief, our conversations were long enough for me to ascertain her incapacitation was relating to cognition and memory. She seemed resigned and possibly had sufficient mental capability to recognize her plight. I've often wondered which is worse: being aware you're losing your mind or having lost it.

One quiet afternoon while I sat with Mom in her room, my attention was commandeered by an eardrum-shattering cacophony surging through the hall; it sounded similar to a peacock. Peacocks have a shrill, sometimes pulsating call resembling a loud party horn. Great for stopping traffic, but not conducive for the maintenance of a peaceful coexistence with fellow residents. Mom heard it, a sure-fire indication the decibels were of sufficient dynamism to charge through her failing ears. I jokingly mentioned that a bird must be loose in the building.

Sure enough, the "peacock" screamed again with untiring ferocity. I easily traced the sound to the "bird's nest," which was in a room two doors down from Mom. The "bird" had apparently been reincarnated into human form. A disheveled elderly woman was the source of the attention-grabbing calls that bounced off the walls and invaded hallways. "Somebody get me out of here," she squawked repeatedly. "Why am I here?" was an incantation sandwiched between her calls to the wild. Eventually, she settled down, giving her well-exercised vocal cords time to recharge. The next day she was gone. I surmised she had been relocated to suitable environs, possibly an aviary. Who she was, why she was in skilled nursing, or how long she had been there remained a mystery. Her vocal peculiarity and penchant for creating a disturbance will always remain a remnant in my mental scrapbook of Forest Meadows.

Forest Meadows Observations and Takeaways

Consistent with my previous observations of various nursing facilities, most of the populace was female, elderly, and many were long-term residents—they weren't there for rehab. That phase of their confinement had long passed and their conditions required 24/7 care. Most were fixtures confined to wheelchairs or were bedridden. Varying degrees of debilitation ranging from paralysis to dementia, or both, was the rule. It was sobering to witness the cruelty of life's final stages for those whose existence was framed by misery, hopelessness, and no one to care. I was reminded of the musical composition, "Come, Sweet Death," which was written by Johann Sebastian Bach in 1736. I could well understand the sentiment behind Bach's work.

Bambi, Forest Meadows' thoroughly engaged activity director, was outstanding. She was youthfully bubbly and relentless in her mission to provide meaningful distractions from the inherent mundaneness of the institutional walls. She took time to determine what made Mom tick and provided opportunities matching Mom's interests. On multiple occasions, Bambi attempted to tap Mom's artistic talent by offering sketch sheets and pencils that Mom could easily employ in her room. Additionally, watercolor sessions were frequently available in the recreation/dining room. To my disappointment, Mom seldom participated in either activity. I suspected she was depressed, but she insisted not. In retrospect, I think she probably felt too poorly to engage.

Most Forest Meadows employees worked tirelessly and were conscientious. They seemed well-equipped to deal with a mishmash of patients, some of whom were less than pleasant. Plainly, the CNAs were overburdened. The foundational role they played in patient care made them indispensable. At times, there were too few of them for the number of patients in the facility. Their work was taxing and thankless. In the facility's defense, I understand staffing projections are based on average workload, not "rush hour."

Mom's overall condition remained tenuous for most of her stay, which accounted for my reluctance to leave her. Emotionally, I was Mom's primary caregiver. At times I felt I couldn't bear another day. The ship was taking on water and I needed a lifeboat … but *I* was the lifeboat and had to continue rowing while bailing out water. With deep gratitude, I accepted lifelines thrown at critical moments, keeping me from becoming shark bait.

The physical therapists lived up to their billing and did an outstanding job for Mom. They were highly trained, professional, and displayed a keen understanding of the psychological components underscoring the success of physical therapy. The physical therapy unit where many of Mom's rehab sessions were conducted was clean, spacious, and bright. Forest Meadows wasn't the Taj Mahal; yet I felt the choice was validated by the outcome—Mom's hard-won recovery.

The food was typically institutional and unimaginative though palatable—I ate there enough to make the call. Mom turned her head to most of it. Her taste buds weren't receptive for much of anything prepared outside of a frying pan, unless baptized in gravy. Most entrées weren't necessarily designed to accommodate Mom's Southern taste buds. Remember, most parts of Florida have a Northern accent. Since many of Mom's days were plagued by persistent appetite-killing intestinal problems, food preparation didn't seem to matter anyway.

Mom's twenty-eight-day stay at Forest Meadows, from September 19 to October 17, 2018, totaled $12,284, including physical therapy costs. My calculator confirms this to be a daily rate of $438 per day—a hefty sum. Medicare covered the lion's share since short-term physical therapy (rehabilitation) had been authorized for Mom's entire stay. To further explain, rehabilitative physical therapy in a skilled nursing facility can be for *up to one hundred days—subject to Medicare authorization.* This caveat can't be dismissed. Most patients aren't authorized for such lengthy stays since they're often judged to have reached their maximum potential for rehabilitation well before a hundred days. Mom was a classic example.

Additional information can be found in Medicare publication #10153 (*Medicare Coverage of Skilled Nursing Facility Care*). This booklet is available online at ***https://www.medicare.gov/publications/10153-medicare-coverage-of-skilled-nursing-facility-care.pdf.*** It's important to note that many individuals are enrolled in Medicare Advantage plans instead of Original Medicare. These plans adhere to Medicare guidelines but differences apply. Any given plan must be contacted for specifics, including cost share.

What happens when an individual remains in a skilled nursing facility after Medicare rehabilitation benefits cease? What if their condition is unsound and self-care at home isn't an option? To make matters worse, many patients have nowhere else to go nor have anyone who can provide care. What a dilemma! It's increasingly commonplace as an aging, financially unprepared population moves down the assembly line.

It all boils down to money. Who pays for continuing care when rehab stops? There are three primary payment avenues for long-term care in a nursing facility: pay out of pocket for the full cost, which few can afford; purchase long-term care insurance well in advance, which is expensive; or apply for Medicaid. Medicaid is government assistance provided to individuals with limited income and assets. Guidelines and administration vary from state to state. I imagine Medicaid was paying the tab for many long-term-care residents at Forest Meadows.

According to the American Council on Aging (*https://www.medicaidplanningassistance.org*), in 2022 the average cost in the U.S. for a shared room in a nursing facility was $260 per day (rehab therapy has been extracted from the cost), which equals a whopping $94,900 annually. Some states are lower, some higher. Additionally, since qualifying for Medicaid varies from state to state, any given state's Medicaid office must be contacted to initiate an application for assistance. The above-referenced website is an excellent resource, jam-packed with useful information and contacts for each state.

CHAPTER 6

A NEW JOURNEY BEGINS

On Thursday morning, October 18, 2018, I brought Mom home to continue her recuperation with Thomas and me. Strangely, it was a relief to have Mom home with us—at least in the beginning. In some ways, life was easier to manage since my daily routine was no longer dictated by Forest Meadows. I wasn't blind to reality and discerned Mom's care might be daunting at times. Duty and gratitude for both parents were my drivers to bring Mom home. It was a mission Thomas and I took seriously. Even so, I wasn't prepared for the rapids and waterfalls that appeared as distant, unidentified specks in placid water.

We set Mom up in a guest bedroom with easy access to the bathroom. My bedroom was close and I could expeditiously attend to her when help was needed during the night, which was twice each night. To account for times when I wasn't nearby or was asleep, I had the perfect solution—a bicycle air horn. I obtained a lightweight model with a squeeze bulb Mom could easily manage. It had a voice similar to the "peacock" at Forest Meadows and was loud enough to rally troops anywhere in the house. Six bucks, no battery required.

Mom's authorization for short-term home health care made the transition less scary. She received one-hour visits three times per week, from a home health therapist or nurse. Some days seemed to be a step backwards, but her overall progress when measured by the week was recognizable. Therapy at home was necessary to address her balance and monitor her recovery from the fractures. Mom's malfunctioning "gyroscope" sometimes jumped off its axis, putting her at risk to topple without warning.

The therapist had multiple conversations with Mom about the urgency to rely on the walker at all times. Admonitions were analogous to wet paint; when the paint dried, the impact dimmed. Mom contended, "My falls have always been backwards and the walker won't prevent that kind of fall." This was exactly the same argument she had proposed a couple of years prior. The therapist's response was a repeat of what Mom had been told previously: "Canes and walkers will force your body to tilt forward and reduce the chance of falling backwards." I had doubts about Mom's willingness to heed the call to action.

Convincing Mom to use the walker remained an uphill battle since she couldn't see or feel herself wobble like a duck when walking without it. I frequently reminded her, "Mom, it's necessary for you to use the walker." Her usual reply was, "Honey, I don't think I need it all the time. It gets in the way and sometimes I forget to use it." It was a daily battle that I grew to resent. Mom's ego and refusal to accept a new normal was at my expense if she fell. I tried to not dwell on it, but it haunted me.

A new rhythm to life for Mom, Thomas, and me was accompanied by significant challenges. Interruptions to interruptions gave new meaning to flexibility, which made planning anything of consequence difficult at best. Mom's improving mobility created yet another concern; she perceived the walker to be an impediment, preventing her from walking "normally." The walker *was* cumbersome and Mom *could* walk faster without it. However, it was an invaluable safeguard and made managing her care less worrisome. At times, my disgruntlement overcame me and I boiled over.

As a result of Mom's penchant for nonchalance, I closely monitored her moves when I could. On one occasion while I was preparing lunch, I got a glimpse of Mom when she got up from a chair and started to walk across the room. I could see she was wobbly and I ran toward her just as she precipitously careened sideways. I caught her before she could kiss the hard-as-a-rock tiled floor.

I said loudly, "Mama, what would have happened if I hadn't been here to catch you? I could have been in the bathroom or outside to retrieve the mail. Please, please, please use your cane or walker! I'm not looking forward to spending my time in the hospital or in rehab for something that's preventable." I was angry. There was no room for debate; Mom would have fallen and fallen hard. The incident seemed to have wised her up, and she initially made efforts to comply with the stated objective to practice safety first.

I resigned myself to the possibility that Mom would fall again. Still, I couldn't remain glued to her side every minute since I had to take care of myself as well. It's the nature of caregiving—you can't be everywhere at the same time. Losing sight of one's own needs or dismissing them goes with the territory, and it *will* lead to trouble. I learned this lesson over and again. Even so, there are times when tough lessons and situations are unavoidable.

Finally, Mom adjusted to the idea that she could no longer live in her home in Jacksonville. It was the bitterest of all pills. She sorely missed her friends, hairdresser, grocery store, and most of all, her church. I regretted Mom's world had turned upside down and her day-to-day sources of familiarity and support had vanished. When her condition improved and car rides were less taxing, she became insistent her hair appointments *in Jacksonville* be resumed. I located an excellent beautician in St. Augustine that Mom's sister had used years before. Mom wasn't interested. She wanted *her* beautician and the associated camaraderie with friends in the Jacksonville shop. It wasn't lost on me.

Mom's resistance wasn't limited to the beauty shop. She put up a fight when I suggested a primary care physician in St. Augustine should be selected. Initially, Max or I attempted to accommodate Mom's requests since twice-a-week jaunts to Jacksonville were necessary to check on her house, yard, and to gather mail that hadn't been forwarded. Mom piggybacked with either Max or me, which turned out to be an unworkable arrangement. Her doctor visits and hair appointments frequently conflicted with our schedules, and additional trips to Jacksonville couldn't be justified. Much to Mom's disappointment, the Jacksonville hair appointments were brought to a halt, and arrangements with a beautician in St. Augustine were confirmed.

The St. Augustine Hair Palace (as I named it) was a plenitude of opportunity. It served as a habitat for shampooing, coloring (but not for Mom), trimming, rolling, twirling, swirling, drying, teasing, and cementing creations with industrial-grade hairspray. This old-fashioned mecca—a throwback to an all-but-extinct era—was also *the* hub for the exchange of information and news among devotees. All were mostly in their 80s and above. Before the final application of hairspray had engulfed Mom's hair and anything else within six feet, I had been transformed into a true believer in the power of this institution. What initially had been viewed as a weekly chore transitioned into an anticipated event … for me. I learned who had died, divorced, married, had endometriosis, was selling their house, been admitted to the hospital, or was living in sin. I confess it was impossible to turn a deaf ear to these empowerment sessions, and I wasn't the only male in attendance taking it all in.

Whoever coined the phrase *knowledge is power* must have been acquainted with a hair palace somewhere. The palace was a unique slice of Americana I'll always recall when a gust of *White Rain* invades my nostrils.

A stroke of welcome news was received when Mom's retinologist in Jacksonville, who treated her macular degeneration, opened a satellite office in St. Augustine. Shortly thereafter, we found a podiatrist in town who could treat Mom's ingrown toenail, and she liked him. And why not? He was affable, competent, handsome, and sported avant-garde designer socks Mom noted without hesitation. With two physicians and a beautician lined up in St. Augustine, Max and I decided to maintain Mom's primary care physician and cardiologist in Jacksonville. This was a palatable accommodation we thought could be handled with minimal disruption to us. The winds of change blew harder than expected. It was a short-lived concession.

Unsettling Observations

One afternoon, Mom was sitting on the couch watching television when she sensed the seat cushion was wet. She assumed a spilled cup of water was the culprit, but it wasn't. Mom had urinated. When she realized the source of the spill wasn't her cup, she was aghast. I helped Mom with a change of clothes and did my best to assure her there was no harm. Without the slightest complaint, Thomas magically cleaned and dried the fabric. He and I treated the incident as a nonevent and employed a simple fix to handle future pickles. We placed a sheet of thin plastic on top of the cushion where Mom sat and covered it with a towel. No further couch anointings occurred, although urinary leaks, some substantial, beleaguered Mom. She had worn incontinence pads inside her panties for years, but an additional protective measure was suggested by her.

Mom was suffering through sudden and unexplained releases of urine upon standing, sitting, or when walking. The volume was, at times, greater than what her pads could accommodate. The excess spilled into her sheer panties and trousers, creating an uncomfortable and unsightly predicament. There was a viable solution: ditch the panties and replace them with highly absorptive disposable underwear. The new defense—a marvel of urine-trapping engineering—was particularly foolproof with the insertion of an incontinence pad. This double protection saved the day on multiple occasions. It allowed for Mom to maintain her dignity and gave our washing machine a break.

Here's a word of enlightenment concerning disposable underwear: these "unmentionables" frequently display the *Discreet* caption on the package and are dubbed incontinence underwear. Regardless of their proven efficacy, they were a source of embarrassment for Mom. On one occasion when we were shopping, I placed a package in the cart and, after paying for it, left it in the cart without bagging. Mom demanded concealment. Perturbed, I returned to the checkout and bagged it. I didn't understand the cloak of secrecy since most females over the age of 80—and some younger—probably use the product.

Frustrations continued to tally due to a general slide in Mom's alertness. This was complicated by her numb hands. The condition caused her to frequently drop things without her knowledge. On one such slip, she dropped a nearly empty glass of cranberry juice that spilled on a burgundy-and-cream-colored rug. By chance, the splash centered in a burgundy section and didn't create a stain. Thomas scooted off to the dollar store and returned with two spill-proof sippy cups. It didn't take long for the two-dollar investment to be validated. Several days later, I gave Mom a cranberry-juice-filled sippy cup while she roosted on her "hermetically sealed nest" on the couch, watching television. Shortly thereafter, she called out, "Seth, where's my cranberry juice?" She thought I had returned it to the refrigerator. I thought, *Maybe I did.* I ran around in a distracted state half the time. But not this time. The cup, with contents intact, was on the floor by Mom's feet.

Our dog was almost the recipient of another of Mom's miscues, but not from being hit by a sippy cup. I dispensed Mom's pills twice daily, in an easy-to-handle prescription cup. It wasn't easy enough for Mom. Her penchant for spilling things nearly spelled disaster for Bella, whom I believe was a vacuum cleaner in a previous life. One evening, Mom dropped the pill cup on the floor when I handed it to her. In an instant, Bella's sonar issued an urgent all-points bulletin to an awaiting six-pill feast—a potentially lethal one. I caught her when she came running toward the assortment, scooped her up, and shut her in another room while I gathered the potential toxins. Scarily, Mom's pill spills were common occurrences. To protect Bella, I discontinued using the cup and handed Mom each pill, one by one.

Mom and Bella developed an unlikely bond that was heartwarming and unexpected. Mom wasn't a dog lover even though we had a black-as-coal mutt for eleven years when I was a kid. I called the dog Prankster. Don't ask me why. He wasn't allowed inside the house, given Mom's penchant for a spotless environment. Prankster was equipped with an abundance of long hair that shed. This alone was an exclusion for inside dwelling; however, there were two other exclusionary factors: the potential for accidents and the simple fact that he was a dog. Bella brought about a drastic shift in Mom's perspective. Besides Bella being loving, Thomas kept her squeaky-clean and well-groomed, which aided in her ability to reel Mom in.

Bella

Bella was exceedingly attentive toward Mom. She followed Mom from room to room and when Mom was sitting down, Bella invariably lay down at her feet. Mom appreciated the warmth emanating from Bella's pillow-like belly and once stated, "Look at her, she's lying *on top* of my feet. I think she realizes they're cold." I believe Mom was right. Bella sensed when Mom wasn't feeling well and closely watched when Mom was sprawled out on the couch. In essence, Bella was a sitter for Mom, and Mom loved her company. It was a mutually beneficial arrangement.

Too Early

Being Mom's caregiver offered few breaks, and my responsibilities started before the crack of dawn. Her thyroid medication marked the beginning of each day at six o'clock sharp, about an hour earlier than my usual wake time. I preferred to get up when my body clock was activated by the early morning beams of sunlight instead of being shocked from slumber by an agitating alarm. Remaining peacefully asleep while the skies were draped in starry blackness seemed civilized. There was no alternative. Since Mom couldn't hear her alarm, it was necessary for me to be on the receiving end of mine. I grew to disdain its unrelenting, too-early scream blasting my cobwebs and transforming me into a zombie-like creature with questionable coherence. I discovered later the pill didn't have to be dispensed at such an uncivilized hour.

After dispensing Mom's medication, I crawled back into the bed and stayed there until seven, when the day began in earnest. I helped Mom roll out of bed and watched her walk to the bathroom using the walker. She needed no assistance beyond that point, and I slipped away. Silence ensued for at least an hour while she meticulously resuscitated her hair and applied makeup—a positive indication of her ongoing recovery. The hour she spent in the bathroom was a gift. It granted uninterrupted time for me to collect myself.

The daily bathroom session was complete when I heard the *clunk, clunk, clunk,* of the approaching walker showcasing her steps toward the kitchen / family room … what a superb sight to see her using the walker.

Mom's breakfast consisted of a cup of decaf, a piece of toast, and, occasionally, a bowl of grits. But never, never an egg! Her abhorrence for eggs was long-established. Five remaining pills completed the morning fare. Mealtime was a never-ending challenge; coaxing Mom to eat breakfast, lunch, or dinner remained a chore. While preparing what I hoped would be appealing meals each day, I gained an enhanced appreciation for the dietician at Forest Meadows.

Call Me June

For anyone who was tuned in to 1960s television, the name June Cleaver from *Leave It to Beaver* television fame might (or might not) elicit a warm recollection of a quintessential mid-century housewife. June was no longer a mere childhood memory. I had become her reincarnated male equivalent—for the second time. Circumstances were eerily similar to May 2016, when Mom stayed with us four weeks. Washing, drying, and folding her clothes, helping her get dressed and undressed, and planning and preparing three daily meals were much the same as before. I did all of her shopping, managed her medications, and took her to a myriad of appointments. Mom was no longer comfortable handling her bank accounts, and I inherited this detail as well. Her care and general upkeep consumed a heap of time. In effect, she was my kid ... fortunately, there were no soccer games.

In one respect, managing Mom was initially less demanding than it had been when she recuperated with us in 2016. During that "run through," she was in excruciating pain and her care needs were constant. That wasn't the case this time around. Thanks to Mom's month-long recuperation at Forest Meadows, she was in reasonably good shape. Unlike 2016, the time frame for Mom's current stay was open-ended. I couldn't help but project how long she might need to stay with us and what was in store beyond that.

Our lives were upended. It was necessary for me to plan day-to-day activities around Mom's *expected* schedule, and it was always subject to change. Simple errands and outings previously accomplished without much coordination became a game of chess. Tactics, logistics, and planning for a shifting gameboard assumed front and center status in my playbook. Haircuts, runs to the grocery store, gym, hardware store, and other errands could no longer be spur-of-the-moment. Simple things such as visiting local parks, taking walks or bike rides in the neighborhood, going out for dinner, visiting friends, and volunteering took a hit. Occasionally, my brother, Max, and his wife, Lois, were able to pitch in when they weren't consumed with new-house *and* old-house complications as a result of their recent move. A few times we obtained the services of a sitter, *when we could get one.*

I never had kids and was getting a glimpse of how hectic Mom's life must have been when my brother and I were growing up, running her ragged. It's worth noting she had a distinct advantage when she was the parent—she wasn't 70 years old. I expect she was better equipped for parenting than me. Nonetheless, becoming Mom's parent caused me to reflect, reassess priorities, and learn the art of patience. I visualized walking in Mom's shoes and grasped it would be a tall order. My love for Mom didn't change the fact that I felt overwhelmed much of the time.

Annoyances

As we settled into our new routines, day-to-day life became manageable yet challenging. Even though Mom was generally agreeable and courteous, a few of her pronouncements and actions became annoying. Routinely, Mom "forgot" to wear her hearing aids, which prevented her from hearing conversations. Predictably, she asked for most things to be repeated and repeated again. The words, "What did you say?" wore tedious. Consequently, I responded by speaking loudly. Mom reciprocated by directing me to stop yelling. And I probably had been. It didn't take much of an imagination to visualize that I was getting a glimpse of my own future.

The television remote was a related "hot button." Mom wanted the volume turned up while Thomas and I wanted it down. One afternoon, I returned to the house after running a brief errand and could hear the television from inside the garage. The sound was earsplitting. Mom and Bella were alone in the house, but they weren't the only recipients of life-threatening reverberation; the television itself was surely destined to suffer a stroke. Without saying a word (Mom wouldn't have heard it anyway), I stepped into Mom's bedroom and retrieved her hearing aids. With resolute haste, I braved entry into the family room and lowered the television volume to a survivable level. Mom's blasted-out ears were subsequently plugged with the hearing aids. Peace was restored.

The thermostat was another point of discussion. Mom was cold when we were comfortable, and we were hot when she was comfortable. She liked to bake in eighty-degree warmth, whereas our comfort resided about eight degrees lower. We didn't want Mom to succumb to hypothermia and chose the seventy-six-degree setting as a workable compromise. She wore a sweater to account for the remaining temperature shortfall. The house was a bit warm, yet tolerable with the recruitment of ceiling fans.

Simple irritations accompanied each day, which is predictable with any long-term house guest. When the guest is a parent, I think the challenge is magnified. Mom was a seasoned conversationalist and loved to talk. Thomas and I were on the opposite end of the spectrum and we revered our quiet time. Mom frequently offered unsolicited and sometimes off-the-wall commentaries on a variety of topics. Her hearing challenges provided ample opportunity for many of her erroneous slants. Most of the time it was easier to let her remain in left field than to engage in a debate.

On some occasions, Mom's extraordinary pronouncements could not be ignored and required correction. It was my mission to provide necessary education. Here's a classic:

"Seth, they announced on the news that Jacksonville is being evacuated. I think there's a tornado up there. This is terrible. I'm worried about the house."

I was watching the newscast while mashing potatoes, and responded, "No, Mama, that's not what's happening. There's a tornado warning near Jackson, Mississippi, not Jacksonville. And they're advising people who are in the path to take shelter."

Mom's penchant for immaculate housekeeping was an irritation. Had she been a nun, she could have been Sister Immaculata. The "immaculate" gene wasn't passed on to me, although Mom had attempted to convert me into a disciple of fastidiousness. When growing up, I was required to adhere to "extreme" observances, such as assisting with dusting and vacuuming. I maintained that a reasonable deposit of dust protected furniture finishes and reduced room glare. Mom disagreed. My adherence to Mom's rules—and adoption—are different animals. When I lived under my parents' roof, I complied with the adherence part of the equation. Though well-indoctrinated, I declined to take the vows of immaculateness; thus the adoption piece of my education in household fastidiousness didn't stick as Mom had intended.

Thomas and I aren't clean freaks, yet we're clean enough. Mom's training as a registered nurse exposed her to a serious condition, which she contracted: germaphobia. She and I resided in a different jurisdiction. Our relative nonchalance, countered by Mom's preoccupation with germs, wasn't an ideal coupling: not contentious, but grating. Of all things, Mom disapproved of our kitchen sponge and felt obligated to offer the following opinion: "Seth, you shouldn't be using a sponge to wash dishes. It harbors bacteria and can make you sick." Her comment was the equivalent of ripe fruit and I picked it. "Mama, we're not eating sponges and neither are you." We all got a chuckle out of it.

In a subsequent internet search, I found sources that supported her argument. Other references stated the opposite, claiming bacteria found in soapy sponges were generally harmless. Ours must have fallen in the generally harmless category. Thomas and I had peacefully coexisted with our bacteria-laced sponges for years without incident. In my estimation, practical science wins! Accordingly, I didn't allow Mom's concerns to compel me to relegate my top-tier dish-cleaning implement to inglorious bathroom use. I still use sponges to wash dishes without obsessing about them being a bacterial port of call.

Mom mentioned I had circles under my eyes. She was right. I couldn't hide them. Mary Kay, Mom's miracle worker in a tube, probably could have, but the blemishes weren't to the point where a consultation was necessary. Mom's study of the puffy half-moons flanking my eyes was the preamble leading to her underlying concern: "Seth, you have to take better care of yourself. I'm afraid I'm running you to death." I assured her I was fine, even though the response wasn't truthful. Some days were better than others for no apparent reason; I attribute this to getting up on the wrong or right side of the bed. Mom wasn't *that* difficult; the situation was.

She had occasional visitors from Jacksonville and they were always welcome. I incorporated various outings into the week to offer additional diversions. Simple pleasures such as riding around in the car delighted Mom. Nonetheless, she was far less engaged in activities than she had been in Jacksonville. I knew she felt penned, and I would have felt the same. In fact, I did. My own emotions were all over the board and ranged from deep sympathy and compassion to resentment for being tied down. Guilt would serve to correct me as if it were an invisible parent. Even though I deeply loved my mother, I came to accept that my vacillating moods weren't out of the ordinary. I reached this morsel of wisdom while speaking to a close friend who was experiencing much the same type of ordeal with her mother.

Anybody got a quart of vodka or equivalent form of "self-medication"? Truthfully, this was never a consideration for me, a nondrinker and health enthusiast. My preferred avenues for mental relief weren't found in a bottle or vial of pills. Breaks in the gym and chats with Thomas were better alternatives. Brief walks were additional stress relievers. Mom could be left unattended for about a half hour, but not much longer. Before we ventured out, several precautionary steps were taken. Mom was asked to go to the bathroom whether she needed to or not. When she returned, I hung the medical alert pendant around her neck and made sure she was securely seated on the couch. A water-filled sippy cup, the television remote, and her cell phone were all placed on the tray table within easy reach. Mom had few reservations about being alone for short periods and we didn't encounter any snags.

A Bad Penny Turns Up

Mom's occasional diarrhea, lethargy, lack of appetite, and general abdominal discomfort were concerning. It was a continuation of the same scourge she had encountered at Forest Meadows. Based on their protocol, I gave her antidiarrheal pills to cover the once-or-twice-weekly bouts, which weren't severe. Mom was concerned the intestinal obstruction surgically removed in 2015 had returned. It was a simmering worry for her. Oftentimes, Mom stated: "Something isn't right in my intestines. I shouldn't be taking so many pills to control them." She was painfully thin, and I suspected something was off.

The intestinal disturbances escalated in late November. Severe abdominal cramping followed by two explosive releases signaled the worst attack since Forest Meadows. We were grateful the toilet was the sole recipient. Afterwards, I gave Mom two antidiarrheal pills and called her primary care physician in Jacksonville. He couldn't see her for two weeks. He suggested the emergency room if her condition worsened. Mom's response, "Oh Lord, not *that*," required no interpretation. There was no argument. *That* would indeed be a last resort.

Another idea came to me—locate a local physician who could see her. The suggestion would undoubtedly elicit a not-so-veiled protest. At the mention, Mom affirmed she was feeling better and thought it would be okay to wait for the appointment in Jacksonville. Vivid flashbacks of her diarrhea "extravaganza" at Forest Meadows haunted me. I began a quick scouting mission on the internet. It was a fruitful search.

I stumbled across an ad for a group of physicians who had an office a few blocks from our house. I called, pleaded Mom's case, and was encouraged to bring her in. They were in a position to accept her as a walk-in if we didn't delay. We were there in ten minutes. After a relatively short wait, we met with an attentive and affable female physician, perhaps 50 years old, who examined Mom and advised her to continue taking the antidiarrheal pills when needed. We were sent to a nearby lab where Mom's blood was drawn, and we were given a "to-go" bag, fully equipped with stool collection supplies—an exciting activity awaited.

The physician had made a positive impression, though not to the degree hoped. On the way to the lab, Mom speedily returned a verdict:

"I liked her, but I don't want to change doctors." I took a deep breath and kept my mouth shut.

The goodies in the bag were tapped after we got home; Mom's intestines were in full-speed-ahead mode. I followed strict retrieval guidelines to avoid cross-contamination with possible competing impurities. I dared not sneeze or breathe ... this was a delicate procedure. Not breathing diminished the possibility of my throwing up in the middle of an indispensable sample. That would have been disastrous. The specimen was carefully extracted, transferred into the designated plastic container with a screw top, and securely sealed inside the authorized plastic bag. The bag had been provided by the lab as a bonus accessory. An additional step was required: the prized package had to be refrigerated—*in our refrigerator*! A safe spot was found next to a past-its-prime bag of salad greens awaiting disposal. The hoped-for answer to Mom's intestinal problems luxuriated in thirty-eight-degree stability until the following morning, when I rushed the sample back to the lab for analysis.

Two days later, the physician delivered a stunning dart of news. "Mr. Vicarson, your mother tested positive for a potentially serious intestinal infection called *Clostridium difficile*. I've ordered a medication for you to pick up today. It's imperative for your mother to begin taking it immediately. She could end up in the hospital if this isn't promptly controlled." No further explanation was needed. I was familiar with *C. diff* and simmered with anger. This had been my initial suspicion when Mom lost all bowel control at Forest Meadows. And to be clear, my anger didn't stem from Mom having *C. diff*. There was no telling when or where she picked it up and I wasn't blaming anyone. However, I faulted Forest Meadows for dismissing my concerns regarding *C. diff* a few weeks earlier. They should have conducted the test, but didn't.

Protocols

So, another layer to Mom's increasing nursing requirements was added to the list. Our house was transformed into a veritable isolation chamber. Thomas and I had to sanitize, with diluted chlorine bleach, all surfaces in the house Mom might have touched. Of course, she had touched most everything. The roadmap led from her bathroom and bedroom to the kitchen / family room, dining room, living room, and outdoor patio. This included knobs, handles, light switches, countertops, tabletops, chairs, spigots, sippy cups, appliances, and the TV remote control. Frequent hand-washing became a ritual since the bacteria is spread to unsuspecting hands from microscopic spores making their home in poop. Without thorough hand-washing and vigilant housekeeping, the bacteria could inadvertently be hiding anywhere. For instance, if I touched a contaminated surface and picked up an apple and ate it, I could ingest the bacteria and possibly get sick. Fortunately, most healthy people don't get sick. Mom was a sitting duck and she wasn't oblivious that she could be in the firing line.

"I wish I hadn't gotten the pacemaker ... this has turned out to be an ordeal I didn't expect." Mom's out-of-character statement took me by surprise. Yet, I understood. She was tired, frustrated, and had slipped into a rare state of despondency. The pacemaker was performing beautifully, but the collateral fallout following the procedure had all but conquered her. The *C. diff* diagnosis didn't help. Mom remained in a perpetual state of fear and couldn't stop projecting something else was bound to happen. And it did a few hours later. Mom summoned me around two in the morning, with the unmistakable honk of the air horn. I bolted from my bedroom into hers. She frantically exclaimed, "The pacemaker monitor on my dresser has been sending out an alarm! Something is wrong with my pacemaker."

Mom's picture-perfect heart rate was the ultimate confirmation her pacemaker was successfully operating. Even so, this life-sustaining device requires occasional electronic checking by a pacemaker monitor, which periodically and quietly transmits reports to an analyst. Such watchfulness helps to ensure potential problems, such as low battery power, are detected before the recipient is notified by a faltering heart. The monitor is wireless, unobtrusive, portable, and about the size of a cigar box.

It's well-established I'm not a technological heavyweight. However, in this instance my meager proficiency was adequate to determine nothing was out of order. At least with the monitor. I waited in Mom's room for about five minutes and heard nothing. I assumed the mystery sound had been dreamed or imagined by Mom and I returned to my bedroom. I plopped into the bed. Within seconds, I heard faint beeps and got back up before being air-horned. The beeping stopped before I got to Mom's room. So, I waited in her room again. Sure enough, the beeping eventually recurred and, without question, the source was somewhere *in her room*. Two beeps weren't sufficient for me to ascertain the exact location, but *were* enough to avert a middle-of-the-night house-wide search. Another memorable dialogue between Mom and me ensued:

"Mama, was *that* the sound you heard?"

She pointed to the monitor and said, "Yes, it's coming from the pacemaker box."

I was surprised she had heard the beeps at all. They weren't loud. Perhaps it was the high pitch. I wondered if Mom's cell phone might be the culprit.

"The beeping might be coming from your cell phone. Where is it?"

"It's in my purse, but the beeping sound isn't coming from there. I'm telling you the beeps are coming from the monitor. You need to call them now."

"Call who?"

"The pacemaker people! There's a special number to call if there's an emergency with it."

I was confident nothing was wrong with Mom's pacemaker or the monitor. Her pulse was right on cue—sixty beats per minute. The green, normal-operation monitor light was easily visible, even at a distance. Nothing seemed out of kilter, but no amount of convincing could get Mom off the precipice. She remained frightened, insisting her pacemaker wasn't functioning properly. After rifling through Mom's purse to no avail, I continued to hunt and found the cell phone. It was hiding in plain sight, *behind the pacemaker monitor*. Mom's sense of sound direction astounded me. No wonder she thought the beeps were coming from the monitor. In effect, they were. She did a better job than I did, determining where the elusive and agitating sound was originating.

"Mama, I'm taking your cell phone to my room to see if anything happens." My hunch was validated several minutes later when the cell phone discharged two irritating chirps—the battery needed to be charged. I informed Mom and she settled down. It took forever for me to go back to sleep. I wasn't angry, though was annoyed at myself for not doing a better job of monitoring her phone battery.

For the next couple of days, Mom's condition remained status quo with sporadic episodes of diarrhea. While they were concerning, I surmised the medication would take a few days to kick in. Mom became fearful of eating anything, thinking it would cause diarrhea to flare. I could see she had lost more weight—precious weight she didn't have to lose. I was unable to persuade her that starving herself wasn't going to starve the life out of *C. diff.* I encouraged Mom to eat a banana. She ate two or three bites and declined the rest. Her rationale was red-letter. Daily, Mom took a potassium pill and deduced the same mineral naturally present in the banana might cause her to overdose. I hadn't heard of the potassium in a banana being cited as a cause of death until she raised the concern. The chances of tripping over an earthworm were greater.

The doctor had suggested Mom should eat probiotic-rich yogurt, another item on Mom's accumulating "I don't like" list. Undaunted, I introduced several flavors, all reinforced with an abundance of sugar and fat. I reasoned the adulterants might give the yogurt a fighting chance of being swallowed. The yogurt was met with halfhearted approval before ultimately facing rejection. Though not totally—I ate it. In the meantime, I cajoled Mom into trying probiotic capsules in hopes her overworked intestines would benefit.

Back in the Saddle Again

I feared Mom would lose her balance, take a hard tumble, and get her ticket punched for a return trip to the hospital. This didn't happen. Instead, she was ensnared by the tentacles of *C. diff* when the infection assumed out-of-control status a few days after her visit to the doctor. The morning of December 4, 2018, wasn't the benevolent kiss the brilliant late-fall sun suggested. Mom was walloped with fierce abdominal cramping and nausea. A loud air-horn call from her bedroom left no moment to consider its urgency. It was accompanied by her screaming, "Seth, get in here quick. I need to get to the toilet now!" Within seconds, I whisked Mom to the "mercy seat" where she had a vicious and uncontrollable intestinal upheaval. She said the episode was worse than what she had experienced at Forest Meadows on the day she obliterated her bed. There was a major difference: we made it to the bathroom with not a second to spare—an environmental catastrophe had been avoided.

Mom "camped" on the toilet for about fifteen minutes and assumed the attack was over. I got her cleaned up and redressed. Five minutes later she was besieged by another vicious onslaught. It still wasn't over. Three additional blasts over the course of the next half hour belted Mom. After she had burned through four heavy-duty disposable underpants, I left her on the toilet. She managed to drink a tad of Gatorade between bouts, in a futile effort to remain hydrated. Thank God, the blitzkrieg ceased, but not before vestiges of a war zone had been created in the bathroom. Thankfully, it was fairly isolated. Even though high-priority, the mop-up would have to wait.

Slumped back on the toilet seat, Mom was too weak to get off. I couldn't budge her and called 911. Within minutes, a rescue van arrived from the fire station three blocks away. Mom was taken four miles to Flagler Hospital, where she was admitted and placed in isolation. Think of isolation as a super-sanitized private room with restricted entry. Anyone tending to Mom, including physicians and nurses, wore protective gear and followed strict hand-washing protocols when entering and leaving the room. I was required to do the same. No one had any inkling a similar frighteningly alien scene would become commonplace throughout America in the coming year.

Mom barely escaped *C. diff*'s grip. She was released from the hospital after an eight-day stay, her care needs far from over. Rehab, here we come again. With dread, I informed Mom of the necessity for her to go to a skilled nursing facility for rehabilitation and continuing "decontamination." Predictably, she reacted with the speed of a hornet and emphatically stated, "You're not putting me back in Forest Meadows. I'm not going there. You can forget putting me in there right now." We had another option.

Parkside, a nearby skilled nursing facility, had an available isolation room. Thomas had toured this facility three months prior and was favorably impressed even though we settled on Forest Meadows at the time. I took a quick spin over to Parkside, a distance of two miles, and was given a tour. I was impressed with the facility and signed the paperwork. A few hours later, Mom was transferred to a larger-than-expected and bright isolation room with an expansive view of a shaded courtyard. The view more than made up for the room's blandness. The protocols for protective garb, room entry, and sanitation practiced at the hospital were repeated at Parkside. It was serious business taken seriously.

Mom continued to wear her disdain for Forest Meadows on her sleeve—a disdain I didn't share. I hoped her perceptions, experiences, and attitude at Parkside would be better. At least she wasn't battling hallucinations and her fractures had healed. I reasoned Forest Meadows might be an easy act to follow, putting Parkside in a better light from the get-go, at least in Mom's eyes.

My supposition proved to be correct, at least partially. Mom wasn't one to see the world through rose-colored glasses and Parkside was no exception. I visited her daily and made an effort to greet her with an upbeat tone in my voice: "Hello, Mama, don't you love this view? Are you feeling better today?" Sometimes she would mention something encouraging, such as having had an enjoyable breakfast. This didn't happen often. One morning, Mom couldn't resist telling me the CNA didn't place the usual cup of water on the bedside table the night before. When asked why she didn't ask for it, Mom said she did and the CNA brought it. Why Mom felt something trivial deserved recognition became plausible when I thought about it; she had nothing worthwhile to redirect her focus. Her world had been reduced to a cube.

The *C. diff* medications performed a miracle. Mom's discombobulated internal workings took notice and her outlook brightened. She proclaimed the food to be "much better than Forest Meadows" and praised the staff. Mom's residency in a private isolation coop demanded a higher level of care and attention. Therefore, a fair comparison to the shared room she had at Forest Meadows was difficult. Regardless, the curve had been rounded.

Mom's improving condition and favorable response to in-room physical therapy allowed me to spend less hand-holding time with her. Mom's month-long recuperation at Forest Meadows had nearly eaten me up, and the memory was unforgettably fresh. It was a relief to be less encumbered with Mom's care at Parkside. Visits became shorter and less taxing than they had been at Forest Meadows. Even so, her stay wasn't devoid of incidents.

One of Mom's unforgettable capers began at 5:49 a.m. on Wednesday, December 19, when I was rousted from the protective bubble of mindless sleep by my cell phone's chiming bell-tower ringtone. I received the following predawn greeting from a CNA at Parkside: "Mr. Vicarson, I apologize for calling you this early, but your mother has fallen and I'm required to alert you. She got up from her bed without requesting assistance and fell in the bathroom. She appears to be okay. She's walking around without difficulty and hasn't complained of any pain. You're welcome to come over if you wish."

Robotically, I rolled out of bed and drove to Parkside in a half-awake stupor. When Mom saw me walk in, she asked why I was there. I replied, "Because you fell. Why didn't you request assistance to go to the bathroom?" She asserted, "I thought I could do it without calling for help. I must have tripped on something." I ascertained Mom hadn't relied on the walker, her primary piece of safety equipment. It was resting in the same spot where I had parked it the evening before—next to the bed. The fall appeared to have been preventable. It was six fifteen in the morning, too early to lecture Mom on safety protocols. She seemed okay and there was no reason to stick around. While walking out, I pointed to the walker and pleaded, "Please use it."

Christmas 2018 came. It whizzed right past us and we scarcely observed the occasion except to give Mom a few new blouses. My sister-in-law, Lois, brightened Mom's isolation room with a festive tabletop Christmas tree and placed it on the dresser where it could be enjoyed. There was no family Christmas dinner—a first. None of us were up for it. In any event, Mom wouldn't have been allowed to leave Parkside even if invited by the royal family. She handled it in stride and without complaint.

Mom continued to improve despite poor eating habits, which weren't appreciably different from what they had been at Forest Meadows. So much for the food being "much better" at Parkside. As in the past, she was encouraged to eat yogurt but wouldn't. Nutritional shakes such as Boost and Ensure were also snubbed. Irrefutably, Mom's primary concern was far removed from the food pyramid; her preoccupation with hair maintenance remained preeminent. Hence, any immaterial details such as bread and water were relegated to lesser significance. Given Mom's "radioactive" status, urgent needs such as an excursion to the hair palace remained off-limits, much to her dismay.

Where Do We Go from Here?

As Mom's trajectory trended positive, I expected her discharge would be coming soon. The prospects of her returning to live with Thomas and me were concerning. Mom required considerable upkeep and her general condition had weakened. Max and I discussed options and we agreed Mom shouldn't live with Thomas and me. Yet, I wasn't seeking to absolve myself of Mom's care. I couldn't consider "dropping her off in Siberia" without remaining involved on a day-to-day basis. We came to the conclusion that assisted living should be considered. I researched three recommended senior-living options. Two were within five miles of Parkside. The third was within two hundred feet, directly across the courtyard from Mom's hangout in isolation. Assisted living residences were part of the Parkside complex. To avoid potential confusion, I'll refer to Parkside's assisted living facility as Courtside.

I toured the three recommended senior-living facilities and eliminated the first one based on costs and atmosphere. Besides being expensive, it oozed a rarified atmosphere with most residents appearing uncomfortably prim and overdressed. In essence, it was a country club minus the golf—not the right fit for Mom or her pocketbook.

The two finalists were pleasant, well maintained, and equally priced. Both were about half the cost of the "country club." Of the two, I preferred Courtside. It was homelike, not overwhelmingly large, and I liked the manager, Maddie. She was engaging, enthusiastic, and had clinical experience. There was one unresolved talking point: convincing Mom this was an appropriate move. Before this could happen, I had to be convinced first. My comfort level hinged on the degree of independence Mom would enjoy at Courtside and for there to be sufficient activities to keep her engaged. I didn't want Mom to feel marooned. Max was in agreement.

I felt like a parent, meeting Mom's first-grade teacher for the first time. I grilled Maddie, possibly asking too many questions. She expended an abundance of time explaining their services and addressing my concerns. No doubt she sensed I was a textbook "nervous Nellie." She assured me Mom would be in a supportive, active environment and would be given the freedom to do what she wanted when she wanted. Varying degrees of assistance were available when needed. All meals were provided and a well-stocked snack bar was open 24/7.

In-house movies, games, ice cream socials, occasional entertainment, and outings to area restaurants and shopping destinations were included. Courtyard's goal was to keep residents as independent as possible within the context of a protective yet unrestricted atmosphere. By the time Maddie had completed her wrap-up, *I* was ready to move in. Before leaving, I took the opportunity to speak with several residents, all of whom echoed their satisfaction with Courtside. Camp Courtside, here we come! And I decided *that* would be my sales pitch to Mom—senior camp.

As if the Red Sea had parted, the path was cleared before I reached it and a sales pitch to Mom was unnecessary. In fact, when I tap-danced around the possibility of assisted living, she interrupted with: "I've been thinking about it, but don't think I can afford it. I *would* be happier in my own place, though." Mom's statement startled me. It assumed an unexpected dimension when she added, "The handwriting is on the wall. I won't be returning to Jacksonville and probably should think about selling the house." Ironically, instead of shouting "Hallelujah," I wondered, *Did we do something wrong? Had Mom been unhappy staying with Thomas and me?* When questioned, Mom allayed my doubts. It all boiled down to one primary factor: independence. Mom missed her independence and wanted it back. This thrilled me.

I had determined Mom could handle the cost, although it would be necessary for her to dip into her savings each month to make it work. Initially, she was uneasy about it. She became comfortable with the idea when I promised she could do it and not become destitute. Max and I wanted Mom to be contented and comfortable even if her care eventually exhausted her nest egg. Neither Max nor I were eyeing an inheritance, although Mom made it clear her desire was to leave us her life's savings. Max and I were in complete agreement that Mom's money was hers, not ours.

The next morning, Mom was declared free of *C. diff* and advised of her "expulsion" from the isolation chamber in two days. Parkside had done a commendable job with Mom. Overall, I thought they were equal to Forest Meadows and perhaps better in the food category. However, a fair comparison wasn't truly possible since the situations were drastically different.

Mom and I visited the assisted living accommodations at Courtside later in the day and met with Maddie, who assessed Mom's need for assistance. She was classed to be middle-of-the-road when compared to most residents. A few were completely independent, while others needed a slightly higher level of care than Mom. No one in the unit had memory impairments. The monthly fee was $4,000 per month for all meals and a private (not shared) efficiency apartment—a *lot* of money. In lockstep with area facilities I had scouted, cost increases occur when care needs increase. If and when care needs exceed the parameters of the facility, alternate accommodations must be sought.

Two aspects of Mom's care remained: laundry and medications. The facility provided weekly laundry service for $40 per month, and a CNA was available to dispense Mom's eleven daily medications for a cost of $300 per month. We needed to economize where possible. Since I had been dispensing Mom's medications and doing her laundry when she was living with us, I decided to resume those duties. The savings over the course of a year would be enough to cover one month's costs.

After viewing several floor plans, Mom chose a unit with a kitchenette. It was equipped with a sink, microwave, and a personal-size refrigerator. The surrounding counter area and cabinetry were adequate for Mom's needs. Mom had a bountiful collection of clothing, and a surprisingly large closet with sliding double doors was sufficient to house the majority. An ample-sized bathroom completed the space. Two large windows provided views of the attractive courtyard, which was crisscrossed by winding concrete walks and shaded by mature live oak trees. There was one disappointment—no "real" telephone. Landlines had been removed.

Max and I had two days to get her room sufficiently furnished to allow for a relatively seamless move. There was no better source for furniture and related accessories than Mom's house in Jacksonville. She told us what she wanted, what she didn't want, and eliminated what she thought she couldn't have. With Max's Chevy Z71 pickup truck and my Subaru Outback loaded to the gills, the "Beverly Hillbillies" cautiously motored down US 1 with Mom's worldly possessions on display for the world to view. The usual one-hour trip, if on I-95, was stretched by a half hour, thanks to our relatively slow forward progress and an excess of traffic lights, mostly red.

At last, we reached Courtside and hauled the cache, piece by piece, into the empty off-white starkness of Mom's living quarters. Furniture was thoughtfully arranged to maximize the almost 300-square-foot layout. We hung her clothes and stocked the kitchenette with her favorite snacks. When we were finished, it was a microcosm of Mom's house. I was elated.

With excitement, we brought Mom over to behold the "miracle of urban renewal." She was delighted. Better yet was her glee at the sight of her beloved curio cabinet, snuggled into an otherwise dead corner. It was filled with her cherished collectibles, exactly as they were when she last laid eyes on them. Mom had advised us to not bring the curio cabinet after assuming there would be inadequate space to accommodate it. I could *never* have complied. The unobtrusive triangular-shaped cabinet was a treasured anniversary gift from Dad in the 1970s.

It had been a laborious yet rewarding day. I peered across the transformed room and it occurred to me the tangible possessions filling the room were a singular portion of what we had moved. Memories precious to Mom were abundant throughout. Photographs, paintings, lamps, and furniture were imbued with indelible imprints of the life Mom and Dad had shared. In essence, we had brought "home" to Mom. She excitedly looked forward to moving "back home" the next day.

Mom's stay in the skilled nursing facility at Parkside had totaled eighteen days, all in isolation. It terminated on December 30, 2018. I was advised to schedule Mom for a follow-up appointment with her primary care physician within two weeks. Mom was insistent that her primary care physician in Jacksonville should see her. I understood her sentiment. Yet, Max and I agreed such an arrangement would be ill-advised; Mom's primary care should permanently be established in St. Augustine. Subsequently, against Mom's objections, I had her medical records transferred to the St. Augustine physician previously consulted. It was the right decision.

Chapter header

CHAPTER 7

A NEW DAY DAWNS

Sunday morning, December 30, 2018, arrived and Mom's transfer to assisted living was at hand. I excitedly walked into her isolation room at nine thirty, ready to escort her to "Camelot." It was comforting to see the isolation shingle removed from the door. Consistent with Mom's modus operandi, she wasn't ready. What I had expected to be a relatively quick exit, wasn't. I found Mom sitting on the toilet, bent forward with her head cradled in her hands.

"Mama, are you sick?"

"I was awake most of the night coughing."

"Why were you coughing? Are you catching a cold?"

"No. I had a tickle in my throat from a confounded postnasal drip. It's driving me crazy."

"Mama, you took that drive years ago and postnasal drip wasn't the culprit." My attempt to derail her thought pattern was marginally successful.

She smiled, adding, "I had diarrhea this morning. I called Angie [the CNA], and she saw the mess in the toilet. I think I might need to go again, so will sit here another minute or two. I'm afraid the *C. diff* is coming back."

I wanted to run for the nearest exit.

Mom continued to sit, waiting for another event. Angie popped in, hoping Mom was ready to vacate the room. I asked about Mom's diarrhea and was told it was simply a soft stool. In addition, lab results received two days prior confirmed no evidence of *C. diff.*

Eventually, Mom scuttled her fruitless bathroom effort and yelled through the closed door, "We can leave as soon as I wash my hands." I thought, *That will be the day.* Twenty minutes later, she opened the bathroom door. Familiar scents of a female construction zone escaped— hairspray and perfume. Mom cracked a wry smile and declared, "I'm sorry it took so long. We can go now." Mom had completed last-minute hair adjustments and applied finishing touches of makeup to facial areas begging for remediation. She was ready for presentation.

Mom was a bit apprehensive. She hadn't met any of the residents in assisted living, and underlying worries about bowel troubles continued to occupy her thoughts. I followed the CNA as she wheeled Mom to the large outdoor courtyard where we were caressed by glorious seventy-five-degree weather and a brilliant sun. I took it to be a favorable nod from the "gods." We followed a curving, partially shaded concrete walkway leading to the assisted living sector on the opposite side of the courtyard, about a two-minute excursion. When we arrived at the entrance, Mom was greeted by Maddie, the manager, and a resident named Carol, who was the official greeter. She introduced Mom to several residents and the assimilation process began. I closely watched while Mom basked in the warm welcome and easily made connections with residents. It was gratifying to see glimmers of her engaging personality resurfacing; she was in the right place.

I stayed with Mom for most of the morning, making sure she was settled in her room and well-supplied with necessary items. She didn't have to search for anything since we moved her furniture with contents undisturbed. It was lunchtime and I accompanied Mom to the dining room, where she was seated at a table with three ladies: Carol (the aforementioned greeter), Elsie, and Clara. Carol and Clara were in their 80s and Elsie was 95. Their ages and gender closely mirrored what I had observed throughout the facility. Mom, who would be 101 in four weeks, wasn't the oldest in the facility. One lady was 103 and another 109. (This isn't a misprint.) Shortly after Mom was seated, I left the henhouse. There was no need for me to remain.

Mom's adjustment period began and she tackled it with an "onward and upward" attitude. Within the week, she referred to Courtside as home. It was gratifying to watch her take flight, transitioning from surviving to thriving. She enjoyed being surrounded by fellow residents and lost no time tapping into the camaraderie existing among them. Carol and Mom developed a close friendship, though Mom enjoyed special relationships with many other residents. There was no lack of opportunity for conversation, an activity in which Mom excelled. As contented as she appeared to be, I was aware she missed her house, her close friends, and her church. Occasional visitors from Jacksonville eased the "in her face" reality that life had permanently changed.

As perceived, the facility shared commonalities with summer camp. A few well-tailored deviations distinguished Mom's campsite from "Camp Granada." Activities were tamed down to a palatable level of physical exertion. Water aerobics in the community pool served as a substitute for water skiing, and softball was abandoned for walks around the building. Archery? Disappointingly, this wasn't on the agenda. Errant arrows flying around without laser-guided assistance might pierce the activity coordinator's derriere instead of a hay-filled target. Another classic camp favorite, badminton, wasn't on the approved list either. Substandard balance among most residents eliminated this accident-waiting-to-happen competition from consideration. Instead, bingo and gin rummy tournaments made for spirited yet friendly competition. As will be explained, there were a few notable exceptions to the friendly factor.

Evening ghost stories around a campfire weren't part of the setup. Not to be outdone, generous time was allotted for scary stories. Discussions about potentially lethal diagnoses among fellow residents were passed around the circle of ladies huddled in the activity room. To make it worse, there weren't any s'mores to deflect the chilling topic. Fig bars were the stand-in—less mess and fiber-rich.

Mom received daily visits from me, with rare exception. Selfishly, on occasion I preferred to do something else. Unless ill, I didn't let her down and never regretted it. Mom always had a story to tell, usually about people, with her favorite subjects being fellow residents. Many narratives weren't particularly stimulating, which encouraged my thoughts to drift into the clouds while Mom interminably expounded on minutia. I tried to appear tuned-in. For the record, there was a flip side. A few of Mom's stories were *so* memorable she had me mesmerized. These firsthand accounts demanded attentiveness and transformed my mind into a sponge. I feverishly took mental notes, which were put into written form when I returned to my car. Several of these real-life tales are featured in this chapter.

Serious Business

One afternoon a few days after Mom had moved in, I realized I had forgotten to add a new medication to her seven-day pill dispenser. I sprung to action and ten minutes later walked into the Courtside lobby, unannounced, with the medication in my pocket. I saw Mom sitting in the conference room and nudged the glass-paned door open. She and several of her fellow residents were ensconced in a card game. Based on the pennies scattered on the table, it wasn't the game of Old Maid. I sheepishly entered the room to get Mom's room key and to tell her why I was there. Her fellow participants weren't amused at the disruption. If looks could kill, I would've been deader than roadkill. I learned a valuable lesson: Don't dishonor the sanctity of a "high-stakes" card game by interrupting it.

Later when Mom and I were conversing, she told me she had won several consecutive hands during the game I had interrupted. Her wins exceeded probable odds. One of the players, Harriet, was offended by Mom's prowess and complained to several members in her "squad" that she wasn't going to participate in any card game where Mom was present. The implication was clear: Mom was a card shark! The comment got right back to Mom within a nanosecond. Mom rarely got offended by much of anything and this was no different. She laughed it off.

My unaggressive, agreeable, and *very* Baptist mom was far from being a card shark. True, she *was* a better-than-average card player, blessed with a steel-trap memory. Even so, a few other players were equally equipped. Sure enough, Mom's losses at the table began to surpass her wins. The community grapevine buzzed. The news found its way to the farthest reaches of the Courtside universe and Harriet saw fit to return to the table when she felt it was "safe" to do so. All was well with the world.

Bingo, anyone? This staple of entertainment is offered at most senior facilities and Courtside was no exception. Games were scheduled two evenings a week, following the five o'clock meal. A six o'clock start time was routinely honored, with limited deviation. It was a popular, well-orchestrated, and controlled event. On one occasion, civility disintegrated and tempers flared—before the game commenced. A disagreement broke out between two 80-something-year-old ladies, Agnes and Beatrice, who morphed into combatants. In amazement, Mom observed the usually congenial decorum collapse into a swiftly escalating bout. Dumbfounded, the surrounding peanut gallery was fixed on the spectacle in the ring.

The initial spark was provided by Agnes, whose virtues didn't include patience. She was perturbed by a thirty-minute game delay. An expected ten-minute delay had previously been announced. Agnes turned the delay into a personal gripe-a-thon to include derogatory remarks about the conscientious, hardworking, and beloved activity coordinator, Connie. In a worked-up state, Agnes ejected herself from her chair, slammed it backwards against the wall, and steered her rollator-turned-bulldozer through a maze of parked transports. Incidentally, a rollator is a gussied-up walker with four wheels and a seat. Beatrice, who was seated in a wheelchair, wheeled herself to the doorway, blocking Agnes' escape. Beatrice was on a roll and unleashed a verbal shellacking, further enraging Agnes. A shouting match ensued. Two residents on the sidelines got involved and brokered a peace deal, which allowed Agnes to pass through Beatrice's checkpoint and return to her room for a period of self-imposed time-out.

The bingo game commenced, minus Agnes, and Mom's patience was rewarded with a windfall in winnings—four quarters and a memorable story. Not long after, Mom expressed a concern about gambling being a sin and concluded she probably shouldn't be playing games that involved money. I jokingly assured her that a few coins, which, by the way, were provided by outside supporters, were well below God's established sin threshold and she should enjoy playing. Nevertheless, I understood Mom's point of reference and attempted to assuage her guilt. I proposed God would surely forgive the perceived wrongdoing since the intent of the games was to provide fun and fellowship. She stared at the wall and, with a mischievous glint in her eyes, whispered, "It's still not right ... but I'm not going to stop playing." We both laughed.

The excitement from the three-ring bingo should have been sufficient; however, another altercation erupted the next week as Camp Courtside was becoming an incubator for out-of-control emotions reminiscent of elementary schoolkids. Once a week, free fingernail painting was offered by a volunteer to any resident who wanted fingernail ornamentation. Her services were a highly anticipated event, offered on a first-come, first-served basis. Two ladies, Maylene and Ramona, who were fast friends, got into a heated argument over which one of them was *third* in line. There was no quibbling with the two ladies who were indisputably first and second. Maylene *had* been third in line, but briefly vacated her spot to go to the restroom. When she returned, Ramona had arrived and was third in line. An argument ensued and rapidly escalated.

Fists flew wildly in the air. Fortunately, limited reach between the two adversaries and refereeing by Connie, the activity coordinator, prevented punches from finding their intended targets. Stupefied bystanders keenly watched the match, probably with their mouths gaping when these 90-year-old children exchanged verbal barbs. Implausibly, the would-be boxers had been inseparable dining room tablemates for eons. And get this … the altercation boiled up again at the dinner table later in the day. This round didn't include boxing, but the argument continued off and on during the meal. Mom was sitting two tables over. She reported it wouldn't have been surprising to see pork chops sailing through the air. Tempers calmed and there was no food fight. Maylene and Ramona reclaimed their friendship several days later. Incidentally, Mom had been eighth in line to get her nails done. Dead last. She was unchallenged.

Is This Peyton Place?

Unscripted and riveting behavior at Courtside wasn't limited to fights. Remember *Peyton Place*? If not, it's a novel, written in the 1950s, about an outrageously scandalous New England town. Courtside shared similarities on a less impressive yet equally salacious scale. As Mom witnessed, there were times when assisted living was provided by fellow residents in the form of "fraternization" with the opposite sex.

With only a handful of male residents at Courtside, their affections were in demand by the overpopulation of coeds, both on and off the field. Courtships *did* occur for a select few desiring ladies who had made their intentions obvious. The only lacking component of this live theater was buttered popcorn.

The subject of this truth-is-stranger-than-fiction story is a 60-something-year-old "wild child" whom I'll call Ophelia. I didn't understand why she lived in the facility—she needed zero assistance. However, she was generous in extending *her* "assistance" to an 80-year-old, skinny as a rail, and dried-up (Mom's description) Romeo, who appreciated Ophelia's physical attributes. Ophelia was on the short side, overly suntanned, with enough makeup to make Tammy Faye envious, and was graced with a few extra pounds of insulating plumpness. In fact, she was attractive. Her mini "cruiser," parked in a designated spot outside the building, was icing on the cake. The vehicle, and her ability to drive it, assuredly enhanced her deliciousness. Ophelia had wheels and was a willing chauffeur to the lucky suitor.

One Saturday evening while a number of ladies, including my mom, were huddled in the lobby chitchatting, a decidedly unsteady and unaccompanied Ophelia sauntered through the open glass entry doors. She had been out "running errands" for a couple of hours. It was evident that Headwinds, a nearby watering hole where Ophelia was a frequent "guest," had been her primary destination. Slurred speech, a bloodied forehead, and inability to walk a straight line were indicators she had been overserved. The Ophelia comedy could have been a skit on *Saturday Night Live*. She tripped and fell forward into the back of a chair. Unhurt, she pulled herself up and managed to sit in it.

Ophelia and Romeo had been inseparable, which made his absence particularly noteworthy. When asked where he was, Ophelia blurted out, "I haven't seen him and he won't be getting any sugar anytime soon." With alcohol-diminished inhibitions, she "pinned the tail on the donkey" by adding she wasn't going to "put out" again until he treated her like a lady. I can only imagine the facial expressions on the body of witnesses, most of whom were upstanding churchgoers. I asked Mom what she thought about Ophelia's dramatic entrance. Not one for reticence, Mom quipped, "It sure livened the place up and was more entertaining than the movies they show around here."

There was initial concern for Romeo's well-being, given the presence of blood on Ophelia's face, which she attributed to hitting her head on the car's door frame. Plausible … but a drunken brawl with Romeo loomed as a possibility. Daily, the facility provided a sign-out sheet that residents were required to log before leaving the building. Ophelia's signature and time of departure were noted on the sheet, but not Romeo's—evidence he hadn't left Courtside. At least he hadn't been deserted high and dry in the bar. Well, maybe not the dry part. He was located a few minutes later in his room. The next day, the couple reconciled after Ophelia returned from attending Sunday school class at her church. She seldom missed it, yet was far from being pegged a church lady.

Ophelia was a fascinating study in contradiction. She was considerate yet unapologetic, religious yet an anything-goes kind of girl, generally quiet yet an excellent conversationalist, and usually sober except when she occasionally wasn't. To be succinct, she was unafraid to be who she was. I was disappointed when she moved away a few months later to help care for a relative. She was one of my favorites at Courtside.

Other romances at Courtside were less advertised yet still suggested. While nothing could match Ophelia and Romeo for sheer entertainment and spice, I observed another couple who occasionally held hands while closely seated in adjacent chairs at the dinner table. Their exchange of sweet expressions suggested they were in the "going steady" phase. Anything beyond a friendly courtship wasn't alluded to. These two chums, in their early 80s, had been childhood friends when growing up in Vero Beach. They reconnected at Courtside. Both passed away not long thereafter.

Is There an Exterminator in the House?

Elsie was 95 years old, immaculate in dress and appearance, and surprisingly agile. She lived directly across the hall from Mom and was one of her tablemates at meals. At lunch one day, Elsie saw what she thought was a roach basking on the floor under the four-top table where she, Carol, Clara, and Mom sat. Without uttering a syllable, she quietly got out of her chair, pulled off a shoe, and crawled under the table on her hands and knees with the shoe in one hand and a napkin in the other. Whatever was lurking had successfully evaded recent insecticidal applications. Not to fear, the interloper was no match for Elsie's deftness with a shoe. She smashed the critter and inspected the carcass to ensure all life had been extinguished. She had been successful! But her efforts had been in vain. A closer examination revealed she had flattened a bit of mud that had fallen off the bottom of someone's shoe—possibly her own.

While underneath the table, she spotted another suspect—this time a real roach—but allowed it to rest in peace after determining it had been rendered lifeless by prior chemical means. Elsie crawled out. While tightly holding the crumpled napkin in her hand, she proclaimed there was no need for further intervention.

One of Mom's profound heartaches at Courtside was the loss of her close friend, Carol. This occurred about a year after Mom had moved in. She and Mom found much in common. They had enjoyed playing games, visiting each other, and talking about life. Carol was 20 years younger than Mom. When her health began to fail, she moved back to Indiana to live with family. Several months later, Mom received word of Carol's passing away.

The frequent loss of residents in an assisted living facility is a difficult reality. This is inescapable where there's a preponderance of elderly living in any community setting. When a resident passed away at Courtside, a memorial table was set up in the lobby to signify the occurrence. A picture of the deceased and an obituary were displayed. Residents typically placed notes of remembrance on the table. The table remained in the lobby for a week and was taken down until needed again, always too soon. I grew to love many of Mom's friends at Courtside. I watched them valiantly continue living while their close-knit band dealt with frequent loss. They were inspirational.

Mom Gets a New Buick

Max and I hadn't pressed Mom to sell her house or her 1998 Buick LeSabre. However, we felt the time had come. Mom had mentioned selling the house when she moved into Courtside, and it didn't take much of a nudge for her to make the decision to sell it *and* the car. The car had low mileage, and was in excellent condition, thanks to Max's efforts. It sold without being advertised. Max's son bought it for someone else who needed reliable transportation.

Mom and her 1998 Buick LeSabre.

Mom jokingly mentioned she needed a suitable replacement for her recently sold Buick. I had to stop and think about it while waiting for the punchline since she usually had one. She explained: Transportation needs at Courtside were such that her walker, a flagrant downgrade from the LeSabre, needed to be retired. When compared to most chariots whizzing through the facility, it was cumbersome. Mom was exhilarated with her living accommodations but hampered by her slow-moving clunker. She couldn't keep up with residents who owned faster vehicles; they eased past her when traveling up and down the wide halls. The halls were the equivalent of an interstate highway with exits to major points of interest: the library, conference room, courtyard, laundry area, and dining room.

Max's son and his wife assessed the situation and bestowed Mom with a brand-new, shiny, red rollator. Mom was ecstatic. She referred to the rollator as the "Buick," named in honor of her beloved 1998 LeSabre. The rollator was adaptable, maneuverable, and "smoked" the retired walker, which hadn't been graced with a name. The "can't-turn-it-down" new model boasted multiple ergonomically designed enhancements. Features included a seat that doubled as a miniature table or chair, four easy-rolling wheels, two handbrakes to prevent a runaway vehicle, and a handy storage compartment accessible by flipping the seat up. The Buick was fully "tricked out." Mom would have been the envy of her fellow residents—except most of them had traded up as well.

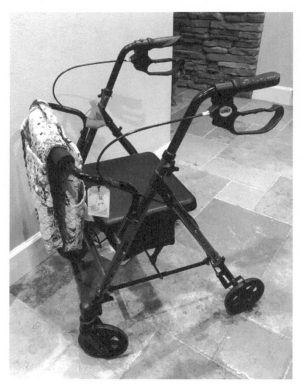

The Replacement Model

Mom's unoccupied house had become a liability. The costs of maintenance, utilities, taxes, insurance, and lawn service were adding up. Additionally, selling the house would provide much of the money needed for her monthly expenses at Courtside. We listed the house in February 2019, three months following her move into Courtside. She hadn't lived in her house for five months. Valuables had previously been removed and any furniture Mom wanted was nestled in her Courtside quarters. We planned to use the remaining furniture in the house for staging purposes and hoped the eventual buyer would keep it. Max and I were willing to make a deal too good to pass up: FREE. Eliminating the burden of moving heavy furniture from the house would be an immense gift for us.

Max and I took Mom to the house when we began the arduous process of rummaging through files, closets, drawers, boxes, and the kitchen. Fifty-six years of accumulation created a passel of God-only-knows. What a menagerie! The task proved a greater challenge than I had imagined. Anything worth repurposing, which constituted the majority of household items, was given away. Worthless junk got tossed. Some of Mom's clothes had been transferred to Courtside, yet much remained in her house.

Mom had a long-standing preference for thin towels. For decorative purposes, she *did* have a few of the plump, thirsty ones, used mostly for company. In her estimation, the thirsty ones took forever to dry and cost a fortune. I'm with her on both points. Remember Breeze detergent and the "free" towel stuffed into each box? Mom was a Tide detergent devotee, so we didn't have any sourced from Breeze. Not to be deterred, the majority of Mom's towels were Breeze-comparable and we kept most of them—some for her, some for me. Max didn't share our appreciation for these vintage keepsakes and declined the opportunity to grab a few.

House treasures weren't limited to Mom's possessions. I came across some she had intentionally held for Max and me in her cedar chest. She had kept all of my formal classroom pictures from kindergarten through seventh grade, all tightly tucked into the original white envelopes protecting them. In an almost hypnotic state, I focused on them, momentarily lost in time, unconcerned about the assignment to clear out the house. Amazingly, I could recall the names of most classmates even though I hadn't seen many since childhood.

The attic was another uncharted fantasyland worthy of deep exploration. There, I found an electronic contraption resembling the guts of a 1950s-era television. This "antique" undoubtedly belonged to Max, whose mind was captured by how things worked. Next I saw a partially crushed box containing ancient, mostly broken Christmas ornaments dating to the 1950s and '60s. I remembered them, but didn't experience any particular regret at their demise. Kind of odd, given my bent toward sentimentality.

Then I came across a slice of history that grabbed my soul ... rolled-up, twine-wrapped newspapers and magazines, hibernating in an oversized plastic bag. The bag had been sealed shut by multiple pieces of crisscrossing masking tape, a mark of Mom's "artistry." She always used masking tape to secure anything in a bag. As tight as her wrapping had initially been, the once airtight plastic bag had been reduced to strips of disintegrated gray rubble from years of baking in extreme attic heat.

Eagerly, I unraveled the rotten twine and unfurled the dust-covered contents, which were still surprisingly legible. Well-remembered late-November and early-December 1963 dates captivated me. The shock of JFK's assassination when I was in the ninth grade was chronicled in pages of print and photographs, some in color, others black-and-white. It was surreal to hold the fragile items I had last touched when they were in mint condition fifty-five years prior. I wondered if my fingerprints on the glossy magazine pages were discernable. Strangely, I felt as if I had leapfrogged in some sort of time warp from being a 14-year-old kid to a 70-year-old man. Yet my emotions felt much the same as they did in 1963 and, for a few moments, I cried. I'm not particularly emotional and my outburst caught me without warning. Possibly, my emotions were predisposed to exposure. It was a sad time.

The attic faithfully guarded revered vestiges from my childhood I assumed had been discarded many years ago. I stumbled upon a few beat-up toy trucks and tractors Dad and Mom had given me when I was perhaps 8 or 10 years old. I effortlessly recalled pushing them around on dirt roads I had graded in the bare sandy soil in the backyard, which was heavily shaded by a grape arbor. Nothing grew beneath it. The arbor was the perfect site for my various road and bridge construction projects.

Assembling scale-model airplanes was another childhood passion when I wasn't into earthbound projects. I had presumed their transfer to the "Mojave Desert" aircraft graveyard was accomplished fifty-plus years prior. This was disproved when an almost missed, dry-rotted corrugated box caught my attention. It began to crumble when I opened the folded-over top flaps, revealing a prized sight—my entire fleet of aircraft. Mom was keenly aware of their significance to me and had Dad store them in the attic. In the bat of an eye, I was transported to the domain of my 14- or 15-year-old self while I carefully extracted the planes, one by one, from their corrugated "hangar." The decals and paint schemes I had meticulously applied in minute detail were remembered. Although I didn't realize it at the time, those planes represented early clues to an eventual career path silently flying in the same wind. The circle was closed when Delta Air Lines employed me for twenty-four years. The aforementioned career in health insurance followed.

My brief attic sojourn wasn't a mere distraction. It was a gift—even if wrapped in grunge—to trip into a once familiar haunt and unexpectedly experience my past *becoming* my present. The kid inside me assumed front and center. During those halcyon moments of inestimable worth, I relived and reflected. My distraction in the attic ended with an inescapable realization: my perspectives were decidedly different than when I was a fledgling. Nonetheless, my long-lost treasures hadn't lost their exquisiteness, even though the years had camouflaged their sheen. Sentimentality does that.

It took multiple trips to Jacksonville for Max, Mom, and me to get the house cleaned up and reasonably staged for the realtor to market the property. The day of our last visit arrived. I dreaded it even though there wasn't an overwhelming workload. I expected it might be emotionally difficult for Mom despite her outward steeliness. She remained focused while we completed the remaining chores. Cleaning baseboards and windowsills, scrubbing the two bathrooms and kitchen, and vacuuming the floors was all that remained. Mom mostly supervised.

There was one last task Mom wanted to accomplish. I watched her carefully negotiate the four-inch step down from the kitchen into the garage and unhook a worn straw broom conveniently hanging on the wall. Countless predecessors had hung on the same hook since the house was built. Mom resisted my attempt to take the broom from her hand, and insisted, "Please let me sweep." It was a comfortable late-winter day, and I felt sure she could do it with me standing close by to catch her if she stumbled. Evidently, she *needed* to sweep, even though the garage floor was fairly clean. The symbolism was clear.

Mom began to methodically and slowly sweep the single-car garage floor, which had the typical irremovable oil stains one might expect to see on old concrete. She continued to sweep a few leaves scattered on the driveway and walkway leading to the front porch. When finished, she handed me the broom and said, "Seth, please hang it up. We can go now." I knew it was the last time. She did too.

"Goodbye, Little House"

When we backed out of the driveway, Mom made a statement that summed it all up. Without shedding a tear and with no emotion in her voice, she bid farewell to her house: "Goodbye, little house, you've been good to me." It was a difficult parting for Mom. She never looked back. Mom was exceptional and I had always been aware of it.

There wasn't much conversation in the car. Silence spoke it all. Mom remained emotionless, with her eyes mostly fixed in a blank stare, occasionally commenting on the beauty of a particular tree or cloud. A flood of memories invaded my thoughts. I battled a lump in my throat and struggled to keep a flood from pouring from my eyes. The cozy house had signified safety, security, and was a place where love had permeated the walls. It was home and always would be, regardless of who bought it.

As I drove, a smile replaced the few errant tears dampening my cheeks while I recalled the house's history. In 1954, Dad and Mom bought a cramped, two-bedroom, one-bath garage apartment and an adjacent vacant lot with the goal to eventually build a new home on it. They occupied one bedroom and Max and I shared the other. I was 5 years old and Max was almost 11. Eight years passed. The lot's primary use as a sandy playground came to a halt in 1962 when the new-house dream took flight. Dad drew the house plans, had them blueprinted, and served as the general contractor. This in itself was impressive when considering he learned how to do it by reading manuals and observing house construction projects in the neighborhood. I can sum up Dad's construction philosophy in one sentence: If the building code requires four nails in a board, eight will be specified. The house was solidly built using construction techniques appropriate for a fort. It was a 1,300-square-foot, concrete block Florida classic consisting of three bedrooms, two bathrooms, and an attached garage—a novelty in our understated neighborhood. Most garages were detached and sat in backyards.

As I continued driving, memories transported me to the time when Dad drafted Max and me into his construction crew by handing a shovel to each of us. Our mission was to help him dig the house foundation trenches. Money was tight and our labor would represent a cost savings. Child labor? Yes, sir! There was much more to it than a cost savings in

Dad's eyes; he thought the experience would instill the importance of teamwork, work ethic, and a sense of pride in the project if we had skin in the game. He was right.

The three of us comprised the "chain gang," and the intolerable July heat and humidity made it a miserable chore. Mom's fresh-squeezed lemonade *was* hydrating, but I would have gleefully traded her elixir for a swimming pool. I didn't feel much pride while digging; however, my attitude received a needed adjustment when the concrete truck backed across the lot and filled the trenches with concrete. Dad "offered" a mixture of construction assignments during the four-month project, yet none approached the unforgettable imprint of digging ditches. We moved into the house in November 1962. It was a *mansion* ... Max and I had separate bedrooms.

We couldn't have imagined Mom would live independently in the house for twenty-six years following Dad's death in late 1992; she had been extraordinarily fortunate.

The house sold quicker than I had speculated. Mom was 101 years old when we turned the keys over to the new owner in April 2019. While selling the house was prudent, it was still emotional for all of us. I feel sure Mom's heartstrings were being strummed, though she didn't allude to it.

A young man around 30 years old was the buyer; it was his first venture into home ownership. Mom, Max, and I were excited to meet him and his partner. With much pride, we showed them every nook and cranny in the house. We shared a number of stories pertaining to the house's history and how Dad had designed the floor plan to maximize every square inch of usable space. With mixed emotions, we conferred the original house plans Dad had drawn. It was emotionally challenging to relinquish something that was so personal to him, but he would have wanted the plans to remain with the house. Much to our delight, the new owner kept the furniture. We didn't have to move it out!

Exasperations

Mom was a treasure, loved by many. Her keen wit, sweetness, outwardly upbeat attitude, caring and giving nature, and abundance of musical and artistic talents drew people in. She was accustomed to having numerous opportunities and associations with countless friends. When the effects of *very* old age finally caught up with her, she was forced to become less involved. Disengagement wasn't in her vocabulary.

Fewer diversions allowed sublimated facets of her personality to surface. She became increasingly negative and complained about things she wouldn't have mentioned a few years before. Most times, I listened and changed the subject.

Too often, Mom called to grumble about insignificant matters occasionally popping up at Courtside. I didn't need to be informed an ant was crawling next to the kitchen sink, or a light bulb was out, or a smudge was on the floor. Concerns of this nature were all within the oversight of the facility and could easily be handled. There was usually a critical piece of information Mom had failed to mention: she hadn't registered her complaint with the facility.

I reasoned with Mom that if housekeeping was unaware of an ant parade or anything else calamitous, they couldn't fix it. When questioned, she was quick to point out she "hadn't had time yet" to tell anyone. Nonetheless, she had found time to call me. Mom had less to divert her attention than ever, and it was only natural for her to focus on what was in front of her. I learned to listen and addressed any of Mom's concerns with the facility. It didn't take much of an effort.

Mom's intestinal engineering was no different than with most senior adults. Irregular bowel function—either constipation or diarrhea—became an obsession. When diarrhea was the aggravation, she concluded the cause was *C. diff.* When constipation distracted her, she assumed another bowel blockage was responsible. Poor eating habits, zero exercise, dehydration, and insufficient sleep weren't considered. I reminded Mom these less threatening, common triggers of irregularity could be blamed. Reassurance usually worked.

One morning, Mom called to request a few cans of ginger ale since the facility kitchen had run out of it. Her bowels were "loose" and she was nauseated. I hurried to the grocery store, picked up a six-pack and took it to her. The Seagram's label caught her attention and she immediately objected. "Seth, Seagram's is an alcohol company and I'm not comfortable drinking this." I did my best to convince her the ginger ale was okay to drink, and thought I had been successful.

The next day, I noticed all six cans were still in the refrigerator where I had left them. I was irritated, given the nature of the "emergency" that had been described the day before. Mom said the ginger ale hadn't been consumed out of fear her throat would fill with phlegm if she drank it. Maybe so. She had made the same comment in the past about carbonated orange beverages. The ginger ale remained untouched, and I left it in the refrigerator to "ferment." I didn't say a word. The steam escaping from my ears told the story. In the meantime, her intestines had returned to normal operation.

"My Life" in Assisted Living

Much of the emotional assistance Mom needed was provided by me. I visited each afternoon for about thirty to forty minutes, which wasn't long enough in Mom's estimation. She seemed to think my availability was unlimited since I was retired and had no pressing responsibilities. In fact, the opposite was true. I sang in my church choir, volunteered in the community, and spent a portion of each day writing. In addition, I expended necessary time completing daily tasks to maintain life. Keeping up with Mom's shopping, laundry, management of her financial affairs, appointments, medications, and correspondence rounded out my list of responsibilities.

The last thing I wanted to do while visiting Mom was to argue about anything. It wasn't worth it ... except when her well-being was jeopardized. The facility had given her a medical alert pendant to wear when she was alone in her room, and I couldn't ignore her continuing failure to wear it. Her rollator was another hassle. She didn't want to use it *in* her room. One afternoon, I walked in to visit and found her standing at the bathroom sink applying makeup. The rollator was fifteen feet away, parked next to her desk, and the pendant was lying *on* the desk. Without saying a word, I retrieved the rollator and placed it next to her. Pendant placement around her neck was next. Mom didn't appreciate the assistance, and barked, "I just finished fixing my hair and that chain you put over my head messed it up." It hadn't. An argument ensued, and I angrily said, "Okay, Mama, have it your way, but at some point you're going to fall. I hope your hair is worth it." This was a never-ending point of contention. She had fallen in her room the week before and, fortunately, wasn't injured—the bed caught her. Mom was a curious study. She advised me of her falls, but wouldn't follow simple safety rules to prevent them.

Got Hearing Aids?

On one of those rare days when I couldn't go visit Mom, I called her instead. I dreaded phone conversations; they were guaranteed to be fraught with complications. To begin with, the phone was an obstacle. Mom could barely operate it. When she managed to answer it, she struggled to hear. In most instances, she wasn't wearing her hearing aids. I expected my attempt to engage Mom in meaningful phone conversation would be futile. My assumption was correct, at least partially. Mom *did* answer the phone. I could tell she had the speaker turned off and her hearing aids were resting somewhere—but not in her ears; thus she couldn't hear. We discontinued the conversation.

Numerous attempts had been made to get Mom "trained" to successfully pilot the phone. Explanations, demonstrations, and practice sessions were guaranteed to be foolproof. They fell short. I appealed to Mom, promising she could conquer the infernal phone: "When the phone rings, all you have to do is open it, press the big 'OK' key to turn the speaker on, and talk." How something so seemingly simple could pose such a challenge was flabbergasting. I could only imagine how diminished Mom must have felt.

Mom called me back in an agitated state and was unable to hear a darn word. After ten minutes of accomplishing nothing, I hung up out of desperation and dragged myself to Courtside. It was eight o'clock. Mom wasn't in the best humor and started complaining about the "lousy" dinner—lasagna. It was a continuation of the one-way phone "conversation" I had jettisoned a few minutes earlier. Her distaste for lasagna was long-standing, yet she hadn't requested an alternative. She admitted to attending an ice cream social at two o'clock and drinking an orange-flavored soft drink at four. She wasn't hungry to begin with. Why she made such a protest over pasta was perplexing. But … it didn't take long to uncover the underlying source of Mom's angst. It wasn't relating to dinner.

Before leaving, I mentioned it would be a good time to change the hearing aid batteries. Unexpectedly, Mom threw a monkey wrench into the suggestion. The usually effortless undertaking was only partially possible. Mom sheepishly informed me the hearing aid for her right ear was missing. I took a deep breath and envisioned a flood of dollar bills floating out the window to replace the one lost. Mom had purchased her pair of hearing aids three years prior at a cost of four thousand dollars. Though ridiculously expensive, in my estimation these weren't top-of-the-line devices.

With no emotion or tone in my voice, I asked, "Mama, what do you mean? Is it really missing?"

She replied, "Well … it's gone. I realized it yesterday and can't find it."

I was surprised she had been wearing them enough to lose one. I probed further. "Do you have any idea where you might have lost it?"

Mom assured me, "It has to be somewhere in this room. I guess it fell out of my ear. That's happened before."

The search began. I expected it would be brief. It wasn't. I conducted a "microscopic" investigation inside and outside the room, including the common areas she had frequented. It was a fruitless endeavor. The hearing aid wasn't found. To top it off, the insurance for loss or damage had expired three weeks prior. Mom mentioned the hearing aid had fit improperly and probably "jumped out" of her ear. I think she was right.

When the hearing aids were initially purchased, Mom was given a ninety-day trial period to identify any problems with fit or defect. None were mentioned. In fact, she proclaimed them "just wonderful." Shortly after the trial period ended, she voiced a complaint—the right hearing aid seemed too large. By that time, it was too late for a free refitting and replacement. I had frequently positioned both hearing aids in her ears, and the right aid required a bit of maneuvering. Since Mom's numb hands were a major impediment to her ability to squarely place them in her ears, I surmised the one lost hadn't been completely inserted. It might have fallen into the toilet or succumbed to a hungry vacuum cleaner.

The hearing aid was replaced to the tune of two thousand dollars. I didn't complain to Mom. After all, it was her money. As her "comptroller," I attentively watched her living expenses relentlessly chiseling down her assets. When she asked about her bank account balances, I always assured her there was no need to worry. (I did enough of that for both of us.)

Letter from St. Vincent's Hospital

About a month after we moved Mom into assisted living, I received an alert letter from St. Vincent's Hospital stating the monitor had stopped generating reports. The letter didn't worry me since Mom's vitals were routinely checked each day at Courtside and her heart rate was normal. Her pacemaker was obviously working, which the stethoscope confirmed. For some reason, the monitor had taken an unscheduled sabbatical. Armed with the 101-page, pocket-size user's guide, I trudged to the facility hoping to find an easy solution and avoid a trip to Jacksonville.

My diagnostic talents enabled me to verify the pacemaker was securely plugged in. I had hoped for a loose plug. I unplugged it anyway and waited thirty seconds before plugging it back in. I extrapolated this might fix the problem since the procedure sometimes worked for cable TV. The green light on the monitor started to pulse and, in a few seconds, it was solidly lit. While it was a positive sign, nothing else happened. I found a page in the user's guide instructing me to push a particular button to generate a manual report. I pushed it and prayed for a miraculous transmission. And a miracle is what would be required, given who was doing the troubleshooting. Blue and yellow lights started flashing and my miracle seemed to be at hand ... until the hoped-for result was sabotaged by one word: failure. Several substitute words for *failure* came to mind, most with four letters. I kept them to myself— Mom was wearing her hearing aids.

I popped open the strangely organized, miniscule-print user's guide. It was written in a geek language I couldn't embrace. I'm sure the writers might counter any perceived strangeness was due to my faulty comprehension and they would be correct. Despite my shortcomings, I delved into the subject matter. After spending twenty minutes trying to uncover any needle in this haystack of confusion, a page of mostly uninterpretable techno-jargon pertaining to a wireless adapter caught my eye. The associated sketch didn't remotely resemble the pendulous apparatus hanging from the back of Mom's monitor. Even though the depiction didn't paint a thousand words, it was enough for me to determine the adapter shown was plugged into the same slot as Mom's gizmo. I deduced the gizmo had to be an adapter of some sort. Almost in passing, the instructions stated a green light on the adapter would flash when a wireless signal was detected. There was no green light, flashing or otherwise. I *did* find an inconspicuous pinpoint-size black hole where a light might hide. Inspired by Inspector Clouseau, I got out a flashlight and magnifying glass to allow for a focused inspection. Even with these state-of-the-art tools, my enhanced sleuthing yielded an unchanged assessment: it still appeared to be a tiny black hole and nothing else.

With an ounce of perseverance remaining and a glimmer of hope, I unplugged the monitor, leaving the affixed impotent adapter dangling from the back. With an eight-foot extension cord trailing, I took the apparatus to the lobby where the internet signal was likely stronger. I claimed an unoccupied electrical socket and inserted the plug. Almost instantaneously, the black hole on the adapter glowed green and began to flash. It was almost imperceptible. Indeed, there was life on Mars! I had my answer: the monitor had ceased functioning because the wireless signal in Mom's room was too weak to wake it up. The solution was apparent. I could initiate a manual transmission from anywhere with a decent wireless signal. I considered the perfect location—Mom's hair palace, the city's inarguable hub of communication. Since Mom was a weekly hair-restoration patron, the palace could function as a port for electronic data transmission while she baked under the hair dryer. It turned out to be a serendipitous marriage. The report was successfully transmitted from the hair palace and became a weekly ritual.

Mom's Neck Problem

Mom's inability to hold her head up posed multiple complications. When eating, she slumped in her chair to the point where her torso was at a forty-five-degree angle. This compensation positioned her head in a semi-upright posture, making eating simpler, at least logistically. It was an imperfect modification. Mom's odd chair posture increased food spillage and, even worse, caused food to get stuck in her throat. It was an invitation for occasional choking episodes that were frightening to witness.

Mom was a significant fall risk, and her inability to hold her head up while walking worsened the condition. Since she always looked down, her perspective was limited. Consequently, she was prone to knock into obstacles residing in her path. On one occasion, I watched Mom bump her rollator into the back end of short-fused Agnes, who had briefly stopped in the hallway. Mom wasn't moving fast enough to cause harm, although Agnes was quick to display disapproval with a scornful look.

Eye injections to slow the advance of Mom's wet-form macular degeneration were always preceded by an optical coherence tomography test. Before you scream, be advised this test is simple and painless. The typical patient sits on a stool, places their head on a chin rest, and focuses on a blue light while the technician takes images of the retina. With Mom, it was less straightforward since she couldn't raise her head enough for an image to be efficiently obtained. There was a work-around. I helped Mom stand up where she could hold on to the side supports of the chin rest. I stood behind her and raised her chin with either hand to the point where she could see the blue light. It was one heck of an ordeal.

Even with Mom standing, I couldn't completely raise her head as a consequence of her deformity. Finding the "sweet spot" where an image could be obtained was a challenge for the technician. This was further complicated by Mom's head tremor, which made imaging difficult. It was a daunting task to keep her stabilized while holding her head in position at the same time. On one occasion, two technicians and the physician were required to obtain a suitable image. On another, the image couldn't be captured. She still received the injection.

Activities Mom once enjoyed were becoming next to impossible for her to accomplish due to numb hands. Nerve compression in her neck was one of several contributors to the debilitating condition. Surgery wasn't an option, and there wasn't a magic bullet to return life into her hands. It saddened me to see Mom abandon the crossword puzzle book when she could no longer nimbly maneuver a pencil. At the same time, she discontinued playing the piano and participating in card games when the cards kept falling from her hands. Her miscues were disruptive to the game flow and embarrassing for Mom.

Casualties of old age were tough for her to accept; however, her loss of writing dexterity was a harsher concession. Mom was renowned for writing beautifully crafted notes. Her handwriting throughout life had effortlessly flowed from her fingertips with barely a ripple. Her penmanship was impeccably old-school, complete with flourishes and perfectly constructed letters. Mom's artistry wasn't limited to cursive mastery. Her skill was evident in carefully worded, heartfelt sentiments. Regrettably, writing became an arduous task and her once majestic penmanship was relegated to scribbles.

Beginning in 2017, Mom had participated in a series of physical therapy sessions with hopes of attaining neck relief. The sessions proved to be worthless. Multiple therapists had doggedly worked to help her regain neck mobility. For added support, various neck braces were tried—all for naught. It was evident there were two unequal sides to the equation: the therapy sessions, and Mom, the unequal partner. I believed Mom was the primary reason physical therapy had failed. She lost interest and didn't follow through with prescribed daily at-home exercises. Mom stated she didn't enjoy doing exercises and doubted their effectiveness. Her logic was confounding given her expressed desire to participate in therapy to begin with.

I wondered, if I were 100-plus years old, would I want to participate in daily neck exercises? Possibly not. The next time physical therapy for Mom's limp neck was suggested, I reasoned it wasn't worth her time, the therapist's time, or Medicare's money. Mom agreed and we declined it. When to say *no* isn't always clear-cut. This time, I felt it was.

Got Prescriptions?

When Mom moved into Courtside, I implored her to *never* sign any forms or give consents without calling me first. Late one morning, I received one of those calls. Mom was upset. A staff member had given her a form to sign and it was relating to prescription drugs. Understandably, Mom was perplexed and the form contents couldn't be correctly established over the phone. So I programmed the TV to record *The Young and the Restless*, which was seldom missed, and drove to the facility.

I perused the form and determined it was an authorization for Mom to change her pharmacy provider to the one with which Courtside was contracted. Such arrangements are standard among senior living facilities to ensure medications are available when needed and easily accessible to facility staff for dispensing. Mom's situation was unique when compared to most residents. Switching her to the facility vendor would not have been cost effective, particularly since I managed and dispensed her medications. Accordingly, I instructed Mom to not sign the form.

Mom Could Be Irritating Yet Entertaining

Consistent with most humans who inhabit our planet, Mom had her share of idiosyncrasies, none of which I inherited. Except for perhaps one or two. Her preoccupation with hair maintenance topped the list. It was the subject of excessive study at home in addition to any ladies' room with a mirror. And I've been advised all of them are well-equipped. And to be fair, the men's rooms aren't lacking in this department either. Vanity isn't gender specific.

Mom's primary weapon in her stockpile of hair equipment was industrial-grade hairspray which was always on call in her purse for emergencies. Calls were frequent. During one of my daily visits, Mom informed me she was almost out of hairspray and needed me to go to the beauty supply store to pick up a *bottle*. I thought she meant a can, until she showed me the nearly empty container. I gasped at the size of it. Indeed, it *was* a bottle, a hefty one about the size of a quart. I had no conception hairspray was available in such gargantuan quantities. Two words stamped in bold letters on the brown plastic container exclaimed the power of the product—*Extreme Hold*. And Mom made sure I took note of these two crucial words, a descriptor signifying a powerhouse of strength. This strength would be necessary to frame an invincible halo of invisible protection around her iconic teased mane.

Recognizing the *extreme* urgency to procure a magnum of sprayable glue, I snared a bottle in the beauty supply outlet posthaste and refilled her pump-action, handheld dispenser. This is the one she parked in her purse. Hold on, this wasn't the end of it. Mom maintained another weapon in her armament. She kept a "regular" *can* of hairspray on the toilet tank lid. This rendition was specified for in-house styling purposes and wasn't to be moved from its place of enshrinement. Mom wouldn't consider setting foot outside the door until a thorough application had been unleashed on her hair and anything else within six feet of the all-encompassing fog.

Mom's penchant for liberal hairspray application was no secret to her stylist at the hair palace. She had to apply baking soda to Mom's hair to release the accumulation of gunk prior to washing. I suppose this was the equivalent of a degreaser applied to birds rescued from an oil slick.

In addition to hairspray, Mom was a loyalist when choosing other products. She was a stickler for name brands and insisted store brands and generics weren't up to acceptable standards. Since I did all of her shopping, her specifications for particular products ran me nuts. Being price sensitive, I tried to pinch nickels and dimes to save her money where possible. There were times when preferred brands weren't available, and I wasn't one to go on a scavenger hunt from store to store to locate a specific item. Not even for myself. In short, shopping was an activity I didn't enjoy and her preferences made it an even greater chore. One of the many annoying stories relating to shopping centered on toothpaste.

Mom's favored brand purportedly whitened, brightened, fought tartar, and did everything else but shine the floors. At times, her shopping requests were given without advance notice. One day she called to let me know she was "almost completely out" of toothpaste and needed me to pick up a tube pronto. Not more than an hour before receiving her call, I had returned from my weekly shopping excursion. The day before, I had advised Mom I was going shopping and asked if she needed anything. She told me, *"No."* Admittedly, I was miffed at the last-minute toothpaste request, but got over it. My centenarian mother deserved allowances.

I trudged back to the store and, of course, they were out of Mom's "got-to-have" brand. There were few alternatives. I happened upon a less familiar yet highly touted niche brand. The box screamed, "Buy me." Each of the virtues Mom requested was boldly inscribed on the box. The price tag, which was two dollars more than the out-of-stock preferred brand, implied a people-pleasing experience. I snatched it and delivered the teeth-saving potion to Mom. It was met with disapproval. She assumed it was an off-brand and didn't want it. She pronounced, "I've never heard of this. I don't see an ADA seal of approval on the box." I informed her my shopping was done until the following week.

Before leaving, I picked up the box of toothpaste and pointed out a hard-to-spot ADA seal. Mom remained unconvinced. I continued "the sell" and brought her up to speed about the product's power to transform her teeth with its all-natural formula of scrubbers and dazzlers. She maintained her skepticism until I informed her of the higher cost. Reluctantly, she relented. Several days later, Mom was singing a different tune and chirped, "This toothpaste is good." Even so, when the three-pack of the preferred brand was back on the shelf a couple of weeks later, I snared it.

CHAPTER 8

2019 BOWS TO A NEW YEAR

The winter months of 2019 and 2020 didn't include any exclamation points. Nonetheless, Mom was anything but boring during this period of relative serenity and continued to supply ample material for inclusion into this "missive."

On Christmas Eve, my silenced cell phone came to life in my pants pocket while ringing church bells heralded the commencement of the seven o'clock evening service. The vibration was easily discounted while I nervously double-checked the music in my crammed choir folder before we processed down the center aisle singing "Hark the Herald Angels Sing." The insistent phone vibrations occurred twice during the hour-and-fifteen-minute service. I had been bombarded with robocalls earlier in the day and assumed it was the same nuisance. I got around to checking phone messages around nine o'clock. A single brief message seized my attention. The assisted living facility had called to advise Mom had fallen but was uninjured. I returned the call and was reassured Mom was fine. This was the third such call I had received during the preceding twelve months. I lived in fear of *the* call ... the one advising Mom was being taken to the hospital.

Unlike the prior Christmas when Mom was in isolation at Parkside, Thomas and I hosted a low-key family Christmas dinner for Mom. We served a spiral-cut honey-glazed ham—her favorite. I contemplated how many more Christmases we would be able to enjoy with her.

The New Year came with scarce observance, although Mom's penchant for creating excitement was unfaltering. I walked into her room around nine in the morning on January 5 and found her slumped forward in her chair. Her arms were crossed on her lap, suggesting she was about to fall headfirst onto the floor. She appeared dead and the sight nearly placed me in the same state. I acted rationally—by screaming loud enough to wake the dead. And it did. Mom raised her head and asked me to lower my voice. Whoa! I witnessed two miracles: Mom was proof of resurrection, and she was wearing hearing aids. She explained her back had been stiff and thought the unorthodox postural position in which I found her would provide comfort.

In addition to any spinal relief her self-prescribed physical therapy provided, it also invoked a nap. Mom had experienced a severe itching spell during the night and she had taken an Ativan pill, which was a recent addition to her prescription arsenal. It knocked out the itching and about knocked *her* out as well.

The pill's sedative properties had kicked in, but not enough to dull Mom's ability to make a comment about Elsie, the "roach-killer" tablemate. She lived directly across the hall from Mom, and I saw her from time to time. Mom asserted, "Elsie has turned into a jack-o'-lantern. The next time you see her, look at her teeth when she smiles. She's missing a tooth right in the front." The comment was classic for Mom and typified her sense of humor. I had seen Elsie earlier in the week but didn't notice her likeness to the aforementioned Halloween decoration. Several days later, I met her in the hallway and was able to confirm Mom's observation—a tooth was indeed missing. I suspected she had fallen, but this wasn't confirmed.

Blame It on Aging

With each passing year Mom became increasingly uninhibited, and this was reflected in her willingness to share thoughts and perceptions, no matter how skewed they might be. Sometimes her higher self seemed to be on hiatus. She didn't hesitate to emphasize the negative components in many situations and this drove me to distraction. Mom didn't intend to be a naysayer, yet this had become a late-in-life trait. Her joy in living seemed to have been extracted and her reaction was a natural response.

Mom was required to have a quarterly blood draw, which had to be completed in the morning while she was fasting (prior to eating breakfast). Her 7:30 a.m. appointment wasn't inordinately early, yet she needed to get up at six o'clock in order to have sufficient time to "put on her face," tame her hair, and get dressed. She called the night before to request a 6:00 a.m. wake-up call from me. She couldn't hear her alarm clock—it wasn't loud enough. A phone call from me was pointless since she wouldn't hear her cell phone ringing either. Incidentally, hearing aids aren't usually worn at night while the recipient is sleeping.

I suggested the on-duty aide could wake her up. No consideration was given to the proposal and Mom responded: "No, I'm not going to waste my time. She'll forget to do it. This happened once before." I insisted that Mom should make the request. She refused. I called the facility and was assured someone would wake her at six in the morning. For grins—though I wasn't grinning—I called Mom at six the following morning and, as expected, she didn't answer. I called the facility and was assured Mom had been awakened. I wondered, *Who has my mother become?*

At 7:10 a.m. I rolled into the covered portico at to retrieve Mom. She wasn't there. She came out at seven twenty; we were going to be a few minutes late for her lab appointment. I got her settled in the car and sped off. The conversation we had in the car makes me snicker now, but didn't at the time.

"Good morning, Mama, how was your night?"

"It wasn't great. I kept waking up out of fear I would oversleep."

I doubted she had overslept, yet still asked, "Did you oversleep?"

"No. Annie got me up and I'm glad she did since you didn't call me. Did you ask her to wake me up?"

"Yes. I made the request last night and I *did* call you this morning."

"I never heard the phone ringing. Are you sure you called the right number?"

"Yes, I'm sure. Your voice mail picked up after the sixth ring. Why are you late?"

"It took longer to get ready than I thought it would. Anyway, being a little late won't kill the lab people. Slow down, you're driving too fast. I hate these early appointments … the place will be mobbed since *everybody* will be in there before going to work. We'll end up waiting an hour. It has *always* been a wait in Jacksonville."

"Mom, we're in St. Augustine and *everybody* is retired. You have an appointment at seven thirty. We won't have to wait a long time … unless we're late and your appointment has been released. This is why it's important to be on time." We walked in the door at seven thirty-five and the tight lobby was filled with people, most without appointments. Our appointment was honored and the wait was short. One minute later and we would have waited "till the cows come home."

Mom revered *Black Pearls* perfume by Elizabeth Taylor and had asked to receive a spray bottle of the scent for her birthday. It was an older fragrance and I couldn't locate the slightest whiff in any brick-and-mortar store despite spending several hours hunting. I was elated to find an online source. There was a downside: the "pearls" were still being harvested and the perfume wouldn't arrive until a week after Mom's birthday. While driving back to Courtside from the lab where Mom's blood had been drawn, I mentioned her perfume was on the way but wouldn't arrive in time for her birthday. I apologized yet expected she would be thrilled even if it was late arriving. Her reaction was, "I probably won't like it. They've probably changed the formula by now."

I about busted a gasket and could feel the hot flash of adrenaline rushing to my face. Before I could count to one, I reacted angrily and said, "I'm sure you won't. It's no different than anything else and we can send it back." Instantly I regretted my anger-fueled sarcasm. It was apparent Mom's "checks and balances" had been eroded by time, and I should have dismissed the disparaging, out-of-character comment. Deafening silence overtook any potential conversation and neither of us apologized. I should have. The remaining five minutes in the car seemed like five hours.

Mom's 102nd birthday arrived a few days later and, per her request, Max, Lois, Thomas, and I took her to Carrabba's for an early dinner. She loved shellfish of any persuasion and was anticipating feasting on shrimp, which was her stated intent. We laboriously pored over the menu selections with her, and she insisted everyone else should order while she contemplated her choice. I was astounded when she settled on wood-grilled tilapia. She had changed her mind at the last minute yet didn't say why. Our dinners were served. Mom picked at her fish and when asked how it was, she unconvincingly responded, "It's fine." In this context, *fine* should be interpreted as "It isn't what I had hoped for." The truth would eventually come out and it did. She admitted her fish was a disappointment. I wasn't surprised; she wanted shrimp. Mom said when no one else at the table ordered it, she changed her mind. Her rationale baffled me.

I was aware my storehouse of patience with my adored mother was becoming depleted and it disturbed me. After examining my feelings and conferring with Thomas, I concluded Mom's frequent complaints and negative comments were akin to fine sandpaper. A rub here and there is tolerable. Over time, the accumulation of rubs surpasses mere irritation and becomes an open wound. With this awareness, I was better able to understand and accept my feelings, which aided in my ability to manage thinly worn patience. Even so, it was a daily battle.

In addition to impatience, persistent conflicting emotions had become minefields when it came to Mom. I experienced exasperation, frustration, sadness, empathy, pity for Mom, pity for myself, guilt, and occasional resentment and anger—these two were the worst of the lot. I was usually successful in channeling internal screams into acquiescence by focusing on the underlying predicament, which was Mom's deteriorating health, over which she had no control.

When I was close to "derailment," an inventory of Mom's frail body caused me to reassess my perspective. This extraordinary woman who gave me life and had been an exemplary parent (along with my dad), was near the end of hers. Her failing sight and hearing, numb hands, urinary incontinence, faltering balance, sputtering heart, slumped stature, impaired sense of taste, sore and swollen legs, blown-out knees, exasperating itching, and deteriorating kidneys were all maddening. Undoubtedly, she was over it. Her closest friends from many years back were long gone, except for one—eleven months younger than Mom—with whom she maintained phone contact. Through it all, Mom managed to muster her trademark sense of humor. Remarkably, her mind remained strong, a blessing beyond measure.

An Unforgettable Day: March 12, 2020

A spectacular, breezy and warm March morning was in progress, and I seized the invitation from nature to take a spin on my fairly new, hundred-dollar, no-frills generic bicycle. The fresh wind created by moving along at fifteen miles per hour smoothed out the wrinkles in my white T-shirt and rendered me placid. Weaving through the curving, cedar- and palm-studded streets characterizing our Davis Shores neighborhood was a joy. I was about five minutes into my restorative sojourn when the peacefulness of the moment was shattered by my ringing cell phone. I could see the call was from Mom. I stopped and answered it. She was distressed and asked me to come to the facility for an impromptu resident meeting starting in forty-five minutes. The meeting had something to do with "a new disease." She needed me there in case she couldn't hear what was being discussed. I exhaled and returned home to put on a decent shirt before driving to Courtside.

The novel coronavirus (COVID-19) had been omnipresent in the media and I expected the meeting would focus on the unfolding catastrophe. My suspicions were validated. The ongoing COVID-19 viral stampede through a Seattle-area nursing facility had killed captive residents with frightening efficiency. News of the horror and the potential for nationwide outbreaks permeated the media. It was a prototype no independent living, assisted living, or skilled nursing community wanted to emulate. When I stepped through the front door of Mom's facility, hastily instituted restrictions for entry astonished me. I was required to complete a brief health and travel questionnaire and submit to a temperature check before earning a "hall pass." It was a minor inconvenience, yet unsettling.

I briskly walked to Mom's room and was impressed to find she was ready to roll, with her Buick idling. I accompanied her at a perceived snail's pace to the community dining room where the meeting would take place. We were among the first to arrive. By the time the meeting commenced, the commodious room resembled a can of packed sardines—residents attended en masse. I stood in the back of the room and could see I was the sole nonresident in attendance.

The winds of change sliced through the crowd as the facility administrator opened the meeting by announcing modifications to daily operations were necessary to ensure the safety of residents, visitors, and staff. The vice president of clinical services, who was also a registered nurse, assumed the podium. Her salient talking points centered on hygiene and facility access. New hand sanitizer dispensers had been installed throughout the building and residents were implored to use them frequently. An explanation as to why the sanitizer was imperative was given, along with a demonstration showing proper application. I could discern some of the residents comprehended the message while the "sawmill whispers" of two residents near me indicated cluelessness. One babbled to the other, "What did she say?" Her friend responded by saying, "I don't know, but why was she washing her hands?"

Facility access for residents had always been without restriction. This was no longer the case. A policy change with an immediate effective date was announced. The word *immediate* had the same effect as smelling salts and captured the attention of those who appeared to be asleep or had migrated to the twilight zone. The facilitator explained to residents they would still be permitted to leave the building using any exit. There was a caveat: the door would automatically lock behind them. Reentry would be allowed only through the main front doors. A booming, shrill voice interrupted the presentation with an objection that floored me: "You *do* realize this procedure discriminates against smokers." Huh? I wanted to go shake the guy into reality. His comment supplied a bit of comic relief for some, although his intent wasn't to be humorous. Incidentally, thirty-five feet separated the front doors from the exit to the smoking area.

In a clipped manner, the facilitator emphatically stated, "Beginning now, facility access is restricted. General visitation has been discontinued. Necessary prescreened visitors will be allowed entry." The word *necessary* caused brief heartburn until defined to include anyone providing needed services including close family. Whew. Max and I were part of the "in crowd." The precautions outlined were plausible and signaled the facility's resolve to protect residents and staff. I conjectured the crisis would pass in a few weeks and a back-to-normal operation would resume shortly thereafter.

The meeting ended. I walked next to Mom while she steered the Buick back to her room. Before I vacated the premises, she asked, "What exactly is going on?" So much for hearing aids.

The Morning After

Courtside was efficiently run by a well-trained, upbeat, and conscientious staff. When I stepped through the front doors of the facility the following morning at nine thirty, it was apparent the usual staff cheerfulness had been supplanted by somber tones and general disquiet. Several of the support staff were in the lobby having a hushed conversation—an unusual circumstance when considering the residents were hearing impaired or close to it. After being screened, I was quietly told by a staff associate to expect additional changes. Nothing else was divulged. It seemed ominous.

A feeling of uneasiness accompanied me as I walked the short distance to Mom's room. Her weekly hair appointment was in a half hour. When I popped into her room, I expected to be quizzed about the rapidly unfolding changes in the facility. Instead, Mom was dialed into another frequency and began grousing about missing breakfast due to oversleeping. As we exited the facility, I snatched a cookie and a banana from the snack bar for her to eat in the car. She definitely didn't have a clear understanding that COVID was about to fling our world on its head. I had an inkling.

It was business as usual in the hair palace. Mom got spiffed up and her pacemaker report was successfully generated. COVID came up in "roundtable" discussions, though minimal concern was expressed. Patrons agreed it would be inconsequential to St. Augustine.

When we returned from Mom's hair revitalization around lunchtime, the facility climate was tense. Storm clouds heralding a shift from business as usual to an alarming paradigm were gathering above the citadel where Mom resided. Ever confident, I thought I was prepared for any eventuality. Subsequently, that assumption was dispelled.

Before leaving Mom's room, I took an inventory of her supplies. Certain toiletry articles, incontinence underwear and pads, bottled water, and snacks needed replenishment. I kissed Mom goodbye and scurried to Target where I gathered the standard complement of basics.

A scant two hours later, I received an urgent text from the facility. My eyes bulged when they came across a particular snippet: *"The facility has transitioned to a lockdown status."* I was expecting something ... but not this. As I continued reading, another zinger was delivered: *"Residents will not be permitted to routinely leave the premises, and only essential visitors will be allowed entry."* Surely, I was an essential visitor. I had to be. What about Mom's weekly hair appointment? This critical need was hardly routine in her book and reigned at the pinnacle of essentialness in her world view. The text concluded by stating an informational meeting would be held the following afternoon, March 14, 2020, in the courtyard. It wasn't in my nature to wait a day to have a few questions answered, particularly when Mom's well-being was at stake. And I didn't.

Nervously, my fumbling fingers managed to tap out the facility phone number on my cell. One of the staff members answered and, at my urging, recited the official definition of *essential visitor*. It was a gut punch—I wasn't essential. The ramifications of this edict were confounding. I politely terminated the call and sat on the living room floor ruminating for an undetermined length of time. Mom depended on me for a myriad of needs, including psychological support. I wondered, *What are we going to do?*

It had taken one day. The evolution from Mom's complete freedom, to a few palatable restrictions, to a lockdown came swiftly. It was the equivalent of a lightning strike. In a dither, I called my brother. Max and Lois agreed we should all attend the meeting the following afternoon.

Use the Side Gate

The courtyard was accessible through the lobby of the facility. This was no longer permissible. An obscure alcove on the western façade of the building sheltered a gate that opened directly to the expansive interior courtyard. Since access through the building was no longer permitted, we were required to use the not-so-secret, secret gate. I had never noticed it.

The three of us arrived early and mingled with a handful of anxious attendees. We sat in chairs neatly assembled under the protective arches of a spreading live oak. Dappled sunlight flitted around us as the breeze rustled the leaves, masking the seriousness of the meeting. It was a perfect Saturday. Except it wasn't.

Regrettably, only a few people attended, perhaps fifteen. It disturbed me to think most residents had no family member or close friend present. The meeting began with an overview given by the vice president of clinical services. She was clear: The facility would employ *all* necessary precautions to protect the residents and staff. Any resident who contracted the virus would be transferred to a nearby hospital, where appropriate staff and equipment to treat the illness were available. This proved impossible to honor when the virus romped with impunity throughout Florida, cramming hospital rooms and their hallways.

The definition of an *essential visitor* was next on the agenda. None of us fell into this coveted category. Though I had previously been apprised of my outcast status, the official pronouncement was a sting. It was a shock for unaware attendees. Open mouths and various mumblings confirmed universal alarm. An alternative solution was offered: Contact with residents could be maintained via cell phones or personal computers. Of course, this provided no consolation. The overview ended with the following statement: Visitation exceptions *might* be made for end-of-life situations. Not an uplifting thought.

Ample time was allotted for questions to be asked and answered. Per Mom's instructions, I asked the most important question first. What about hair appointments? *Sorry, all hair appointments are out.* What about doctor appointments? *No, unless it's urgent.* What about Mom's eye injections for macular degeneration? *Yes, this is considered urgent. She'll be required to be transferred in the facility bus and can't be taken anywhere else.* May I still bring mail, medications, and needed supplies to Mom? *Yes. You'll be required to drop them off at the facility's front door, and we'll deliver them.* Will I be permitted to continue washing Mom's clothes? *Yes. Please call ahead. We'll bring her laundry out to you.* Mom's mail, supplies, and laundry were accommodations I handled. Being able to continue performing routine tasks for Mom slightly ameliorated visitation restrictions. There was one bright spot: Mom could visit with us at any time by coming to the locked front glass doors where we could peer at each other while attempting to communicate on our cell phones.

The meeting lasted forty-five minutes. Mom's room had windows overlooking the courtyard. Before leaving, we were allowed to tap on her window to briefly say hello and exchange looks. There was no time for conversation. We were ushered out. Graciously, a staff member delivered two large bags of supplies I had brought for Mom. We were the last meeting attendees to leave. After being escorted through the open gate, we heard the clanging of metal followed by a *click*—the unmistakable sounds of the gate being closed and padlocked. Max, Lois, and I talked for a minute before leaving. I was downhearted yet felt the communication we had all heard could have been worse.

And It Got Worse

Effective Wednesday, March 18, 2020, Courtside will no longer accept personal items or food from anyone outside of our complex into the facilities. All resident personal laundry will be managed by in-house staff. These measures are recommended by CDC guidelines to further prevent the spread of the COVID-19 virus.

This message was received in the midmorning on the eighteenth. There it was, in black and white. I could sense my face flushing. The latest edict represented another slammed door, leaving me dazed and out of options. At least this was my perception. Shortly thereafter, Mom called to advise me all meals would be delivered to her room for the next two weeks. I suspected this was a dress rehearsal, and Mom concurred. Her 102 years hadn't diminished the registered nurse indoctrination about disease prevention protocols and how germs infiltrate closed environments. She was still free to roam the halls, if masked, and venture into the protected courtyard. This slight concession helped assuage her increasing isolation. No matter how unbelievable, nothing could be done; we were immobilized.

Finding Equilibrium

What a day it had been. My psyche was in overdrive when I dragged myself into bed at ten thirty. There was no tossing and turning—I was too wide awake for that phase of sleeplessness. Thanks to an abundant pillow supply, I constructed a downy fortress at the head of the bed, where I was supported semi-upright, melded into my safe place. I had an unobstructed view across the marsh, to the night-blackened Matanzas River. City lights reflected across the glassy water, creating a peaceful solitude contradicting my contemplations. I hoped Mom was ensconced in the security of sleep.

I abhorred dilemmas. Who doesn't? The intractability of Mom's situation had me rattled and the quietude of the night magnified my worries. Earlier in the day, I had spoken to Maddie, the facility manager, about the logistics of getting supplies to Mom. I was most concerned about medications. She suggested that medications could be shipped directly from the pharmacy provider to Courtside or I could mail them. My overriding concern was the possibility of medications being lost or being delivered late. Additionally, Mom would be subject to the facility's $300 per month dispensing fee.

Each Friday I was accustomed to delivering Mom's weekly pill allotment. They were meticulously arranged in an oversized pill organizer with two rows, each containing seven compartments representing each day of the week. One row was for the morning allotment and the adjacent section accommodated the evening allocation. This easy-to-follow system reduced the chance of Mom getting pills mixed up, forgetting to take them, or spilling large quantities since each compartment had tight-fitting lids. The arrangement had worked well for Mom.

After sleeping on it, I called Maddie in the morning and appealed to her sense of logic. I questioned why it was okay for Courtside to accept a delivery via U.S. Mail, or UPS, or FedEx, where multiple hands had been involved, but couldn't accept a pill organizer from me. After considering my request, she allowed me to continue delivering Mom's pill organizer once a week, with certain requirements. I agreed to sanitize my hands and the organizer. The organizer had to be sealed in a plastic zip-lock bag.

A staff member would meet me outside the building's front door and exchange Mom's empty container for the filled one. I was required to wear disposable gloves and a mask even though the transfer occurred outdoors. A second sanitizing was conducted by the facility prior to it being given to Mom. It was a few extra steps for me, and well worth each one.

Anything else had to be delivered via an approved source. It made no sense to me, but there was no way around it. Mom's daily essentials were shipped when possible and, if not, they were mailed by me. I about choked when it cost nine dollars to mail a single roll of paper towels to Mom—the post office was a mile from Courtside. Due to inordinate processing times, soap, deodorant, toothpaste, tissues, snacks, and other items had to be sent well before Mom ran out. Once items were delivered to the facility by an approved vendor, they were required to sit for three days in a storeroom before they could be taken to Mom. The three-day delay was believed sufficient to allow any COVID germs to die out.

Don't Go to Bed After Watching an Unfolding Disaster on TV

I experienced a series of restless nights, mostly attributable to watching the late news before lumbering upstairs for the night. I'm sure most of America was glued to the same somber newscasts with similar outcomes. The virus galloped across America with an unrelenting flurry of horrifying stories pervading the news, day and night. The most distressing situations were those being played out in nursing facilities and assisted living communities throughout the country. Despondent sons and daughters were interviewed while they held days-long vigils outside a nursing facility turned prison. Inside, a parent lay trapped and mostly deserted, dying alone, cocooned in cold sterility instead of being comforted by the warm embrace of family.

My emotion-charged contemplations had me tossed like a salad, causing me to flounder in bed after watching the news. Any sense of serenity I had mustered beforehand was hijacked. I batted ideas back and forth much of the night, turning my brain into a game of Ping-Pong. Should I bring Mom back home to live with Thomas and me? Would she be better off to remain in assisted living? Was her facility better equipped to keep her safe than I was? If I brought Mom home and she was stricken with the virus, or Thomas and I were, then what? I contemplated COVID-19 was the planet's revenge for overpopulation, environmental rape, or a disjointed world. At this moment it was immaterial. The plate had been served.

The sun's rays awakened me around seven thirty. At some point, sleep must have found me. During the night I contemplated bringing Mom back home, and discussed the idea, ad nauseum, with Thomas. He agreed there were pros and cons and was supportive of the conclusion the family reached. I called Max and Lois to ask their opinions. They believed Mom should remain at Courtside since she preferred being in her own space, was surrounded by friends, and was in capable hands. While all this was true, I remained conflicted and sought additional feedback.

Suzanne, a close friend in Colorado, was facing a similar situation with her father. I called her. She had determined that leaving him in assisted living was the best arrangement and agreed with my brother's assessment: Mom shouldn't be moved. Another friend reached out to me that day. We discussed the pros and cons of taking Mom out of the facility, and the cons were the winner on his ledger as well. This was the third strike and I was out. Almost. Since I wasn't an avid baseball fan (except to gobble up hot dogs in the ballpark), I wasn't through counting and granted myself the opportunity for a fourth strike.

I made a phone call to someone I greatly trusted—Maddie. In addition to being the assisted living manager, she was also a nurse. I had immense respect for her expertise and common-sense approach to health-care management. I knew she would be objective and honest.

No doubt, Maddie had enough to handle without my interjecting questions and concerns into her frenzied day. Generously, she took the time to speak with me. She assured me the facility was strictly following CDC guidelines regarding access, sanitation, and precautions for staff and residents. Their protocols were several steps above what I could attempt at home. The facility had industrial-grade disinfectants, and I couldn't find disinfectants of *any* grade—store shelves were stripped. Got toilet paper? You bet! This was my one ace. I had purchased forty-five rolls of plush-grade toilet paper at Sam's Club the week before the crisis hit. Sheer luck.

I asked Maddie the question that had robbed me of sleep: "Do you think Mom would be better off if I brought her home to live with Thomas and me?" Her crystal ball was no better than mine; however, she cautioned if I took Mom out of the facility, she wouldn't be allowed to come back until the epidemic was over. They had made the decision to not accept new residents during the outbreak, and Mom would be considered a new resident.

With logic regaining preeminence over emotion, it became obvious my brother and friends were correct. Mom should remain in Courtside. And she did.

Cell Phone and Hearing Aid Sagas

I encountered a few glitches getting essential supplies delivered to Mom and occasionally had to find alternatives for out-of-stock items, especially *preferred* incontinence pads. We forged ahead and Mom's life hummed along to the beat of a new normal. As far as I was concerned, communication was the most frustrating facet of her confinement. Mom was experiencing increasing difficulty operating her cell phone—if that was possible—and she claimed the phone was malfunctioning. I figured it wasn't. Soon, I would have a golden opportunity to "confiscate" her cell phone and make a diagnosis. If there was a malfunction, I suspected it was tied to the operator of the phone.

Mom was granted an "exit visa" on March 27 to receive an eye injection in the office of her retina specialist. Max and I had discussed the apparent hazard this appointment posed for Mom. In the final analysis, we decided the possibility of Mom losing her eyesight as a result of not getting injections was greater than contracting the virus in the physician's office.

Because she would be carried via facility bus, I was granted permission to meet her at the physician's office to lend assistance getting her inside. I wore a mask and disposable gloves. When the bus arrived, I helped Mom get off and pushed her in a wheelchair to the office door. The physician's nurse, wearing blue nitrile gloves and garbed in what resembled a hazmat suit, met us at the door and escorted Mom inside. I peered through the glass doors and could see Mom was the only person in the waiting area. My fear of her coming in contact with the virus lessened. The office was empty, eerily so. Patients waiting to be seen had been instructed to remain in their vehicles until called.

I had asked Mom to bring her cell phone to give me a chance to look it over while she was in the physician's office. I requested it when she exited the bus, but she didn't have it. It was a lost opportunity. She advised, "Oh honey, I can't find it in my purse." This was no wonder. Her purse was a portable junk drawer, stuffed with untold treasures for maintaining life support.

Since I wasn't allowed entry into the physician's office, I waited in the car and listened to the radio. A *tap-tap-tap* on the passenger window diverted my attention from Elton John singing "Your Song" on the oldies station. Appropriate, since I was in the "up in years" category. I looked up and was surprised to see the nurse who had ushered Mom into the office a couple of minutes earlier. She had a black object in her hand. It was the equivalent of the "golden egg"—Mom's cell phone. This lady had to be an angel, even though dressed in a Martian-looking costume. I didn't ask what else she had found in Mom's purse.

Mom's vintage yet seemingly functional flip phone was in dire need of cleaning. A dried, syrupy residue was smeared on the front and sides. Supplemental nastiness common to most cell phones decorated the other surfaces. I squeezed my hands into a pair of latex gloves and decontaminated all surfaces of the phone with disinfecting wipes. The resulting transformation was astounding. I wasn't finished. A functionality assessment was next. As disclosed, my lack of proficiency with electronics or mechanics is no secret. To mitigate the deficit, I had the user's manual at my side. It was fairly straightforward, but still challenging for the challenged.

The reason Mom couldn't hear a conversation on her phone was identified. She had inadvertently turned the volume down to the lowest setting and had the speaker cut off. Easy fix, even for me. Next I experimented with ring tones and settled on the old-fashioned yet familiar "dinner bell." It's the quintessential ring baby boomers and their parents remember from way back when. I turned it up to the maximum, run-for-the-hills volume.

Max, who's way smarter than me, had suggested the phone might have programming to allow for hearing aid compatibility. I didn't think it did. Max was right. It did. I discovered specific instructions in the manual and wedded the phone to Mom's hearing aids. This coupling promised to reduce high-pitched feedback Mom had been getting when she used the phone while wearing hearing aids.

I had to test the phone fixes to ensure my tweaks landed where intended and weren't free radicals floating in the cell phone ether. My semi-sterile car laboratory had served its purpose. Using Mom's revamped phone, I called Lou, a close friend who was usually home. In fact, most of America *was* home per CDC directives, except for unobservant spring breakers who hadn't yet been booted off the beach. The phone performed admirably; the conversation between Lou and me was effortless and clear. After disconnecting, he called back to give me a chance to test the ringer. The sound was of striking magnitude. With confidence, I pronounced the initial run-through a success. The phone was once again in first-rate working order ... for the time being.

The venerable Z221 model phone received one final cootie-killing sanitized wipe, and I dropped the revitalized device into a plastic zip-lock bag for customer delivery. Shortly thereafter, Mom was released to the care of the facility bus driver who had pulled into the parking lot. With great pride, I placed the sealed bag containing a germless and functional phone into Mom's purse when she boarded. She asked, "Is it working?" I was pleased to proclaim it was and asked her to call me when she got back to Courtside. She called back in fifteen minutes.

"Hello, Mama. Thanks for calling me back so fast."

"Hello, Seth. What was wrong with my phone?"

"Mama, nothing was wrong. It needed adjusting. Did you understand what I said?"

"Yes, I did."

I was doubtful. "Mom, are you wearing your hearing aids?"

"What did you say?"

I spoke louder. "Are you wearing your hearing aids?"

"No. And you don't have to yell."

"Mama, will you please put them in?"

"Why? I can hear you fine without them."

"I need to see if the hearing aid phone adjustment works."

She didn't understand me and thought her hearing aids needed adjusting. So I punted and revisited the previous question, speaking slower and louder.

"Please put in your hearing aids."

"Seth, they're in my purse and it's hidden under the bed. It's going to take a minute for me to get them. You'll have to wait."

My request had made its mark!

While waiting for what seemed like forever, I could hear vague noises in the background confirming life. I wondered, *Did she fall?* Five or six minutes later, she came back with her hearing aids installed. She could hear me clearly, and a rare "normal" phone conversation ensued. A miracle! I explained that she hadn't been able to hear anyone on the phone because the speaker function had inadvertently been cut off and the volume turned to the lowest volume. Mom was happy the phone's desired settings had been restored. She didn't mention any squealing, and I concluded the hearing aid marriage to the cell phone had been a success. Of course, the next day would present opportunities for my efforts to be undone.

Mom called later that evening. She began the conversation by asking, "Did you call me?"

I responded, "No. Why did you think I did?"

She didn't hear me. Her TV was blaring.

After I yelled three times, "Mama, turn down your TV," her impenetrable sound barrier was penetrated.

She responded, "Okay, but I'll have to look for the remote. It's usually right here in the chair, but I don't see it."

She found it. Pat Sajak's voice began fading on the *Wheel of Fortune.* Mom came back on the line. "Okay, it's turned down."

With competition removed, I answered her initial question. "Mama, I don't know who called you, but it wasn't me."

"Well, my phone rang and I thought it was probably you."

"Why didn't you answer it?"

"Because I couldn't get to the phone fast enough."

"Why not? I thought you kept it in your lap."

"It *was* in my lap, but I only heard it ring once."

There was no need to ask why the rings weren't heard. Pat Sajak had answered the question. I asked why she hadn't looked at the recent call list in her phone to see who had called. She commented it was easier to press the #2 speed-dial key, which auto-dialed me. I couldn't blame her.

She ended the conversation by saying, "It was probably your brother. I'll call him."

Max buzzed me later. The call Mom had missed wasn't from him.

Mom and I talked daily. In addition, we visited twice a week, gazing through the glass doors of the facility's entrance. We were no different than zoo animals—safe at a distance. Phone conversations were a bit easier during these visits since we could see lips moving. Occasionally, the noise of lawn equipment and passing vehicles made hearing on my end difficult. It was the best we had.

About a week after I had fixed her phone, Mom called to tell me it was broken again. Surely, this was a stretch, and I suggested someone in the facility could check the settings. There was nothing I could do until her next eye injection in six weeks. In the meantime, we continued to converse with questionable success. Mom generally heard every other word and got things so mixed up she rivaled a food blender. Our conversations were mostly monologues. For the majority of the time I listened and answered most questions with a simple *yes* or *no*, unless Mom was having a better-than-usual "hearing day." During those rare occasions, we had honest-to-goodness conversations.

Peripheral Consequences

Being under "house arrest" due to the COVID lockdown was no picnic for Mom. She didn't attend the Friday afternoon socials, in-house movies, or bingo games. Most residents didn't. The fear factor kept them in self-imposed isolation. How frightening to think social activity might render a death sentence. There was another deterrent to community gatherings—masks. Nobody liked having to wear them when they weren't in their rooms. Mom was no different. A social animal, she remained bored in her room. Her mostly solitary existence worried me. Since meals were no longer served in the dining room, her social life was nonexistent.

To fill the void, Mom frequently called and talked incessantly about minutiae. She expounded on inconsequential trivialities such as the color of the presidential helicopter and anything else she had seen or thought she had seen on the news. Cold coffee, overcooked broccoli, and delicious cherry pie were examples of what filled her world. On the comical side, she loved to comment about how deaf most folks were at Courtside. There was no debate on that one.

Mom's discourses sometimes spanned forty mind-numbing minutes, requiring me to lasso every ounce of patience at my disposal to keep from imploding. But I managed. I imagined how difficult it had to be on *Mom's* end of things. There wasn't much to keep *her* from imploding. Max received the same calls I did and there was no variation. What she had told him was exactly what she had told me, proving her memory was exceptional. Her fortitude and internal strength were a continual source of amazement and inspiration.

COVID was the ultimate distraction, and the necessity to generate Mom's pacemaker reports got lost in the shuffle. Since visits to the hair palace had been scuttled, I forgot about the reports. St. Vincent's Cardiology hadn't. They called to advise me the transmission was overdue. I spoke to Maddie, and she agreed to bring Mom into her office where a signal was strong enough to generate the report. This should have been an easy solution. It wasn't. Maddie scampered to Mom's room and explained the new process, expecting Mom's full cooperation. She didn't get it. Mom refused to participate until she spoke with me. I was mystified. We had generated pacemaker reports from various locations multiple times. After being "counseled" by me, Mom submitted to the change in venue even though hairstyling wasn't included.

The COVID dynamic forced a spate of edicts and updates to be belched from Courtside, all citing ever-evolving CDC guidelines as the ultimate authority. I read a few and remained confused. It was predestined that facility interpretations bordered on the nonsensical since the "CDC mother ship" itself seemed to be regularly switching gears. Of course, the

CDC had no choice but to adjust guidelines as their knowledge of the disease evolved from week to week and month to month.

Mom was a generous user of aerosolized air freshener to maintain her room as a fragrance oasis. I shipped two cans and shortly thereafter received astonishing news from the facility: aerosolized air freshener was off-limits. I was given no plausible reason and later was told it was a fire hazard. It was puzzling. Mom had been using it for well over a year with no protests from any staff member at the facility. For some reason, COVID seemed to be the impetus for the fire hazard concern.

Curiously, hairspray carried no such prohibition. Perhaps it was considered critically important to the overwhelmingly female populace and was granted an exemption. I asked for a list of all restricted items and was tersely advised by someone in Courtside's "disease control" office that no such list was available. I concluded "you can't fight city hall" and didn't. The air-freshener edict prompted me to call a friend whose mother was in a nearby assisted living facility. He told me he wasn't aware of any such regulation in his mother's facility.

As the weeks became months, a handful of COVID cases were reported in Parkside (the skilled nursing wing of the complex), though none popped up in Courtside. A few CNAs, some of whom had been in contact with Mom, got infected. Much to my astonishment, no residents were ensnared. The mask requirement and related safety protocols seemed to have made a difference. I learned to appreciate the obtuse guidelines and concluded they had prevented a rampant spread of the disease in each facility.

Worry and the constant juggling to hold Mom afloat in increasingly turbulent water kept me swirling. Stomach problems and acid reflux became unwanted companions. My first acquaintance with them was in high school. At the time, Dad shared a bit of wisdom I have remembered. He told me: "Seth, what you're eating isn't the problem, but whatever is *eating on you* is." He hit the bull's-eye.

CHAPTER 9

BREAKS IN THE CLOUDS

September 2020 brought an early Christmas present. The Florida governor ordered nursing and assisted living facilities to loosen the bolts from their doors. Limited visitation from individuals who were considered compassionate caregivers was allowed. I was ecstatic. Max and I were among the "ordained." Following a brief training session on safety protocols, we were allowed to begin visiting Mom in the latter part of the month. Each of us was allowed a single thirty-minute visit each week, though not at the same time. It had been six months since either of us had stepped foot into Mom's room.

Our visits were scheduled in advance, and adherence to strict safety precautions was nonnegotiable. The covered drive-thru and adjacent portico leading to the front building entrance were converted into a makeshift visitor check-in area. Occasional blowing rains managed to transform the usually dry "al fresco" reception area into a rainforest. During those inclement weather events, visitors waiting to be processed received a dampening. There was no running for cover—we were under it.

Whether I was dripping or dry, the hand sanitizer station was the first stop in the chain of protocols required for passage. I extracted copious amounts of COVID-killing gunk from the dispenser and over-applied it to my germy hands. The path to the "Emerald City" continued to a table containing a box of sterile disposable gloves and masks. Per unalterable guidelines, I put on a pair of gloves and a mask in that order. Next, I was invited to the screener's desk for a thorough grilling. The screener perfunctorily asked a batch of questions from a preprinted form regarding my activities for the previous fourteen days. After answering each question to the screener's satisfaction, I took a sterilized pen from the designated box and signed the form attesting my responses were truthful. Once those hurdles were cleared and I was deemed not to be a threat to society, I was given a gown to wear.

Last, I was asked to remove the gloves, throw them in a garbage can, and reapply hand sanitizer. Entry was granted! After entering the doorway leading to the resident "bubble," I was directed to walk across a sanitized pad to de-germ the bottoms of my shoes before proceeding to Mom's room. It wasn't always this simple. On one visit, I was wearing sandals and my entry was denied. Jesus might have approved of my footwear, but the on-duty staff sergeant was less forgiving. Thomas (my partner, not the apostle) happened to be home. He met me at the halfway point in between our house and the facility with a pair of "real" shoes. The exchange took five seconds, perhaps less, and I rushed back. The shoes were on my feet two minutes before my time slot expired.

As cumbersome as entry requirements were, I respected the other-worldly measures instituted to protect the residents and staff. Much to my disappointment, getting supplies to Mom remained a major hassle. I wasn't allowed to bring *anything* inside the building, even to place next to the door leading to the designated holding area for supplies. This arcane policy had no logical explanation. Relaxation of rules regarding acceptance of supplies came shortly thereafter. Glory, glory, hallelujah!

My weekly visits were all the same—too short. The first and foremost item on my visitation agenda was to hug Mom and check on her general well-being. Her resiliency was extraordinary. My plan included a number of housekeeping items, the first of which was to check her pill organizer to see if she had missed taking a pill or two. Her cell phone was next on the to-do list. There were always missed calls and unheard voice mails. Phone settings had to be checked. Invariably, the volume had been inadvertently turned down. This was unavoidable. The volume toggle on the side of the phone was obscure and Mom couldn't feel it. She usually kept the phone battery charged but, if low, I hooked the charger up. Hearing aid batteries were changed at the same time.

Though Mom enjoyed nurturing several plants on the windowsill, they were a bit difficult for her to manage. I watered them when they were thirsty. She was consistently running low on various supplies, which prompted me to routinely inventory her soap, snacks, incontinence essentials, tissues, lotions, balms, hairspray, and anything else I noticed. During one visit, I noticed floor stains, most likely from orange juice, and cleaned them up with her nearly exhausted supply of paper towels. They were added to the list.

During another visit, Mom mentioned she needed her hair trimmed. Clueless, I promised to trim it or attempt to trim it at some point in the future. Admittedly, her hair was longer than it had ever been and, for once, I agreed with one of her prior assessments: it was an "absolute mess." She loved the term and had frequently used it to describe anything disheveled or out of place. I reached for the scissors, but a *tap-tap-tap* on the door preempted me. The taps signaled the thirty-minute clock was out of ticks. Thirty minutes was cruelly short.

I trimmed Mom's hair the following week. The haircut was nothing short of a butcher job. Anyone who might have viewed the final "styling" could have concluded my chosen implement had been a pair of hedge clippers. There was a saving grace: most of my "work" was in the back of her head and she couldn't see the unnatural disaster I had created. It was *that* atrocious. If the "powers in charge" had viewed Mom's hair, they would have expanded the definition of compassionate caregivers to include beauticians.

Mom had several prescriptions with no refills remaining, and requests for their renewal had been rejected by the physician. Ugh! She was down to a three-week supply, and the COVID pandemic didn't offer any wiggle room for a simple process. Lab work and a subsequent office visit to the prescribing physician were required. I understood the rationale, yet hoped a viable alternative could be found. One alternative was to switch Mom from her current physician to an on-call nurse practitioner at Courtside. This wasn't advisable for numerous reasons and might be fraught with unforeseen complications.

Taking Mom to an offsite lab would border on insanity, given the mass of humanity flooding their lobbies for COVID tests. Once again, I sought Maddie's advice. She was hesitant to let Mom leave the "pen" for a visit to an outside lab, but offered the perfect solution: the blood draw could be done at Courtside. It worked seamlessly. The following week I was allowed to take Mom to her physician, who performed an examination and reviewed lab results in her nearly deserted office. She changed the dosage on one of the prescriptions and discontinued another altogether. The necessary refills were authorized and the world returned to its axis.

In spite of my frustrations, Mom kept me chuckling at times. She called one evening and asked for the name of the "good-looking doctor" who was on CNN. I gathered it was Sanjay Gupta. I repeated his name several times at varying decibel intensities and voice intonations. All I got from Mom was "Huh?" Moving forward, she asked me if his brother was the mayor of New York City. I told her "No," which she heard. Mom's inquisition continued with the statement: "I think the blue-eyed man on the show might be related to the mayor. He's a good-looking rascal too. What's his name?" She was referring to Chris Cuomo. To avoid an exhaustive explanation, I kept my answer simple and explained, "The man's name is Chris, and *his* brother is the *governor* of New York."

Mom asked no questions regarding the news item being discussed by the two men and I conjectured she hadn't absorbed much. It was evident she was less riveted by the "meat and potatoes" being served during the telecast than with the "eye-candy" serving it. Her centenarian status had in no way diminished her admiration of attractive men.

Another humorous incident involved a "news program" Mom was watching. She called to tell me: "The TV station where Joe Namath works announced all visitation restrictions in nursing facilities have been lifted." I promised to check it out, yet doubted the accuracy of her understanding. After some online sleuthing, I uncovered the morsel of evidence I was searching for—and Mom was mostly right! I shouldn't have been surprised. I found a significant *however*. The visitation relaxation wasn't instantaneous and wouldn't be an "everyone welcome, y'all come on in invitation." Significant entry requirements would still be the order of the day for months to come.

I was aware Joe Namath didn't work for the TV station airing the attention-grabbing news. He was a spokesman for Medicare Advantage commercials often aired on one of the networks Mom watched. It was understandable why she assumed he was a newscaster. I didn't touch that detail; it was immaterial.

Prior to the 2020 Thanksgiving holiday period, Courtside reinstituted serving meals in the dining room, following a several-months-long cessation. It surprised me that Mom seldom took advantage of the opportunity and continued to receive most meals in her room.

The dining room opportunity had a drawback: seating was limited to one person per table. This arrangement made reasonable conversation difficult among diners, who were *all* hearing-impaired. Reinstituting community dining, though less than ideal, was an encouraging step.

Got Incontinence Pads?

The topic of incontinence pads is an unlikely candidate to be granted air time. This particular necessity caused such a stir between Mom and me that it merits special attention. Finding the *right* pads for Mom was a source of frustration spanning several years. Regrettably, it also resulted in useless arguments. This bizarre source of irritation worsened during Mom's COVID lockup at Courtside; she had few diversions to distract her.

Mom was specific when giving instructions relating to the purchase of anything. I didn't fault her for having preferences. I have them too. Yet, her specificity made my shopping task a royal pain. Pads shared a commonality with compression stockings: they were equally perplexing.

Per Mom's directive, I forged ahead to Walmart in search of a particular type of pad she had seen in an advertisement. She hadn't previously tried the prescribed model and perceived it might be *the one*. Following an exhaustive search, I spotted the elusive package in an ocean of competitors. The size, absorptive strength, and pad length matched Mom's specifications. My hopes were high when I threw the bright pink package containing forty-eight pads into the shopping cart and whizzed through the self-checkout. To make identification easier for Mom, I circled the pertinent attributes stamped on the outside of the package with a black marker pen residing in my Subaru-turned-office. My shopping extravaganza culminated in a beeline trip to Courtside, where I dropped off the package for its three-day cooling-off period.

During my weekly visit three days later, I noticed the pink package on her bed. I asked, "Is this what you wanted?"

She answered, "Yes, I think it's what I need."

I opened the package and handed two incontinence pads to Mom. I commented they were thicker than the models she had previously dismissed for being too thin. She agreed. The next day, I asked about her impressions. They were positive. This bumpy road had been traveled multiple times and, while skeptical, I was delightfully surprised.

Five days later, Mom called to report she was out of pads. In disbelief, I questioned how this was possible. She informed me I had bought the wrong size; the pads were too thick and uncomfortable for her to wear. Mom maintained I had bought pads with an absorption factor of six instead of five. I asked her to get the package and read what I had circled.

"It says number five, maximum, regular length."

It was exactly what she had asked for. She asked me to go back to the store and get the number fours. These had been tried previously and received a thumbs-down verdict—they were declared too thin.

An argument ensued when I stated, "The pads are expensive and no matter what I've gotten, it's never been right. Incontinence pads don't come with options for customization. They are sold *as is*. You can't have it your way like a Whopper burger."

She shot back, "Oh yes, I can."

Later, I thought how stupid of me to let something this inane become a point of contention. Contrite, I got the number fours the next day. It was a fourteen-dollar investment in my sanity and, hopefully, her comfort.

Mom complained about every pad that had graced her underwear and she was acquainted with all makes and models. Besides being frustrating, it was sometimes comical. In addition to thickness dislikes, Mom had rejected various pads for other reasons: they were too long, too short, irregular, improperly sized, or were dressed with wings—this is really a thing. Be assured, they don't support flight. To Mom's defense, I discovered her claims pertaining to irregulars weren't imagined. I found some oddballs noticeably thinner than the rest in the same package.

Store brands? Not on your life! Mom was a card-carrying brand-name devotee. Anything else was judged unworthy before the jury was selected. Inferior or not, these alternatives didn't make it from the store shelf to the shopping cart. Since I tightly managed Mom's money, I sought ways to stretch it. Hence, her buying preferences were a challenge for me, a value shopper who will experiment with a store brand prior to pronouncing a verdict.

COVID Vaccine, Anyone?

As Mom approached her 103rd birthday, she was increasingly unable to reach logical conclusions when given straightforward information. It was mostly attributable to her deteriorating hearing, but not always. Sometimes her hearing aids *were* in her ears. Generally, Mom correctly gleaned about fifty percent of what she heard and extrapolated the rest. Her skewed reception was potent fertilizer for the garden of misinformation she unwittingly cultivated … misinformation prompting her to initially decline the COVID vaccine. When I asked her why, she informed me: "They said on the news a lot of people had dropped dead after getting the shot." To make matters worse, wild rumors pertaining to vaccine dangers were fodder for locked-down residents who had nothing to do except pass erroneous suppositions. This person-to-person social powerhouse was indisputably a highly effective in-house "web."

Coincidentally, Mom had a friend in Parkside's skilled nursing facility who had died from COVID a few days before vaccines were scheduled to be administered. I expected Mom would be clamoring to receive the shot after hearing of Sadie's fate. This wasn't the case. She dug her feet in and firmly stated: "No one is going to vaccinate me." Mom continued to be swayed by resident chatter. Perhaps a reasonable approach should be tried … present the facts.

I proposed two scenarios to Mom. First, she could get the vaccine and possibly feel lousy for a day or two. Second, she could decline it and risk getting COVID, with possible ominous consequences. It didn't work. She "reasoned" that remaining locked up, as she had been for ten months, was preferable to being injected with an unproven agent. I understood her misgivings and acknowledged her concerns, some of which I shared. Yet my own uneasiness was overridden by a fear of contracting COVID. Statistics were hard to refute; individuals who were fully vaccinated had a much lower incidence of dying from the disease than those who weren't.

After much pleading, convincing, and peer pressure from well-informed residents, Mom was injected with the Pfizer vaccine at her facility, on Wednesday, January 20, 2021. Fact had triumphed over fiction throughout the facility and most residents eventually rolled up their sleeves. Three days later, Mom called to report she had hallucinated during the afternoon when she was trying to nap. She declared, "The vaccine caused it and I'm afraid to take the second shot. It might make me go nuts again."

I expected to hear Mom's latest escape from reality had tapped into the talents of former actors—spiders and kids running wild. It hadn't. Instead, her imagination had beamed her to a former neighbor's house in Jacksonville. She couldn't figure out why she was there or how she had gotten there. She wasn't aware of how long her departure from reality had persisted, and returned to sanity when a CNA delivered the evening meal at five. I did a bit of research and found no instance of vaccine side effects resembling what Mom had described. In all probability, she had fallen asleep and had a dream.

On Friday, January 29, I walked into Mom's room for my weekly half-hour visit and found her precariously standing at the kitchenette sink; her rollator wasn't in the vicinity. She had obviously been ambling around the room without it. I reminded her that safety was *her* primary responsibility and underscored the need for the rollator to be positioned close behind her with brakes locked. When asked what would catch her if she fell, she assured me: "I'm not going to fall. I usually have the Buick with me, but got busy and forgot it." Aside from Mom's usual disregard for safety protocols, a few wires seemed crossed. I recalled her recent hallucination or dream, or whatever it was, and wondered if something was going on.

One week later I walked into Mom's room for my scheduled visit and was mortified to find her sprawled out on the floor, lying on her back with her legs straight out. Her head was slightly cocked and her eyes were wide open, appearing fixed. She didn't react to my entry; I thought she was dead. Though initially unnoticed, a folded blanket was positioned under her head. Surely, not the work of a corpse.

My initial reaction was to yell, and I did. "Mom! What are you doing on the floor?"

With no hesitation or apparent concern, she said, "I lost my balance while standing at the sink and fell."

In a flash I turned to run out of the room for assistance and Mom tried to stop me.

She ordered, "No, you don't. They'll haul me to Flagler Hospital. I think I'm all right. ... I'm *not* going to Flagler."

I disregarded her directive and, within seconds, roped in Rachel and Hattie, both CNAs.

When quizzed, Mom guessed she had been on the floor forty-five minutes, perhaps longer. She swore she hadn't hit her head. Such an admission would have earned an automatic ticket to the Flagler ER, a frequent destination for residents. With help from Rachel and Hattie, Mom rose to her feet, dusted off her trousers, and walked around. All moving parts seemed to be in working order. I exhaled with relief. Mom was okay, but complained of a sore shoulder.

Stones weren't left unturned and a portable X-ray machine was rolled into the room. It captured several pictures of Mom's shoulder. Once again, she had been lucky—the images showed nothing was broken. Before Rachel exited the room, she informed me that Mom had been given a urine test two days prior and the results had come back earlier in the day. It was positive for a UTI. We'd been on this merry-go-round so many times I could name each horse on the carousel. Mom was placed on a familiar tour of antibiotic debugging and, in a few days, she reclaimed mental clarity. Her perceived visit to her former neighbor was attributed to the UTI.

Once the hubbub of the morning's excitement had faded, I asked Mom about her nowhere-to-be-seen medical alert pendant. She pointed to the top of the dresser. It wasn't there. I eventually found it in the seat pocket of the rollator.

An Exchange Worth Framing

Some conversations with Mom were humdingers. It was a little past seven in the morning when my cell phone rang. The display on the readout read *Mama*. I didn't want to answer it, but did. Though awake, I was still in bed and in an unfocused state. The amniotic-like sea of serenity embracing me ruptured when Mom excitedly reported, "I've lost two pills."

An expedition was assuredly in the works. I got out of bed and began to pace back and forth across the room. I asked Mom which pills were lost and she responded, "The little ones." She took several pills fitting this description. Her UTI pills were removed from the investigation based on their large size.

I attempted to narrow the field and asked, "What do you take them for?"

Mom responded, "I take them twice a day."

While helpful, it wasn't what I was looking for. I repeated the question: "*What* do you take them for?"

The emphasis on *what* hit the target and Mom informed me: "Oh, my blood pressure, I think."

Mom took three blood pressure medications: propranolol, HCTZ, and losartan. I eliminated propranolol since it was a capsule and larger than the rest. HCTZ's size fit the bill, but she only took it once daily. I deduced she had lost two losartan pills, which were slightly larger than HCTZ.

I asked, "Did you lose some losartan pills?"

Again, Mom was wandering in another ballpark and responded: "I had them in my hand and don't know *where* they went."

Slower and louder, I repeated the question in Mom's indigenous language—Southern drawl.

There was silence; she still hadn't understood me.

With urgency, I pleaded: "Please ... put ... in ... your ... hearing ... aids."

Miraculously, the plea penetrated an eardrum and Mom declared: "They're not working."

No doubt, the batteries needed to be changed since I had forgotten to change them when I was last with her. They were tiny and seriously challenging for Mom. Negotiating them was a pain, even for me.

I mustered another attempt: "Mom, the losartan is white and oval-shaped. Is that what you lost?"

After another long pause, she stated: "I don't know who Opal is."

And neither did I. I took a deep breath. In a slow and deliberate tone, I asked, "Are the pills white and shaped like a football? Look at the color-coded chart. It has pictures of all the pills you take." One thing was certain. I wasn't revisiting *oval*.

Mom got part of it and asked, "Huh? What chart?"

I attempted another revision of the question while aimlessly pacing from room to room: "Mom, look at the pill chart I made you. It's in the top drawer of your desk."

Mom asked, "Extra pills are in my desk?"

Undone—actually fully baked—I dropped the cell phone to my hip and shouted toward the ceiling, "God, have mercy!"

Mom heard the *God* part of the utterance and with a tone of disapproval, asked, "What did you say?"

Ignoring her question, I continued with the interrogation. After a twenty-two-minute conversation, the goal line was reached. I was convinced Mom had lost two losartan pills and they were likely on the floor. Prior to COVID visitation restrictions, I could have driven to Courtside, located the lost pills, and returned home in less time.

My scheduled Friday visitation was coming up in two days, and I promised, "Mama, I'll bring replacement pills on Friday."

She comprehended what I had said and asked, "You're bringing me the pills on Friday?"

I answered with an enthusiastic "Yes."

Eureka! We were on the same page regardless of the circuitous path taken. In the meantime, Hattie called to report the lost pills were on Mom's desk and the hearing aid batteries had been changed. My previously drawn conclusions were proved wrong. The pills hadn't been on the floor, and Mom had lost one losartan and one HCTZ.

In the early 1970s, Carly Simon sang a very popular song titled "Anticipation." I decided to write a sequel—"Exasperation."

Act Two

Mom called again later that evening. Her greeting was upbeat. "Hello, honey. You'll be pleased to know I'm wearing my hearing aids. By the way, I'm out of eye drops."

I thought, *She ain't out,* and stated, "Mom, they were in the carton of supplies you received less than two weeks ago. How can you be out? I sent two bottles, enough for a month."

Mom countered: "I must have used them. And while you're at it, could you please get me a box of Puffs tissues?"

Dumbfounded, I drilled deeper. "Mom, they were in the same carton containing the eyedrops, toothpaste, incontinence pads, and soap. They have to be in your room."

She insisted they weren't.

Mom had another concern: "Seth, one other thing … I can't remember if I took my antibiotic for the UTI tonight. I took everything else, though. Should I take one now, just in case I missed taking it?"

There was an easy mathematical solution. I suggested, "Count the pills. If you took tonight's pill, you should have eight remaining. If nine are left, you haven't taken it. Get Hattie to help count them if you need to."

Mom resisted the suggestion: "It's almost ten o'clock and I don't want to bother her this late. Besides, I'm quite capable of counting … I'm not *that* far gone. I'll call you back after I go to the bathroom."

She called back a few minutes later to report eight pills were remaining. Problem solved. When I visited Mom on Friday, I located the Puffs and eyedrops in a carton sitting on the floor.

Extra! Extra! Read All about It: Courtside Prisoners Offered Parole

As the COVID outbreak continued to moderate in baby steps, Courtside residents were granted releases to leave the premises on occasion. Since Mom and I were both fully vaccinated, the process was straightforward. I was required to notify facility administration when Mom would be exiting the building and advise them when she returned.

To my disappointment, in-house visitation remained unchanged; Max and I were limited to one weekly visit each.

In mid-February, after a two-year hiatus, the swelling in Mom's legs began again. I credited the pacemaker for the two-year break. With permission granted by Courtside's medical gurus, I drove Mom to her physician, who informed us compression stockings would be necessary. I thought, *Oh no, not that again.* Yes, again.

Each day, a CNA would be required to apply Mom's stockings in the morning and remove them in the evening. This added level of assistance computed to a different kind of pain—a quantifiable one equaling $450 per month. The increase in Mom's monthly outlay for assistance was due to two factors: the stockings, and Mom's recent need for hands-on bathing assistance. The upward cost trajectory was concerning yet inevitable. It had been expected.

Mom's first hair appointment since the advent of the COVID lockdown occurred on February 26, 2021, nearly a year since her previous styling. This red-letter occasion was cause for celebration. Mom's hair had become lifeless and appeared to have been run over with a steamroller—flat, straight, combed back. Mom wasn't alone; the COVID hairstyle, as I called it, had been adopted throughout the "kingdom." Over the course of the ninety-minute reclamation project, Mom's hair was washed, cut, rolled, dried, teased to the maximum degree allowed by law, and sprayed with enough lacquer to withstand hurricane-force winds. The visit to the hair palace was well worth the investment in time and money. Two uplifts were the result: one involving hair, and the other, attitudinal. A jubilant woman with refound dignity walked out of the "restoration room." It had been a momentous day.

Got Teeth?

Mom hadn't "enjoyed" a routine dental visit in over a year, and the pause in professional care preyed on her mind. Though out of the ordinary, Mom still had *all* of her teeth. Not a single one was missing. She had been a patient of an esteemed dental practice in Jacksonville for over sixty years and remained loyal through inevitable staff changes. Her revered dentist was a delightful young professional who waived her fees for established patients 100 years of age or older. Regardless of this over-the-top accommodation, Mom was married to the practice. Wisely, I wouldn't have been the impetus for a dental divorce.

Mom's long-anticipated mid-April appointment had been booked six weeks prior. Per her request, I picked up an orchid with purple blooms the day before the visit for Mom to give the dentist. At last, the day arrived. I had arranged to pick up Mom at eleven. Her appointment was at two o'clock. We had planned to grab hamburgers, eat them at home, and Mom could brush her teeth afterwards. It was all set.

I arrived a few minutes before eleven and attempted to call Mom to advise her I was waiting in the portico. I sensed she had opened her flip phone, but there was silence.

I waited a couple of seconds before speaking. "Hey, Mom. I'm here."

The phone blanked out. Mom had inadvertently disconnected me and probably was unaware. I called back and it went straight to voice mail. Success came at seven minutes after eleven, when Mom answered.

She hurriedly stated, "I've been *real sick*. It's going to be several minutes before I'm ready."

She had my attention. I sought clarification, asking, "What do you mean by *real sick*?"

Click. Disconnected again. I didn't call back and waited for the next news bulletin.

At eleven twenty-five, a CNA appeared from the inner sanctum and reported Mom had experienced a spell of diarrhea moments before I had arrived. Mom was in the process of changing her pants *and* shoes. Not being allowed inside to talk with Mom was a hindrance. I had no idea how sick she was. Based on Mom's *real sick* description and thirty-minute cleanup, it was reasonable to assume the event was significant.

I weighed the possibility of a second siege. Such an occurrence would be dreadful while motoring down the road or, even worse, in the hygienist's or dentist's chair. It wasn't worth the risk for the sake of a noncritical dental prophylaxis. I asked the CNA to tell Mom I would cancel the appointment and we would make the trip at another time. I called the dentist's office before leaving and rescheduled the appointment.

At eleven thirty-five, Mom called while I was driving home. She asked, "Seth, where are you? I'm waiting at the front door and don't see your car."

She hadn't received my message. In retrospect, I should have waited a bit longer before leaving. I advised her I had cancelled the appointment and was on the way home. There was a pause while the gravity of *cancelled* sank in.

Mom was upset. Emphatically, she growled, "You cancelled it? Why? I'm ready to go and we have time to get there! This has been planned a long time and there's no telling how long we'll have to wait to get another appointment."

She was partially right. We *did* have time to get there, particularly if we skipped lunch. However, the possibility of a second intestinal uprising overrode all else. And generally, Mom's intestinal history strongly implied "one and done" wasn't usually the case.

I reiterated, "Mom, I canceled it because you had diarrhea, and was concerned it might return."

My explanation didn't mitigate her disappointment, and she insisted she hadn't said she was *real sick*. She was angry at me, and I understood why she felt let down.

Abruptly she stated, "I'll go to the dining room and eat lunch."

I attempted to tell her the appointment had been rebooked, but the message overshot the runway. Mom wasn't interested in hearing anything else, and I didn't have the emotional bandwidth for further conversation.

Later in the evening, I spoke to Mom and her earlier disgruntlement had evaporated. She wasn't one to hold on to disappointments and had always moved beyond them with ease. Perhaps this was a contributor to her longevity. I advised her the dental appointment was rescheduled for May 10, three weeks out. She was placated. As it turned out, Mom was right about her morning intestinal episode. It was a single event.

Dodging Bullets

When I was a kid, I loved playing dodgeball despite being frequently struck by balls thrown by someone more accurate in targeting than I was in avoidance. I wondered, *Could this kids' game be a prep for fending off unpredictable and uninvited events later in life?* Mom was a seasoned player in real-life dodgeball—far better than me—and she always managed to get back up when hit.

A week following the dental visit snafu, Mom's physician called to advise me a urinalysis performed two days prior, at Courtside, revealed the presence of yet another UTI. In keeping with the script, Mom had become batty, which had necessitated the test. It had been six weeks since Mom cleared the prior UTI, and I assumed the bout was a resurgence of the previous infection. My presumption was erroneous. The UTI strain this go-around was from a different planet and required an intergalactic pharmaceutical combatant.

Mom was offered a tray of medicinal hors d'oeuvres that included antibiotics, probiotics, and any additional "otics" to treat her condition. The days passed and she completed the prescribed course. Mom's symptoms disappeared and she fully recovered without any dire side effects.

She had barely consumed the last antibiotic pill when yet another near calamity befell her. She called one morning to report she had gotten out of bed to go to the bathroom at 2:00 a.m. and lost her balance. She slipped from the edge of the bed to the carpeted floor and remained sandwiched between the bed and dresser for about an hour. Her pleas for help weren't loud enough to escape the walls.

Mom lay trapped and helpless on the floor … until remembering the alert pendant was on the edge of the dresser. It wasn't within her field of vision, yet it was reachable. While sliding her hand across the top of the dresser edge, the pendant fell into her hand. Sheer luck! Mom pressed the button and, within seconds, the CNA came rushing in. Mom didn't have a scratch and the decision was made to not call me. Thank you for that favor! All the lecturing she had gotten regarding the importance of wearing the pendant hadn't made a dent and never would.

Welcome and Unwelcome Changes

Monday, June 7, 2021, was a day worth celebrating. I received an email announcing that deliveries of personal items to Courtside residents would no longer be subject to cumbersome drop-off restrictions and subsequent waits. The fifteen-month-long pain-in-the-ass procedures were history. I would be allowed to drop off deliveries to Mom any day or bring them on my designated visitation day. Got toothpaste, toothpicks, or chocolate-covered cherries? Indeed! Mom's starved sweet tooth wasn't disregarded.

Other entrenched policies kept my eyebrows furrowed. Visits to Mom in the facility remained limited and highly regulated. I would be kicked to the curb if any one of several screening questions pertaining to my day-to-day activities was answered *yes*. This included being in a group of ten or more people in the last fourteen days. Nothing new here. I had no objections with screening or the requirement to wear a mask while inside the building. Yet, Mom could leave the premises for virtually any purpose, when she wished … and wasn't screened upon her return. Inconsistent rules were a paradox.

The dismantling of the supply-chain roadblock at Courtside was a win for all parties. I was basking in this ray of freedom when a new annoyance took its place. This time it wasn't from Courtside—it came from AT&T. Mom received a letter in mid-June stating her cellular flip phone would need to be replaced prior to February 22, 2022. This unwelcome message was softened by the eight-month advance notice. Mom's phone operated on the 3G network, which was being retired.

There was reason for optimism. In a few weeks, a replacement flip phone compatible with the newer network would be sent, free of charge. Upgraded features and additional functionality promised to heighten customer experience and satisfaction. The words *additional functionality* gave me the willies. It was apparent the writer of the letter hadn't been introduced to Miss Dot. Upgrades and improvements, no matter how sensational to the inventors, would likely spell exasperation for many users. Assuredly, a high percentage of flip phone owners were seniors who weren't technological athletes. Skeptical, I wondered what the heightened customer experience might entail.

As previously disclosed, Mom was seriously challenged by the basic functions of her soon-to-be-defunct flip phone. On most days, she could barely make or receive calls. The replacement phone was described to be similar to Mom's current phone in appearance and use. It sounded encouraging, but not enough for me to dive into an unfamiliar digital pool until I had to. Waiting until the last possible minute seemed prudent. A lot could happen in eight months.

Circumstances can change on a dime and they did in *two weeks*, making eight months a moot point. Before the dust had a chance to settle on the letter from AT&T, Mom dropped her vintage cell phone on the unforgiving ceramic tile floor in her bathroom. A CNA called to report the cellular carnage. I retrieved the lifeless phone and rushed it to the "electronics hospital," hoping for a miracle. My hopes were shattered. The phone was declared dead on arrival by the attending techno-geek. Since Mom had no PC and no landline phone in her room, she was cut off from the outside world. With urgency, I began a quest for a new phone—one that was Mom-compatible. My task was comparable to a search for the Holy Grail.

I considered five or six flip phone models, all with bells and whistles capable of running Mom nuts, and me with her. It didn't take long to conclude Mom was in for an adjustment, regardless of the phone selected. I slept on it. The following morning, I took a deep breath and traveled to the AT&T retail outlet where I was introduced to the "official" replacement phone—the same model scheduled to be sent in a few weeks. It was similar in appearance to the deceased model. The phone was engineered with an instant dissatisfier: Mom's lengthy contact list couldn't be transferred from the old phone to the new. Time was a pressing factor and we didn't have the luxury of waiting an unspecified number of weeks to get the free phone. Feeling compelled to make a decision, I bought the "new and improved" replacement after receiving a five-minute overview by the sales rep. The phone cost seventy dollars— not a cause for heartburn. The purchase apparently cancelled shipment of the "free" phone. It was never received, and I didn't pursue it.

Now came the tough part, learning the basics. When I returned home, I rifled through the box containing the cell phone and associated gadgetry, but couldn't locate the instruction manual. There wasn't one. My user experience was trending downward even before the phone had been popped open. I returned to the AT&T store and was advised the manuals weren't available in print. With a smile, the wet-behind-the-ears clerk proudly referred me to the website where online manuals resided. Summarily, she sent me on my way.

With a clear mission but not a clear mind, I returned home and fired up my laptop, promptly locating the online users' manual. It was an encouraging start; however, discouragement overtook me as I found myself lost in a digital haystack. I discovered that the new phone, which had been billed as similar to the old one, wasn't similar enough. It was overengineered with capabilities overshadowing the original intent of a phone—talking. I spent several mind-blowing hours learning how to use the "cellular device." The online instructions displayed on the PC screen kept disappearing into dark oblivion while I attempted to operate the phone. Or the phone went dark while I tried to digest the gobbledygook on the PC screen. Coordinating the two was a fight. My first impulse was to hurl the phone against the wall. Instead, I settled on verbal slanders. Persistence paid off and, prior to the sun setting, I had developed an acceptable degree of proficiency. With extraneous phone functionality disabled and Mom's contact list manually loaded, a formidable assignment awaited me: tutoring Mom.

She was 103 years of age, hence Mom's cognition wasn't what it used to be. Numb hands, diminished hearing, and failing eyesight were menacing impediments. These deterrents had to be overcome for her to resume communication in the cellular universe. A smartphone wasn't a consideration. It would have been a "bridge too far."

Undaunted, I introduced Mom to my surefire training solution: "Seth's Simplified Learning Module." Mom struggled. My "seamless" educational prototype was less simple than I had envisioned. To complicate matters, the phone was rife with its own preprogrammed roadblocks. Uninvited, out-of-the-blue messaging, some of which couldn't be muzzled, were sand traps. My "classroom" was interrupted by a flow of pesky notifications and useless updates. At times they commandeered the phone. In some instances the only way out was to shut the phone completely down and start over. And God forbid if Mom glanced a wrong key with a wayward finger. This happened numerous times, sending the phone's programming into a far-flung galaxy. Recovery was difficult since the manual didn't address cellular escapes to distant realms. In those instances, forums and blogs became a last-ditch resource.

My mantra for learning was repetition, repetition, repetition, and practice, practice, practice. This was met with marginal success. Mom never became proficient, even with simple cheat sheets at her disposal. At least she could usually answer the phone if she heard it ring *and* it was nearby. She could make an outgoing call after several attempts. The odds were stacked against my poor mother. She couldn't efficiently operate the phone and it wasn't the phone's fault. I wished a thousand times the landlines, or as they were called, *real phones*, hadn't been ripped out.

A Fizzling Fourth

It was late in the afternoon of Thursday, July 1, 2021. Thomas and I were busily preparing for the arrival of his brother, sister-in-law, niece, and two-month-old great-niece. They were arriving the next afternoon from Atlanta, for a long-planned holiday weekend. A few minutes shy of six o'clock, I received an alarming call from a CNA at Mom's facility. Mom had fallen in the bathroom and rescue was on the way. She was in considerable back and hip pain. The news rattled me while I contemplated another prolonged, miserable ordeal.

The CNA explained that Mom fell while attempting to walk the short distance from the toilet to the sink. I inquired about the rollator's whereabouts ... it wasn't in the bathroom. As with all but one of her previous incidents, the fall was probably preventable. Mom's affinity for "timing mishaps" to coincide with well-planned activities or trips simmered under my skin. Of course her falls weren't intentional, but her failure to use the rollator to mitigate them seemingly was. And therein was the source of my ire. Saying anything to Mom about this "oversight" would have served no purpose.

Mom was taken to Flagler Hospital where she, Max, and I were squeezed into an emergency room cubicle for six tiresome hours. Mom was miserable, and test results revealed the reason: she had two fractured ribs and another fracture in her spine. Mom's rib fracture tally since 2016 now totaled ten. Remarkably, her hips were unscathed.

With no overriding concerns for noise abatement or privacy, we left the cubicle door open. Mom's groans were blunted somewhat by conversation among nurses in the hall. "Hey, Sybil, where's the urine sample in cubicle six?" We were in four. A response echoed throughout. "It was spilled … we have to get another one." "Entertainment" came in various other forms: stretchers with occupants passing by, clunky equipment being pushed up and down the hall, and the sound of coins feeding vending machines. All were diversions.

Mom's blood pressure, clocked at 210 over 100 at one point, all but blew the cuff off her arm. This was high enough to induce a stroke. High-pitched beeps discharged from the monitor every so often, signaling the latest reading. Mom's inquiring mind wasn't the least bit dimmed by pain, and she insisted on being told the numbers after each string of beeps. So I disclosed them after applying a downward adjustment. The medications eventually trimmed Mom's blood pressure, eliminating the need for me to be a creative purveyor of white lies.

Her beleaguered body was under assault, and we were advised she would be admitted into the hospital when a room became available. At midnight, the room was assigned and I left. Max stayed until the transfer was complete—two hours later. Hospitals operate in a time zone understood only to them. Probably a good thing.

Why Mom lost her balance and fell was anyone's guess, and pinning down the cause required further testing. After a multitude of tests were run and serious causes ruled out, it was determined her sudden loss of balance was likely attributable to an inner ear disorder. Spells can occur at any time without warning and cause a fall. Seniors are particularly susceptible, which explains why many of them are affixed to walkers and rollators.

It was the Fourth of July weekend and the hospital was quiet. Mom began her recuperation in an eighth-floor room with a southerly view, offering peeks of the Matanzas River through partially opened blinds. Physical therapy was prominently featured on the daily agenda. Mom wasn't thrilled, yet mustered a cooperative attitude.

The hospital's visitation guidelines required masking and were otherwise relaxed. Max and I were allowed to visit Mom when we wanted to. This facet of her confinement was an upgrade when compared to the head-scratching protocols still enforced at her assisted living facility. Since I was only ten minutes away, I visited Mom twice daily, limiting visits to an hour or less. This gave me the freedom to spend quality time with Thomas' family.

Mom's hospitalization spanned five days. Though she was plagued by pain and discomfort, she voiced few complaints. This alone was a victory. Flagler rendered concerted compassionate care and positioned Mom for a successful transition to a skilled nursing rehab facility of our choice. We chose Parkside. It was familiar and convenient.

Mom was released from the hospital at 5:45 p.m. on Tuesday, July 6, and transferred via medical transit to Parkside. Max and I drove ahead, arriving first; it was six o'clock and offices were closed. We had Mom's belongings and were primed to begin setting them up in her room beforehand. Our conscientiousness was rewarded with locked doors and no sign of human habitation. Repeated doorbell rings were unanswered. Five minutes later the transport van arrived, with Mom securely strapped in "steerage class" directly behind the driver's seat. A burly, cheerful driver bounded out, flew open the rear doors, and deftly extracted Mom from her tight lodging. A harried on-duty and in-charge "mother superior" appeared within seconds. The message was clear: doorbells don't carry the same sense of urgency as a van driver dropping off a special delivery.

I assumed our passage across the border crossing would be automatic once we were garbed with protective gear and our "visas" stamped. Since Mom was a resident in the assisted living wing, and Max and I were on the official visitors' list, it was a no-brainer. Additionally, similar facilities in the area had begun to relax their entry requirements. But ... the law of the land, as strictly interpreted by after-hours Parkside staff, stopped us in our tracks. There was no mercy, no exception, not even for humanitarian considerations. I was primed to call Amnesty International, but didn't think their focus would include the likes of Parkside.

Barred from entering, we hastily piled Mom's belongings on a rickety hotel-style luggage cart. I held my breath, praying the payload would reach the intended destination. Max and I were given assurances Mom's clothes and toiletry articles would be unpacked and appropriately handled. The glass doors automatically shut when Mom's stretcher and teetering luggage cart cleared the threshold. I watched until the rear ends of the assistants who were pushing the two-float parade disappeared into dimness. I carried anger and exasperation with me when I turned around and walked off.

Mom called later that night to report her belongings had survived the trip but were sitting on the floor in the closet. At least they were in the right room. Mom didn't know her room number or the phone number of the nurses station. Minimally, we should have been given the information when she arrived at the facility. I didn't think to ask for it.

The next day when I arrived for an authorized thirty-minute visit, all of Mom's belongings were still on the floor. I hung the "hangables," set up Mom's toiletries in the bathroom, and placed anything remaining in dresser drawers. Her roommate, Blanche, was delightful and mentally sharp. She was an 80-year-old "youngster" who was wheelchair bound, on continuous oxygen, and a permanent facility resident.

At Flagler Hospital, we had enjoyed unrestricted access to Mom during normal visiting hours. This wasn't the case at Parkside. She was allowed a single thirty-minute visit each day during her first week. Subsequent weeks followed a different schedule. The thirty-minute visit was allowed on Monday, Wednesday, Friday, Saturday, and Sunday. A cumbersome appointment process had to be navigated a week in advance of each desired visitation day, and available timeslots varied from one day to the next. The process had to be an administrative nightmare for the facility. Max and I were grateful for any visits we could get, regardless of when they were scheduled.

The template for Mom's rehabilitation closely mirrored the procedures and therapies employed during her 2016 and 2018 flirts with disaster. Even though her injuries were less severe than those experienced with prior physical breakdowns, she was considerably weaker. Physical therapy was a steep climb. Mom's worsening balance problems didn't help; on most days she appeared to be a candidate for a breathalyzer test. Loss of balance and generalized weakness were a dangerous combo. If and when Mom might fall again lingered in my thoughts.

The Sky Is Falling

Mom's experience in the skilled nursing facility turned out to be exasperating. This was partially attributable to COVID—the gift that kept on giving—and Mom, the unwilling patient. With restricted visitation, it was difficult to gauge whether or not her accounts of "being neglected" were valid. Long wait times to receive bathroom assistance topped Mom's complaint list. Thirty-minute waits were commonplace, which was corroborated by Blanche. I met with the director of social services two days following Mom's admission and was told the state required them to meet minimum standards. Thirty minutes didn't fall within established guidelines.

Parkside was short-staffed due to sick-outs, in addition to an exodus of workers who had left the industry. This was in lockstep with facilities throughout the country. To counteract the shortage, the facility had reduced the number of patients. I wondered if the ratio of staff to patients was still less than it should be. Circumstances were extraordinary, so I took a wait-and-see attitude.

Communication with facility employees was difficult. Phone calls were frequently unanswered, although messages left on voice mail were typically returned the same day. The CNAs were overworked and had to be worn to a frazzle. Many were drowning in a sea of double shifts, covering for sick colleagues.

My frustration reached the boiling point when Mom called on Wednesday morning, July 14. She was fuming and by the end of the call, I was too ... mostly at her. Here's the context of our conversation:

"Seth, I cannot get anyone in here to help me."

"Mama, what's wrong?"

"I need to go to the bathroom."

"How long has it been since you pushed the button?"

"I can't find the button. I think it's behind my shoulder."

"Is Blanche in her bed? Ask her to push her button."

Mom fired back, "*She* doesn't need help, I do."

"I understand that, but Blanche can get someone in the room *who can come to you*. Ask her to push her button."

The suggestion seemed to go into outer space and Mom got increasingly belligerent, saying, "You lie in this bed and try to get help. *You'll* see how awful this place is. I want to get out of here and go back to my apartment in Courtside. You need to get me out of here and I mean *now*. I'd rather be dead than stay here."

She meant every word except for the last statement, which was added for effect. Regardless of her demands, I couldn't change the orbit of the planets.

Mom refused to ask Blanche to request help. Yet, as urgently as Mom needed to go to the bathroom, she continued to discharge criticism from her bazooka and wouldn't listen to my suggestions.

She ranted, "I've been in here for seven days and haven't had a shower. All they've done is wipe me down. This is the worst place I've ever seen. They're mistreating me."

The last remark was unsettling, yet I didn't believe Mom's characterization was an accurate assessment. From the moment Mom was placed in the rehab facility, she was predisposed to abhor it.

I was on the edge of implosion or explosion and my frustration level was to the point where I got lightheaded. This used to be a rare state for me. I was angry with Mom, at the facility, at COVID, at God, and anything else while I was at it.

I couldn't get anywhere with Mom. I fumbled through a stack of papers until I found the one containing the phone number to the nurses station, which I had obtained during my first visit earlier in the week. I called it and my cry for help was answered on the first ring. The CNA who answered was unaware Mom needed help and promptly provided it.

Ralph Waldo Emerson stated: "For every minute you remain angry, you give up sixty seconds of peace of mind." I had far exceeded Mr. Emerson's directive and placed myself into mental detoxification by falling into the arms of the Soundscapes music channel on cable TV. I chilled to mood-altering, New-Age "sedatives," coupled with inspirational quotes on the screen. My blood pressure came down.

Having regained symmetry, I skedaddled to the facility and spoke to the director of social services. This was my second meeting with her. She seemed surprised to hear lengthy waits for bathroom assistance were still a problem and wasn't aware of Mom's food and shower complaints. She was apologetic and put me in contact with the manager of food services. He tweaked menu options based on Mom's many dislikes, which should have been known since Mom was a permanent resident at Courtside.

No promises were made about bathroom wait times except for the assurance they were closely monitored. Mom's chart was brought in during our meeting and it contained a revealing notation: Mom had declined a shower—not once, but twice. When the showers had been offered, she stated she was too tired and opted for sponge baths instead. What a revelation!

My next visit with Mom was at five o'clock the following afternoon. The timing was perfect. The "awful" food she had frequently maligned was delivered before I walked in. It was well-prepared and smelled appetizing. I commented, "The cut-up roast beef, mashed potatoes, and carrots should be delicious." Mom disapprovingly pointed to the carrots and pronounced: "They're tasteless and need salt." I found some salt and doused the carrots. She ate one. I asked Blanche what she thought about the dinner and she gave it a thumbs-up. She also said the lunch served at noon was excellent and thought Mom had enjoyed it. There had been no mention of it. I asked Mom what had been served for breakfast, expecting she had been offered grits and bacon, per my request ... and that's what she got. However, it hadn't pleased her; the bacon was too salty and the grits were described as rubbery. She didn't have to say another word. I was as steamed as the uneaten carrots on her plate.

I concluded Mom needed an attitude adjustment and had a stern conversation with her, similar to the ones I had been given by Dad when I was a kid. "Mama, if you want to go back to Courtside, you're going to have to cooperate. This place is doing the best they can, given the lousy deck of COVID cards they've been dealt. It's essential for you to do what they ask, when they ask, and do whatever it takes to get strong enough to get out of here. You're not leaving until they certify you're ready, and this isn't going to happen without your help. This is no different than your two prior stints in rehab. You don't want to hear this, but you're going to be in here another week or two. It's in your hands."

I could only hope my lecture had landed on a fertile plain rather than a minefield. Though quiet, Mom had listened and didn't recoil. Incidentally, she received a shower following the evening meal. Mom had assumed a persona I didn't recognize, yet I understood the dynamics at play. Repeated injury and pain, illness, loss of dignity, loss of control, and evaporation of a once-vibrant life had exacted an enormous toll. All were disabling blows.

The following morning, Max and I attended a weekly scheduled phone conference with representatives from Physical Therapy, Social Services, Dining Services, Insurance, and Nursing. We discussed Mom's list of previously aired complaints and were assured they had been addressed. We were pleased to hear Mom had been cooperative and sweet, had done everything as asked, and was making progress in physical therapy. In fact, no one had encountered any problems with her. Max and I concluded Mom wore two hats: one for us and one for the facility. What she told us wasn't necessarily what she told the staff. She wouldn't complain directly to them, yet readily called Max or me to "get things fixed."

I visited Mom at five o'clock the same afternoon. It was her tenth day in skilled nursing. Her color had brightened, and I hoped to find an improving attitude. This wasn't the case.

"Hello, Mama, how's it going? Are things better?"

With deeply furrowed eyebrows, she responded, "This place is awful." Angrily, she highlighted each item featured on her list of objections.

I asked, "Weren't you given a shower yesterday?"

She responded "Yes," but complained it was given too late in the evening.

I continued. "What about breakfast this morning? You requested toast and grits. Is that what you got?"

Again, her answer was "Yes." Her evening dinner tray was sitting in front of her. The salmon, stewed tomatoes, and rice were among the items she typically liked. She ate perhaps five or six bites and pushed the rest away while declaring, "This is lousy."

I put the fish through my own taste test, chomping down on an adequately sized sample. A few seconds was all I needed to assess the entrée. It was dry and tasteless, and the rice was barely edible. Mom's disapproval for the lifeless dinner was legitimate. Anyone not hungry to begin with would have been tempted to throw the fish to the alligators. Don't do it! You might get eaten in the process—not to mention feeding them is illegal.

On many days I wanted to scream, but Mom surely wanted to scream louder. Understandably, she was in despair. There was nothing to bring any real joy in her life. In essence, Mom was a prisoner to herself and the facility. It could be argued that Mom had been shielded from COVID, but the trade-off was her mental health. The following account points to her mental slide.

During a scheduled thirty-minute visit the next morning, Mom told a tall tale reminiscent of her hallucinogenic traipses several years prior. With certainty, she described a "serious, life-threatening situation" that had occurred in the middle of the night. Mom insisted a male employee, who she couldn't see, was about to kill her when another employee discovered the plot. The two got into a noisy scuffle and the attack was thwarted. Shortly thereafter, Mom alleged a man came into the room and whispered in her ear, "You're lucky to be alive." Mom was convinced she had barely escaped being stabbed or shot, and wanted me to call the police.

There was a better option: question Blanche. And why not? She was alert and had excellent hearing. I asked her if anything out of the ordinary had occurred during the night. She responded, "No, nothing happened." A calamitous disruption in the quietude of the night would have been noticed by Blanche, and I believed Mom's fright was borne from a nightmare. She wasn't open to the suggestion, and I wasn't open to calling the police.

I assumed we were done with it, but Mom couldn't let it go. She called around nine o'clock, afraid to remain in her room. She whispered, "They might be coming back for me tonight. I don't think it's a safe place." Even though Mom's paranoia was likely the result of a dream, she thought otherwise. I managed to walk her back from the cliff's edge by reasoning, assuring, and convincing her she was in the best of hands. I insisted, "Nothing bad is going to happen." I asked her to trust me and she did. Mom didn't mention it again.

Mom remained in the skilled nursing facility four additional days, for a total of nineteen. From her perspective, it had been nineteen days in hell. She couldn't acclimate to the environment and was overjoyed to be transferred back to Courtside. Hopefully, physical therapy's emphasis on the need for Mom to employ personal safety measures had made a lasting impression. I held my breath.

So, how did Parkside fare on my ledger? Aside from Mom's abhorrence for skilled nursing facilities in general, I concluded her care had been acceptable. We were fortunate Blanche had been her roommate; she was observant, communicative, and kept me informed. And Parkside had proved to be a satisfactory choice, based on the most important parameter—Mom's positive response to therapy.

I think the food was better than Mom claimed, most of the time. Many of her complaints were probably exaggerated or even unfounded; Mom's emotional nosedive surely colored her perceptions. Though, one of her recurring complaints—long waits for bathroom assistance—seemed warranted. Mom was a clock watcher, and a large, easily readable clock was mounted on the wall directly in front of both beds. Monitoring wait times required minimal effort. While recognizing Mom had moments of confusion, I believe this wasn't one of them. Furthermore, Blanche concurred with Mom's estimates on wait times.

My previous experiences dealing with Mom's health care taught me the importance of being an involved patient advocate. Getting a handle on who does what is crucial to understanding how a skilled nursing facility operates and how to address problems when they arise. And they will. My touch points with the social worker, nurse practitioner, and director of dining services were highly satisfactory. These professionals were competent, keenly aware of patient welfare, and appreciative of honest feedback.

Mom's attitude was disappointing and remained steadfast until her discharge. She frustrated me to the point of distraction. However, she was my mother and I could never have left her defenseless and solely dependent on the whims of fate.

Back Home with the Assisted Living Gang

Mom returned to Courtside on Monday morning, July 26, 2021, uneasy and unsure of her physical capability. It was apparent she could use an injection of reassurance and encouragement, and I was allowed to remain with her for a couple of hours. Mom needed to move around and I prevailed upon her to fire up the Buick. Her self-confidence needed a boost, and driving the rollator in familiar surroundings was an ideal jump-start. We ambled to the dining room, about a hundred feet away. It was perhaps an overly ambitious journey for a first attempt; Mom was drained when we entered the dining room. Even so, it was a pivotal moment. A mental and physical hurdle had been removed. The return itinerary included a rest stop, which made the trip back to her room less taxing.

The ensuing days became less onerous and, once again, Mom bounced back from her most recent tussle with gravity. The bounce was less vigorous than with previous recuperations. She moved slower than ever, had a poor appetite except for sugar-laced desserts, and pushed away opportunities to participate in community activities. All were disconcerting, though my overriding concern was her balance. And for reasons only the cosmos can answer, Mom continued to ignore numerous urgings to follow safety protocols.

Visitation restrictions remained an impediment until November 12, 2021. The light of reason broke through the clouds on this momentous day when the CDC mandated a major policy change. The edict stated facilities could no longer limit the number and length of visits to a resident or require advance appointments. When visitation restrictions were initiated in March 2020, no one imagined a twenty-month nightmare was in store. Screening questions, a temperature check, and masking were still required prior to being granted entry. No big deal. As fate dictated, we benefited from relaxed guidelines at Courtside for less than a week.

Four Months and Seventeen Days

My cell phone rang at 7:08 a.m. on Thursday, November 18, 2021. I wasn't asleep and had been contemplating crawling out of the bed. I leaned up from my pillow and glanced at the cell phone resting on the bedside table. I could see the call wasn't from spam, or Mom. Spontaneously, I tensed up, fearing someone was calling from Courtside. After all, no one else of sound mind would ordinarily be calling at such an ungodly hour. My hunch was correct.

The CNA who called, said that while she was passing Mom's room, she heard a call for help. She opened the door and found Mom lying on the floor, unable to move. Mom wasn't wearing her alert pendant and the rollator wasn't nearby. She had been sprawled out for an undetermined amount of time. Mom later told me she had been on the floor for around twenty minutes. It had been four months and seventeen days since July 1. That's when Mom's orbit was last dislodged as the result of a fall. Mom was taken by paramedics to the Flagler Hospital ER, where MRIs and X-rays did their requisite inspections while Max and I waited.

My emotions roamed the range and were familiar accompaniments to the boxed-in ER cubicle. Max and I had been here before. There was no escape. Anger, worry, exasperation, and pity for Mom were intermingled into one package, though my anger with Mom seemed to be in the driver's seat. I couldn't get beyond her refusal to wear the alert pendant or rely on the rollator. More than likely, her fall was preventable. This extended-play record had multiple cracks and scratches, yet the music still played. I simmered in silence, knowing there was nothing I could say or do to change what had happened—or change Mom's behavior.

We were elated when advised that Mom had no internal injuries or broken bones. However, a severely sprained neck and spine, which were responsible for her fierce pain and immobilization, could keep her down for weeks. The news was appended by a significant unsettling footnote: Mom didn't meet the criteria for admission to the hospital.

I tensed up. We were faced with one whale of a problem because her care needs were clearly outside Courtside's purview. There was another option: Mom qualified for rehab in a skilled nursing facility. Parkside, here we come! Again.

Déjà vu!

Mom's less-than-triumphant return to Parkside was a continuation of where she had left off four months prior, except she was in a different room. She was less than pleased to find herself back in the rehab unit and didn't hesitate to offer her commentaries. Mom called early Friday morning, the day after her admission, in a highly agitated state, with this eruption: "This is the absolute worst place I've ever been in my life … it's terrible, just awful, and I'm telling the truth. I had to wait an hour and a half last night to get some help to go to the bathroom, and *you* need to do something about it." Other than a few twists, the script was much the same as I had heard during her previous admission at Parkside.

I felt as if a shotgun blast had slammed me. I could feel my heart fluttering. The described bathroom wait was hard to believe. Additionally, the nurses station was close to her room, ten or twelve steps away. I was confident the CNAs hadn't ignored Mom for ninety minutes. Mom's demanding tone pushed me to the edge and scraped a raw nerve. Emphatically, I reacted: "Mama, they're doing their best to care for you. I'll be up there later in the morning, but can't come this second." I tried to reason with her … unsuccessfully. Mom ended the conversation by saying, "If you won't help me, I'll call your brother and he'll get things straightened out in a hurry."

True to her word, Mom called Max. A few minutes later, Max called me with the lowdown. Mom told him I had been mean and refused to take charge. For sure I had been firm, but not mean. Mom's conversation with Max was a carbon copy of the one she'd had with me. She insisted he needed to "Get the facility staff straightened out *right now.*" Max and I discussed it and we believed Mom had dreamed the bathroom incident. She had a colorful history of distorted perceptions when she had been under the influence of painkillers.

I visited Mom later in the day and stayed with her for several hours. She had calmed down, and insisted she was ready to return to her assisted living apartment. This in itself suggested she was "wandering in a hayfield." Before leaving, I observed Mom having a problem operating the call button. It occurred to me her inability to locate and press the button would be a deterrent to getting bathroom assistance. I spoke to one of the staff members about it, and she agreed to periodically check on Mom.

A True Dilemma

The timing of Mom's latest woes couldn't have come at a less convenient time. Of course, is *any* time *ever* convenient? Thomas and I had planned to visit his family in Mississippi and were scheduled to leave on Sunday. Two days out. His mother was in the throes of a long-term illness and his sisters had been saddled with her care for a number of months. They needed relief and we had planned to help out during Thanksgiving week. Of equal concern, Thomas had a tendency to get drowsy on road trips. He could use my assistance with the drive—a hypnotic, ten- to eleven-hour slog to Vicksburg.

What a dilemma! Should I stay in St. Augustine? Or should I go to Mississippi? I had two days to make a decision. Thomas made it clear he didn't expect me to accompany him to Mississippi. Max and Lois strongly felt I *should* take the trip. Mom's overall health was stable, and they would keep tabs on her in my absence. I talked to Mom about it, and she encouraged me to go.

On Saturday morning, Mom told me she had been to Jacksonville the evening before to visit with her next-door neighbor. When asked how she got there, she responded, "I think someone from the church took me." The same account was shared with Max, with no variations in the story. I asked several leading questions, hoping she would realize the trip hadn't occurred. This didn't work and I dropped it.

I recalled Mom had experienced the same delusion earlier in the year, and I supposed this second neighborly visit was a follow-up. Both visits were impossibilities. The neighbor Mom visited had passed away in 2014, and time travel wasn't available in our zip code. Something was "a bit" off and Mom was tested for a UTI. The outcome was according to plan. Once again, she was prescribed her favorite appetizer—an antibiotic. Her refusal to drink sufficient liquids was the primary culprit paving the way for frequent UTIs, but she didn't care. I was at the point where I didn't either.

Early Sunday morning, November 21, Thomas, Bella, and I headed west to Vicksburg. We found Thomas' mother painfully thin, fragile, and with deep-set circles under her eyes. Migraine headaches and lethargy kept her confined to the bed most of the time we were there. Her appetite was similar to my mother's—seriously lacking—and she was living on an assortment of pills. Bathroom assistance during the day and night was required due to her high risk for falling. She seldom ventured outside the house, was no longer able to drive, and was dependent on family members to provide support with most daily tasks.

The parallels with my mom were glaring. It was heartbreaking for Thomas and me to see his 88-year-old, beautiful mother significantly weakened. She was spiritless. Thanksgiving Day was a bright exception. She mustered the strength to get "prettied up," dressed, and attend a family gathering. For a few short hours she flashed snippets of her former self.

Max maintained a close watch on Mom during my absence, and we communicated daily. He and Lois took her out of the facility on Thanksgiving Day—Mom's favorite holiday—for family festivities at the home of Lois' daughter and son-in-law. Mom handled the day with grace, but felt poorly. It had wiped her out.

Mom detested physical therapy sessions each day and wasn't hesitant to say so. She was beginning to show some hard-won results when a secondary infection—ESBL—hit her. I hadn't heard of it. No need to get into the details, but this highly contagious assailant landed her in an isolation room the day after Thanksgiving. One of the positive side effects, in Mom's estimation, was a pause in physical therapy sessions; she was too sick to participate. Parkside allowed Max to continue daily visits provided he suited up in a protective facility-provided "costume" appropriate for the occasion.

We returned from Mississippi on Sunday, November 28, arriving late evening in a road-weary and depleted state. I visited Mom the following morning and was disheartened to see she had regressed. Her less than enthusiastic, subdued greeting was troubling. She was glad to see me, but resembled a forlorn bloodhound and was leashed to oxygen tubes. Mom was gaunt, had sunken eyes, and was confused. I wondered if she would return to her beloved assisted living apartment, which was a stone's throw across the courtyard.

Mom always had stories to tell and was eager to recount two preposterous events she was certain had occurred while I was in Mississippi. Her latest delusions were first-run, not previously described incidents. Mom imagined taking a trip on the Atlantic Coast Line Railroad (now CSX), up to South Carolina, even though she had no close friends there and had no idea how she had gotten to or from the train station in Jacksonville. She gushed about having had a "marvelous" time on the trip. I didn't challenge her … the imagined excursion brought her joy.

Mom's second narrative was "off the rails" and blew the rails completely off the track. Unlike her tranquil South Carolina tour, her tale assumed horrific proportions. She claimed that an "obese man" who introduced himself as Bill, had entered her room one night and raped her. She maintained he returned the next day to pay her a visit and promised to come back. I did my best to reassure her: "Mama, this isn't real and didn't happen. You dreamed or imagined it. You have to believe me. This … did … not … happen." She seemed to doubt me, though eventually quieted down. I began to wonder why Mom's subconscious mind would have conjured up such an unspeakable event. Was she reliving a long-repressed or forgotten incident from childhood? The thought was disturbing. Nothing had been hinted by her or anyone else in the family. I let it go.

Although I attempted to feed her baby-spoonful doses of food each day, Mom had no appetite. The scowl on her face was sufficient. She wanted none of it, no matter what was on the plate, except for a bite or two of dessert. I imagined being fed by her when I was a baby, spilling food, creating a mess on myself and the floor. Now the roles were reversed—she was *our* "baby." Max and I had become her parents, and we were in our 70s. I wondered how much time might be remaining in Mom's reservoir.

Over the course of a few days, Mom's voice diminished to a whisper and her breaths were short. Her delusions expanded and she asked if her parents, who had died sixty years prior, were angry at her. I assured her they weren't and that their love for her was forever. In childlike fashion, Mom smiled and murmured, "Oh, I'm so glad to hear this." In a heartbeat, she regained lucidity and apologized for being a burden on the family. I choked back tears while promising she wasn't. To anyone else, there was no denying her care was taxing and a continual worry.

Convinced additional physical therapy and medications couldn't effectuate a miraculous comeback, I prayed for Mom to pass away. The pharmaceuticals continually thrown into her primarily served to extend her misery, delaying the inevitable. For what? For Mom to tell Max and me how much she loved us and how sorry she was to be a burden on the family? There was an overriding, hard-to-come-to-terms-with truth: Medical interventions were increasingly pointless. At times, I felt guilty for being honest with myself.

Chapter 10

The Final Lifeline?

Mom's deterioration seemed to be accelerating, and Medicare rules were clear. Her lack of progress dictated an end to rehab benefits in two days. This looming certainty was downright frightening on multiple fronts. If Mom remained in the facility as a resident after Medicare rehab benefits were cut off, the cost would be exorbitant. She would be paying a fortune to be miserable. This scenario seemed eerily familiar: a flashback to December 2018 when assisted living had been Mom's salvation. This time around, it was apparent Courtside would no longer be an option.

Max and I had spent untold hours at Mom's side, watching her swirl aimlessly in a steady downward spiral. It seemed cruel, even inhumane, yet was innately human. The care Mom received in the Parkside rehab unit had been adequate and I had few complaints. Nonetheless, it wasn't where we wanted Mom to spend her last days. Finding a personal, warmth-filled environment was our goal. Max and I met with the social worker at the facility to discuss post-discharge options. There wasn't an "Easy Street" to be found. Mom wasn't well enough to return to assisted living. Now what? There was one possible option I wished to explore—hospice. Hospice is covered by Medicare and is provided to individuals with an estimated life expectancy of less than six months. Mom? Considerably less than this, perhaps a few weeks. I held hopes she might qualify for admission into a hospice facility.

A hospice nurse assessed Mom the following day and submitted paperwork for her enrollment into the hospice program. Approval came within a day. Mom didn't qualify for admission into a hospice facility— her needs were less urgent. Instead, she qualified for a moderate degree of services rendered in a home setting. No interpretation was needed. In order for this to work, Mom would need to move in with Thomas and me. It would be our last gift to Mom. We discussed it and agreed it was the *right* thing to do. I expected Mom's stay would be of short duration, manageable with hospice assistance. I had no clue of the roller coaster ride awaiting.

The time came. I had to inform Mom her rehab benefits were ending … and she couldn't return to her Courtside assisted living hideaway. Ever tell a young girl her beloved dollhouse had been given away? It was like that. Call me "the Grinch who stole Christmas." Mom was unable to grasp why she wouldn't be returning to her cherished assisted living domain. This was mitigated when I assured her she would be returning to live with Thomas and me.

The failure of Mom to recognize the precariousness of her condition was puzzling. It seemed apparent her misfiring spark plugs impaired her ability to objectively assess much of anything. We debated whether or not to tell Mom she had been enrolled in the hospice program. After much discussion, we decided to not tell her out of concern the news might put her in a spin. It was the right decision at the time. Later, that changed.

Mom's "recuperation" in rehab had spanned twenty-three mind-blowing days, from November 18 to December 11, 2021. Since a return to Courtside wasn't a possibility, Max and I were under the gun to empty her efficiency apartment to avoid accumulating charges. Clearing it out seemed surreal. Three years had zoomed by since we moved Mom in.

We spent the better part of two days cleaning out Mom's compact yet packed kingdom. Her cedar chest, brimming with treasures from another era, required deep probing. The contents were well organized and neatly placed, a testament to Mom's preciseness. I uncovered an abundance of memorabilia, some dating to my childhood. A slew of vintage black-and-white photographs, some a hundred years old, filled a cream-colored shirt-size box. It wasn't an ordinary box, but a *real* one, made of polished cardboard with firm, non-collapsible edges, fitting as originally designed. The box came from an area department store and likely had contained a Christmas or birthday gift. It possibly dated from the 1940s or 1950s when such boxes were commonplace. I shuffled through the jumble and stumbled across several black-and-white photographs of Mom and Dad taken when they were young and fresh-faced. The photos drew me in. I couldn't stop staring. Brief moments in time were frozen, showcasing the spring of their lives for posterity. The photos were reminders that youth is fleeting and the aging process bypasses no one.

Mom and Dad gave me a brown teddy bear when I was 4 or 5 years old. I found it hibernating in the bottom of the chest. Seeing it again, after being separated for perhaps sixty-plus years, was analogous to being reunited with a forgotten friend. The most poignant find was a Bulova watch Dad had given Mom in 1940, when she graduated from the Erlanger Hospital nursing school in Chattanooga. I remembered the watch well. Mom wore it for forty years, until it could no longer be serviced. She had written a note detailing the watch's history and her sentiments. It was attached to the watch. In some respects, cleaning out Mom's assisted living space was more emotional than cleaning out her house had been. It signaled finality.

The watch Dad (Johnny) gave Mom in 1940, her nursing school graduation photo, and her note about the watch.

Mom Comes Home

Before I could bring Mom home, a number of essentials had to be obtained: a hospital bed, oxygen generator, oxygen tubing, wheelchair with a reclining back, and a host of medical supplies. I felt overwhelmed, but Community Hospice of Northeast Florida filled in the blanks, providing *everything* needed, including delivery and setup. We were fortunate our house had two primary bedrooms. There was ample room for Mom's medical equipment and hospital bed to be placed next to my bed. My long-suffering partner, Thomas, spent two days prior to Mom's arrival getting the house ready. All of her clothes, collectibles, and memorabilia were kept, thanks to his superior organizational skills. He rearranged closets and moved furniture, creating spaces to accommodate Mom's accumulation. When space ran out, her jumble of clutter filled up the guest bedroom, transforming it into a storage facility.

I drove Mom home from Parkside on Saturday afternoon, December 11, 2021, opting to forego the windowless institutional transport. The thought crossed my mind that the ten-minute transit could be Mom's last. It was a stunning day with temps punching the eighty-degree mark, ideal for a scenic ride in the car, even if short. Mom was painfully quiet as we motored down Avenida Menendez, which is adjacent to the seawall, and crossed the Bridge of Lions spanning the greenish water of the Matanzas River. Our last jog took us down the winding neighborhood streets that led to our house. Mom's silence during the ride was a major departure from her usually chatty self. Though frail, uncomfortable, and dejected, she seemed to have absorbed the beauty surrounding us. I couldn't help but note that three years had passed since Mom had moved into her assisted living apartment. That was a happier day.

Moving Mom into our home was the easy part. Adjusting to a new living situation was anything but. Mom needed considerable support and could walk no farther than a few steps before getting winded. She was wheelchair bound and on oxygen when needed. She couldn't get in or out of bed by herself and required assistance with toileting, bathing, and dressing. Mom could barely feed herself and showed no inclination to eat anything. Her propensity to choke and spill food exacerbated an unfortunate set of circumstances, turning mealtime into a potentially hazardous affair.

The entire dynamic of managing Mom's care required an unrelenting 24/7 commitment. I understood her care would be a major challenge, though expected a short-term assignment—perhaps two or three weeks. Surely, I could handle it; I had to.

To alleviate the inescapable nature of the job, I hired sitters to stay with Mom for three to four hours, three days a week. Max or Lois filled in during times when sitters weren't available. This prized respite paved the way for me to run errands, go to the gym, and clear my head in the process. And it needed a lot of decluttering. Additionally, Community

Hospice of Northeast Florida provided an individual to give Mom a shower twice a week and an RN to check on Mom once a week. These visits were relatively short, typically a half hour, and provided much-needed and appreciated services I wasn't equipped to handle.

Mom Defies the Odds

Mom's overall condition began to slightly improve after her first week with us. Her appetite ticked up, while she consumed woefully slim quantities. The hospice workers were compassionate and supportive. They explained a lack of appetite was part of the end-of-life process and advised me to refrain from pushing Mom to eat. I complied.

Even with help, my days were demanding. The nights were worse. Three hours of sleep, sometimes less, were frequently my allotment. Mom coughed sporadically during most nights, and she *always* needed to visit the bathroom once or twice, usually around 1:00 a.m. and 4:00 a.m. Her sleep-shattering plea, "Seth, I need to go to the bathroom *now*," catapulted me from the bed. With a firefighter's urgency, I responded to Mom's appeal, hoping to reach the toilet before she sprang a leak.

Specific protocols had to be followed:

Position the wheelchair next to Mom's bed and lock the brakes.

Help Mom edge to the side of the bed.

Hold her under both arms, assisting her to stand and align with the wheelchair.

Ease her down to the chair seat, unlock the brakes, and push her into the bathroom.

Lock the brakes. Help Mom stand long enough to get her pajama pants and incontinence underwear slid down while keeping her stabilized.

Lower Mom to the toilet seat and let her do the rest.

Mom's occasional need for oxygen necessitated additional scrambling. With or without oxygen, the roundtrip bathroom jaunt became a well-practiced ten-to-twelve-minute sprint. This tour, though relatively short, left me wide awake. There were times when I couldn't go back to sleep for an hour.

Preserving Mom's dignity was a constant goal, whether in the bathroom or when providing assistance to dress and undress her. She was acutely aware of the sometimes uncomfortable dynamic and frequently expressed regret my involvement was necessary. I became adept at tending to her needs in an uncompromising fashion; however, I would be committing literary malfeasance to not disclose an incident involving her bra. All decorum was lost when a shocking "malfunction" was caused by my subpar understanding of bra application. Mom's bras had rear fasteners—with the exception of one rogue outlier, a front-fastener model. The rear-fastener design allowed Mom to slip on the undergarment and get everything tucked in with minimal effort. Once this step had been accomplished, she gave me the all-clear signal to secure the fasteners in the back. I hadn't encountered failure until …

One morning, I hastily yanked the aforementioned unorthodox model from Mom's underwear stash. Unsuspecting and clueless, I handed the oddly constructed, "front-loading" device to Mom, who was seated in the wheelchair. I stood behind her, fully expecting a problem-free application. Ordinarily, it would have been a simple procedure, but her numb hands were no match for the tiny front-mounted fasteners. I was still standing behind her, and she handed the object back to me. It was necessary for me to figure out an efficient application process. *Obviously*, the contraption needed to be buckled up in advance, so I fastened it. This surely would place Mom one step ahead of the game. It seemed simple enough.

I discovered this thingamajig wasn't an ordinary holster, and there was no sheet of instructions to validate my preassembly solution. After I handed the fastened-up apparatus back to Mom, she attempted to fashion it, though probably not as the manufacturer intended. Somehow, the side straps got hopelessly crossed on top of her head. I had to scoot in front of her in an attempt to untangle the strangulating disarray when it happened. The hooks came loose and the internal pressure was too great; Mom's "appointments" burst out of their corral! Thank God they didn't hit me. I jumped back and screamed, "Oh Lord," while running back to the bra vault to retrieve a simpler configuration. Embarrassment aside, I laughed so hard that I cried. Mom was amused as well. Consider this word of warning: Stay away from front loaders, except when considering a washing machine.

Maintaining Mom's dignity while bathing wasn't possible. This invaluable support was provided by female hospice aides. However, one activity posed an inescapable challenge—cleanup after toileting; it was necessary for me to service Mom's back end. She and I both abhorred it. Unavoidably, duty called and dignity got flushed down the toilet with everything else. We both got over it; we had to. In any event, taking care of Mom's personal janitorial requirements wasn't a gleeful experience. Mom wasn't completely helpless; she was able to clean her front parts.

"Experience is the best teacher" and "Necessity is the mother of invention." I remembered these two proverbs for reasons unclear to me. These sage axioms became personally noteworthy while I grappled with the challenges of getting Mom sufficiently clean following a bowel movement. Despite using copious amounts of toilet paper and wipes, there was always a "little something" left behind hiding in a crevice. There had to be a better way.

When the next opportunity came along, I fetched a pitcher of water and poured it over Mom's problem zone while she was bent forward on the toilet. I deduced it would be effective and efficient. It wasn't. The gush of water from the cumbersome vessel splashed everything in sight while missing the intended target. After discussing the matter with Thomas, he suggested a solution might be found in the dollar store. And based on his prior successes at this cornucopia of clutter, some useful, I trusted him. To my delight, he netted two plastic squirt containers with pointed tips. They're commonly seen at hot dog stands for community use and are usually filled with ketchup and mustard. An assortment of hand-passed germs is typically included as an invisible bonus. With superior sanitation in mind, Thomas gifted me with a package of plastic gloves to complement the squirters.

I filled the containers with water, located the bull's-eye, and squeezed. What a success! Mom was the recipient of a spic-and-span bottom. As hoped, the surrounding environment, including me, remained unbaptized. Thomas' better idea for superior hygiene required minimal toilet paper and qualified for an environmentally green designation. I imagined the manufacturers of those mustard and ketchup squirters never envisioned them being transformed into portable bidets.

My excitement was tempered when an unforeseen complication sent me back to the drawing board. I'm still drawing. Mom discovered the water from the hand-held bidet had a tendency to transport unwanted items into unintended, forbidden places—a neighborhood I wouldn't dare trespass. Given the delicate nature of this discussion and my desire to keep it for general audiences, I'll leave the rest for your interpretation. The better idea for personal sanitation had to be scuttled. However, it's worth noting that I continued to experiment and found the bidet useful for my own needs. In fact, I don't travel without it.

Mom talked in her sleep, mostly mumbling. Occasionally, her mumblings ratcheted up to a cry for help. "Someone please help me. Please, I need help." This was repeated over and over on many nights.

Each time, I woke her up and offered reassurance. It was the best help I could offer. She could never tell me what help she needed. It was unsettling that somewhere, deep in her spirit, she was unexplainably troubled.

After a week of caring for Mom, I had established a rhythm and found ways to make caregiving a bit less complicated, primarily with smart scheduling and sequencing. It was essential for me to get up an hour before Mom awakened each morning. This treasured period was *my time*: time to get dressed, eat breakfast, brush my teeth, pray, and catch up on emails without interruptions. It was surprising how a few tweaks here and there could make a major difference in the day's flow. Even so, I wondered how anyone could provide care for a severely compromised loved one without outside help. And there are many caregivers acting as a "team of one," struggling to provide care while attempting to keep themselves from drowning. Even with help, the daily rigors of the job eventually caught up with me.

"My Hair's an Absolute Mess"

Mom was notorious for issuing this declaration and her most recent pronouncement was irrefutable. Her naturally thick hair *was* well past its zenith. Her needs far exceeded a trim. It had been two months since professional hands had tended to what was now a "true mess." Mom was unrelenting in her ardent disapproval of the "flattened mop" on top of her head and insisted on getting a hair appointment at the palace. I had reservations about taking her, but couldn't refute an intervention was called for. So, on Friday morning, which was Christmas Eve 2021, I packed the portable oxygen tank, Mom's wheelchair, and Mom into the car for the appointment. It was one of Mom's Christmas gifts.

She couldn't hold her head up enough for Glenda, Mom's hair magician, to easily wash, cut, and roll her hair. I volunteered to assist. What a production! The hair dryer was another battle. It was one of those helmet-shaped things from outer space and Mom had to sit under it. Sounds pretty straightforward, right? It wasn't. I held her head up for thirty-five minutes to allow the hot air a chance to cook her hair and not the back of her neck. The human head is heavy; envision the weight of a bowling ball. My duty wasn't over. Unrolling, combing, teasing, and applying finishing touches took Glenda another fifteen minutes, with my assistance. The entire reclamation consumed well over an hour, and Mom's energy reserves were spent. When we returned home, she collapsed into the bed and slept for four hours. You can guess what happened. Her coif didn't sleep as well as Mom. The back of her hair had flattened out—unmistakable bedhead. It was fortuitous she couldn't see it, and I surely didn't advise her.

Christmas Day was subdued, though we observed it. None of us were really into the holiday, yet wanted it to be as normal as possible for Mom. We got a spiral-cut ham and Thomas made his signature cornbread dressing. Max and Lois brought a squash casserole and a green-bean dish. Of course, we had a few gifts for Mom to open. She would be 104 years old in a month, if she lived to see it. Her overall condition had slightly improved and it appeared she might reach that milestone. I was aware that in many instances, terminally ill individuals experienced a rebound before succumbing.

Adjustments

Since Mom was unable to care for herself and couldn't be left unattended, I was on call for anything she might require. This facet of caregiving kept me hopping and mostly confined to the house. Out of incontinence supplies, disinfectant, or toilet paper? Don't fret, this didn't happen. I learned to shop for necessities three weeks or more before they ran out. And with erratic COVID-related shortages, defensive shopping and stockpiling made me a convert to this survivalist tactic.

Thomas and I periodically received impromptu invitations for dinner, which invariably had to be declined. Advance planning was essential in order to secure a sitter. Many times, one wasn't available. Our situation was a replay, with additional complications, of Mom's previous residence with us in late 2018. I was reminded of a familiar quote from the writer Allen Saunders: "Life is what happens to us while we are making other plans."

Mom maintained a determined quest to continue fighting for life in spite of her discomfort and dilapidated physical state. Her spirit was indomitable. She refused to give in or give up, no matter how poor the odds seemed. Mom's lifelong concerns regarding her health were unfailing. Out-of-the-ordinary aches and pains were analyzed—once a nurse, always a nurse. She tended to extrapolate the worst possible cause for any perceived or actual physical irregularity. Mom often repeated a familiar refrain: "I need you to make an appointment with a specialist. We need to get this checked out." To clarify, enrollment in hospice doesn't restrict a patient from obtaining outside medical advice or treatment; however, hospice doesn't pay for such costs. The hospice nurse who visited each week was an exceptional listener and was generally successful in allaying Mom's worries.

Much to our surprise, Mom continued to improve and celebrated her 104th birthday in late January. She was buoyed by cards and notes, and received visits and phone calls from her Jacksonville friends. At this point, Thomas and I had been caring for Mom for six weeks.

With my help, Mom continued to religiously apply anti-wrinkle cream to her face and neck each night. I thought, *For what? This daily ritual can't mitigate the inevitable creases and spots that come from living 104 years.* Or could it? There was no denying Mom had flawless facial skin, and perhaps her diligent skin maintenance was why. I learned to keep smiling and reordered the "magic serum" before it ran out. If nothing else, Mom's self-image was enhanced. This alone made it worthwhile.

When Thomas and I decided to bring Mom home to "spend her last days" with us, we expected she would live a couple of weeks, perhaps three. The thought of her dying in a facility, possibly alone, had troubled both of us. This was a major factor in our decision. Now that we were at the six-week mark, it was apparent our commitment was evolving into a longer-term arrangement. I was bewildered, not knowing what to do if this went on much longer. I was almost 73 and my steam was running out.

At about the same time, the evil COVID winds wreaked havoc yet again, when the Omicron variant set its sights on Mom's caregivers and sitters. No mercy was shown. The hospice aides who gave Mom twice-weekly showers were knocked out of commission and no one else was available. Back to square one. At one point, Mom had gone twelve days without a shower. Imagine that. In the meantime, she was minimally able to take care of necessary "spot cleaning" with some assistance from me. Since Mom's sitters were unavailable, Thomas sat with Mom, allowing me to run errands. Max and Lois also pitched in when asked, even though they lived forty minutes away.

We were elated when one of Thomas' nieces confirmed she was coming to visit in a few weeks. There was a problem. The spare bedroom-turned-storage-facility was uninhabitable. We needed to reclaim the space. Multiple boxes and ten large plastic bins brimming with Mom's many-years-long accumulation of photographs, knickknacks, and ephemera occupied every square inch of usable space. The result was an obstacle course and eyesore. The bedroom fortification of "land mines" would be ideal in a theater of war, but this theater was designed for sleeping, not combat. The closet was another impediment to habitation; it had to be partially cleaned out before we could host a houseguest.

Mom had more clothes than the law should have allowed, and her unwillingness to part with *any* of them thrust us into a real-life family feud. Her dresses, slacks, blouses, sweaters, and coats crammed two of our closets, one of them in the spare bedroom. Some of her outfits were historic and had never been introduced to 21st-century sunlight—too old to keep, in my not-so-humble opinion. Though Mom had parted with a few clothing items when her house was sold, the purge barely scratched the surface.

A thoughtful culling had to take place, beginning with the packed closets. Mom's stance on most things had usually been reasonable. *But.* She had a streak of intractability coursing through her veins when the topic of excess clothing was raised. Mom taught me a valuable lesson: sacred objects weren't necessarily confined to the dominion of the church. We had one option: a painstaking "fire sale." One by one, I extracted outfits begging to be released from years of uninterrupted darkness and placed them in a *going, going, almost gone* pile in the living room. The heap of clothes appeared to be a sacrificial pyre, although a torch party wasn't on the agenda.

Prior to taking the bonanza to a nearby thrift center, it was only fair for Mom to view what I had pulled for repurposing. We perused item after item, one at a time. A debate ensued on some selections and I agreed to keep a few. Mom relinquished a few without discussion. In the end, about a quarter of Mom's clothes was released from bondage, opening up enough space to accommodate the needs of a houseguest.

The boxes and plastic bins were next on my blitz. Mom was none too thrilled at the continuing purge, but renting a storage unit for mostly junk wasn't a consideration. Thomas and I carefully examined an abundance of items in each box, making sure to separate anything of value. Photographs on top of photographs, close to two thousand, slowed my progress. Duplicates and triplicates were summarily discarded. Photos of people who were unfamiliar to Mom or me weren't kept. Some photos were passed on to people who I thought would want them, primarily cousins and children of Mom's deceased friends.

Many hours were spent over the course of several days to accomplish the task. Anything sentimental to Mom, valuable or not, was kept. And much of what she had, fell into the bucket of sentimentality. When the downsizing was complete, there was still enough merchandise to open a gift shop. We housed the remaining hodgepodge of clutter underneath beds, on top of kitchen cabinets (out of sight), and in the attic.

Mom continued to rebound. At the two-month mark she no longer needed oxygen and was doing better feeding herself, with some assistance. Meat had to be cut into bite-sized pieces to lessen the possibility of her choking, which remained a constant hazard. It was necessary for Thomas or me to remain with Mom during all meals even though she consumed meager amounts. This was the tip of the iceberg; she needed considerable help with *everything* else. At about the same time, Mom's strength started to return, allowing her to walk short distances. This was unexpected. Though encouraging, her balance hadn't improved one iota. Mom needed stabilization and didn't take a step unless Thomas or I was at her side. Not even the rollator was trusted.

Appointments for Mom—or me—were tentative. It goes with the landscape when caring for someone trapped in a precarious medical condition. As was the case in late 2018 when Mom lived with us for two months, the word *tentative* became a bold-print entry in my dictionary. One might think anyone receiving hospice benefits wouldn't need to worry much with appointments. After all, if close to the end of life, why bother? In many instances this may well be the case. With Mom, a rewrite of prevailing "protocols for the dying" was in order. Her improving condition dictated the resumption of eye injections, pacemaker checks, care for painful ingrown toenails and, of utmost importance, hairstyling. This last one still makes me smile. Though hospice didn't pay for any of these medical needs, Medicare did—except for the surgical cuts on Mom's hair.

I've always been drawn to philosophers. Socrates, Plato, and Aristotle are among the obvious ancient wise guys. These Greek navel-gazers are inarguably notable. Yet, there's one non-Greek whose contemporary wisdom outshone them all: Roseanne Roseannadanna. What a beacon of brilliance! Even now she speaks to me with her quote: "It's always something. If it's not one thing, it's another." I concluded the best way for me to keep my wits was to accept Roseanne's axiom. For the unacquainted, Roseanne Roseannadanna, played by the late comedian Gilda Radner, gained fame as a *Saturday Night Live* personality in the late-'70s.

There were positives to having Mom with us. Her sharp wit hadn't faltered, and we shared quality time together that couldn't be recaptured when she was gone. She was a wealth of information and her memory remained keen. I was one of many beneficiaries of this living and breathing archive. Mom offered a unique opportunity for me to tap her mind. To maximize the experience, I took copious notes for future reference.

Unexpected Heartbreak

It was early February 2022. We never thought Thomas' mother would pass away prior to my mom. His mother was much younger (88). Although her health had been failing for some time, her death came as a surprise. It had been slightly over two months since we spent Thanksgiving with Thomas' family in Mississippi. I'm grateful to have made the trip with Thomas.

I was now faced with a quandary: Mom couldn't fend for herself and had nowhere else to go. There was insufficient time to get her into Parkside even for a relatively brief stay, not to mention their staff had been decimated by the COVID resurgence. An acquaintance who worked in health care told me *all* the nursing facilities in the area were in a state of disarray for the same reason. Based on my own challenges in finding dependable sitter assistance, this wasn't surprising. What a mess. I had no choice but to remain home.

Being placed in a position where I couldn't fully support Thomas during such an emotionally trying period in his life was deeply troubling. He and his family were generous to a fault in expressing their understanding for my absence. I was less generous with myself. Guilt girdled me. I felt I had abandoned him. He had no choice but to drive to Mississippi without me. We came up with an out-of-the-way work-around to keep him from driving such a long distance alone and potentially falling asleep at the wheel. Thomas drove seven hours to Atlanta where his brother lived, and they drove the remaining distance together, another six hours.

Week Nine Meltdown

My contemplations caught up with me on Monday morning, February 21. The subdued sounds of my cell phone clock alarm were loud enough to awaken me but soft enough to keep Mom sleeping. If there was a positive side to Mom's hearing loss, this might be it. Still, it was an unwelcome six thirty in the morning siren. I wanted to stay in bed, longing to hug my pillow until the dance of sunbeams tapped me on the shoulder.

The alarm *did* signal my chance to greet the morning and enjoy sweet solitude before waking Mom. It was a coveted hour of quiet restoration. This day was different. My hour of "restoration" left me detached, even dejected. The unmistakable pangs of depression had set up shop. Not the jump-off-the-cliff variety, but a nagging cloud of despair. It was unwelcome, familiar. I had a history of transient depression dating back to high school, although it had been many years since an episode to this degree had harassed me. I considered the universe had something dreadful in store … perhaps an asteroid. Doom and gloom are a characteristic of depression.

The day before, I had taken Mom on an outing in the car. Both of us needed to get out of the house. It was a sun-splashed afternoon, splendidly ventilated by a chilly breeze coming off the winter-cooled ocean. With car windows lowered a couple of inches, the heavenly air filtered in while we motored down the iconic A1A strip which hugs Florida's Atlantic shoreline for more than 300 miles. We moseyed south from St. Augustine for thirty miles, to Flagler Beach, and turned around to enjoy the same views while traveling in the opposite direction.

Returning home was blunt confirmation the two-hour respite was over. The brief sojourn amplified my awareness of how pinned down I had been. Selfishly, I immersed in self-pity and dwelled on my perceived entrapment. When the day was over I took my woes to bed, hugging them like a teddy bear. And I stewed. Deeper depression found me the following morning. It took several days to shake the worst of it, yet remnants simmered in the background.

Mom's urinary incontinence and occasional bowel irregularities, which are common among the elderly, kept her in a state of apprehension. Bowel movements were of primary concern, and any deviation from what she considered normal was cause for alarm. She quizzed me after each one. "Seth, is there any blood? Is it well formed?" Regardless of what I saw, my answer didn't deviate: "It's normal. You should be the envy of the neighborhood." And heaven help us if she missed a couple of days without a "delivery." Time for diagnostic tests! (Max and I didn't consent to them.) Advanced age and infirmity were no match for her will to keep marching forward.

The truth was irrefutable. Mom's batteries were running out of juice and not much could be done to recharge them. She seemed to be encountering difficulty coming to terms with her life ending, possibly soon, but remained quiet on the subject. Even though she resided in discomfort and boredom, she sought life extensions. I wondered if I would be any different when it was my turn. Possibly not.

Mom's care consumed an untold amount of time, and there was no such thing as an eight-hour shift. Mom's needs weren't "shift sensitive" and my assistance might be required at any hour. Whether she needed to go to the bathroom, have me pick up the sippy cup she knocked to the floor, find a dropped pencil or tissue, retrieve her coloring book, open and read her mail, dispense medications, prepare her meals, wash her dishes, or change her hearing aid batteries, it seemed to never stop. Because it didn't. Washing and drying her clothes and linens, and handling her financial and insurance affairs added onto a heaping plate. I had been through this before, but the intensity was now ratcheted up and all-encompassing. Reminding myself of Mom's unwavering love for me and being grateful were constants that occasionally got lost in the dust.

Thomas' niece, Merry, who lived in Columbus, Georgia, worked in sales and her territory included Jacksonville and St. Augustine. We were delighted when she arrived for a planned four-day work stint. One might think hosting a visitor while overwhelmed with caregiving wasn't the best idea. The opposite was the case. Merry provided a much-needed diversion and brought joy into the house. She was an undemanding houseguest, and Mom instantly bonded with her. Merry was sweet, pretty, youthful, and made a point to spend time with Mom. We were all brightened by her presence.

Supplementary beams of sunshine lightened our days. A neighbor I called Saint Cindy, who was a registered nurse, frequently brought us baked items and thoughtfully prepared dishes. She frequently took time to visit with Mom, swap nursing stories, and offer encouragement. And she wasn't alone. Our aforementioned Colorado friend, Suzanne, and her partner, Alana, were in Jacksonville Beach to escape winter and drove an hour to bring us dinner from our favorite barbeque spot. These and many other uncelebrated acts of compassion left lasting impressions, amplifying the importance to "pay it forward" when an opportunity presented itself.

The opportunity came unexpectedly in an unbelievable and hard-to-fathom twist of fate. Our much-loved and vivacious neighbor, Saint Cindy, whose life blessed myriads of people through selfless volunteer work, was diagnosed with pancreatic cancer in late spring 2022. She passed away six months later, at the age of 61. Her husband was shattered.

It was our turn to listen, to take a meal, or cry with him. Cindy's death seemed unfair and pointless. Many times, there are no answers, just questions. This was one of them. I was taught faith must be allowed to do its work. Sometimes, that's a tall order.

Gimme a Break

I'm fond of Kit Kat bars. But I needed a longer-lasting break than the crunchy chocolate confections could provide. There was hope. COVID's Omicron surge began to abate in early March, returning health care to a semblance of normalcy. I began to consider respite care for Mom. This type of care is typically provided by skilled nursing and assisted living facilities for short stays, to give caregivers a break from the daily grind. Mom could be admitted as a short-term patient in a skilled nursing facility for a few days or even longer, giving me the opportunity to de-stress and rejuvenate. The average cost for respite care varies widely, depending on the level of care needed. The average quote I was given by several skilled nursing facilities in the St. Augustine area was $300 per night. Assisted living would have been less, but Mom's substantial care needs eliminated the possibility.

I mentioned to Mom's hospice nurse I was considering respite care for Mom. She informed me hospice would cover up to five days in an approved facility once Mom had passed the three-month mark as a hospice patient. That box was checked. If additional days were needed, they could be purchased at prevailing rates—$300 per day. There was a fly in the ointment. Respite care is based on bed availability, and confirmation wouldn't be available until one week in advance of requested dates. If space wasn't available in a preferred facility, I was told alternate locations *might* be available. *Might* gave me heartburn. In my book, *might not* deserves equal consideration.

Thomas and I had planned to travel to Mississippi in early July 2022 to attend his nephew's wedding. It would be a logical time to tap the respite benefit, *if available*. Forget the qualifier. I took off my pessimist hat and assumed the trip *would* take place. The *possibility* of going gave me a lift.

The respite benefit was generally offered in three local nursing facilities, the most likely being Forest Meadows. I expected Mom wouldn't welcome being placed in *any* facility, and Forest Meadows would be an even harder sell. This time around, her situation was drastically different than in 2018 when her objectivity was clouded by unrelenting foes:

delusions, hallucinations, extreme pain, and exhausting rehabilitation sessions. Mom wouldn't have to contend with any of those bedevilments, and I felt she could handle it for a week. With trepidation, I broached the subject. Mom wasn't overjoyed, yet there was cause for optimism. She reacted with less negativity than anticipated and encouraged me to take the trip.

Unexpected Ray of Sunshine

As I became immersed with the ins and outs of concerted caregiving, I discovered a potential source of relief—adult daycare. This change in latitude might boost Mom's spirits while opening up some free time for me. I should have investigated daycare sooner, but it didn't register. Perhaps I had wandered so deep into the woods I lost the trail. After surfing the web and exploring various options, I contacted the local Council on Aging. They maintained an on-site adult daycare facility less than ten minutes away. I took Mom over to be assessed and for her to preview the facility. After we completed paperwork, provided proof of COVID vaccines, subjected Mom to a chest X-ray to check for tuberculosis, and obtained an authorization from her physician, the program accepted Mom.

The center was open Monday through Friday, from 9:00 a.m. to 4:00 p.m. We selected Tuesdays and Thursdays. Seven hours per day would be too much for Mom, so I scheduled her for five: 10:30 a.m. to 3:30 p.m. The cost was $15 an hour and included lunch. For some attendees, the cost was lower or even free of charge, based on meeting low-income guidelines.

Mom's first day at "Camp Sunshine" was Tuesday, March 22, 2022. Oddly, I was a bit uneasy when dropping her off, desperately hoping she would enjoy it. And she did! Predictably, her assessment of the lunch was less than flattering. Smothered chicken sounded great to me, but not to Mom. Even the camouflaging gravy disguising the chicken couldn't conquer it. There's a scientific reason that explains why older adults find many foods tasteless—diminishing taste buds. Take heart. It happens to all of us as we age. Here's a reference on the topic: *https://www.usatoday. com/story/life/2016/03/06/smell-taste-loss-aging/81105980/*.

There were seven attendees at the "day camp," plus an abundance of volunteers and workers. Mom was well-cared-for while there. She participated in a designed-for-seniors, chair-based exercise program, played a word game with her campmates, and took a nap in one of the easy chairs. It had been a worthwhile day for Mom, and I was overjoyed. Five hours of freedom for me was a godsend!

Even though Mom's care requirements remained taxing, I was managing her situation better, thanks to outside help and unflappable support from Thomas. This was reflected by my improving attitude and subsiding depression.

Irrespective of Mom's overwhelming challenges causing her to reside in a shell of discomfort and physical compromise, there were bright spots. Occasional visitors always lifted her spirits. She especially anticipated visits from Max, Lois, and friends from her church in Jacksonville. Mom no longer had the dexterity to paint, yet she found joy bringing vitality to lifeless coloring book pictures with artist-quality colored pencils. Mom's artistic eye was keen, evidenced by her spot-on sense of color and attention to detail. Her ability to stay mostly within the lines with shaking hands validated her fortitude.

In Florida, the billowing cloud formations framed against azure skies are well-known to those of us who are sky watchers. Mom savored sitting outside on the breeze-washed back deck where views across the marsh afforded unobstructed vistas of the ever-changing heavens and spectacular sunsets. Mom was awed by the grandeur of nature's canvas. In her younger years, she had painted scenes with cloud formations prominently captured. The birdlife in the marsh was another of Mom's favorite observations. She and I gazed at great blue herons, egrets, roseate spoonbills, ibis, storks, redwing blackbirds, pelicans, ospreys, and kingfishers. All were frequent visitors supplying a potpourri of unique entertainment while they floated and darted over the marsh grasses and mangroves.

Keeping Mom engaged with something meaningful for at least an hour or two was a daily quest. On many days she didn't want to do anything. Her default was to watch a couple of afternoon TV shows or doze on the couch for hours to give her neck some relief. I accepted it was part of the process. When we crossed the four-month mark of her living with us, I couldn't help but project, wondering how long Mom's ordeal might go on. I wasn't hoping for her death, yet recognized it was the only portal out … for her and for me. I grappled with this.

Mom had mentioned on several occasions that she loved the "home health people" who tended to her needs each week. She knew them by name and looked forward to seeing them. When she began to feel better and had an improved sense of her surroundings, she noticed the

Community Hospice logo on the purple blouse of the hospice RN and asked about it.

I confessed: "Mama, it's true, the care you've received has been provided by hospice."

With a shocked look on her face, she said, "Hospice is for people who are about to die."

I paused to collect my thoughts, and said, "Mama, your perceptions are *not* correct. Hospice care varies from person to person, depending on the need. Initially, we thought you weren't going to live long, but, thankfully, this isn't the case. Fortunately, hospice doesn't kick you out of the program once you're enrolled, and I can't handle your care without them."

She didn't bring it up again.

The Cruelty of It All

It was heartbreaking to watch Mom descend on a slow yet unstoppable glide path leading to her final destination. Surely, she contemplated her trajectory, yet seemed uncomfortable to talk about it. In a rare divulgence several months prior to her death, she matter-of-factly stated, "Nobody really wants to die." She thanked me for the care Thomas and I were providing and acknowledged caregiving wasn't easy. She added, "Never forget, your mother is your best friend. I've always loved you." I kissed her on the cheek and expressed my love and gratitude for all she had done for me. Though I sometimes felt shackled by her care requirements, the thought of losing her was painful.

A busy Tuesday was on tap. Thomas and I had scheduled a lunch engagement in Jacksonville with an 85-year-old friend whom we hadn't seen in months. Since Mom's daycare visits were on Tuesdays and Thursdays, anything I needed or wanted to do was scheduled on those days. My haircuts, doctor appointments, lunches with friends, shopping, and anything else presenting itself were slotted in. The system worked well. Usually.

When I attempted to get Mom out of bed on Tuesday morning, May 24, she was out of sorts, even adamant when she screeched, "I'm not going to that place today." The reference was to daycare. Initially, I thought Mom wanted to stay home for no valid reason. When challenged, she became insistent and started to cry—an uncommon occurrence. Mom told me she felt awful and asked me to get "all of those marbles out of her bed." Marbles? None were on the bed; even so, she continued to insist. I took her to the bathroom and noticed her urine was cloudy and reeking to high heaven.

I called the hospice nurse, who expeditiously dropped off a simple-to-use urine test kit. Mom eventually made the necessary contribution in the provided "collectoratus" I had positioned over the toilet seat. The instruction sheet directed me to insert the bottom third of the official litmus stick into the urine for a few seconds. The procedure was comparable to the science experiments conducted in junior high (middle) school, except for the bodily fluid component. Within seconds, bright pink and purple colors glowed on the stick. Mom had a "red-hot" UTI. God help us! I wanted to run. I took a picture of the lit-up litmus stick and forwarded it to the nurse. She concurred with my diagnosis. The lunch engagement with our friend in Jacksonville was rescheduled.

As previously shared, Mom was no stranger to UTIs and didn't need to be introduced to the array of antibiotics waiting to wipe them out. She was acquainted with them all on a first-name basis. Before the sun had set, she began taking a broad-spectrum antibiotic. It was prescribed for ten days. Within four days, Mom's symptoms were gone. Although tempted to discontinue the pills, we could not relent. A handful of surviving critters were likely present, lurking in the background for a counterattack. And they might easily return with a vengeance if not completely eliminated, rendering Mom sicker than ever. So, ten days meant ten days.

Mom experienced bouts of diarrhea while on the antibiotic regimen. This side effect was always a fear, yet I had hoped she wouldn't have to deal with it. Experience taught me to be prepared, and I was. With hospice approval, I dispensed Imodium, probiotic pills, and yogurt from our household arsenal. And it took all three on a daily basis to control Mom's intestinal response to the antibiotic. She ate the yogurt, which was a major deviation from prior rejections. It was apparent that her distaste for it was overshadowed by the alternative. Mom survived the UTI, the diarrhea, and the yogurt.

"I Need New Glasses"

When Mom initiated the topic of new eyeglasses in June 2022, I cringed. Her need for them was likely, but I suspected her compromised stature and shaking head would predispose any eye test to inaccuracies. In spite of my concerns, I made an appointment with a local optometrist, expecting it might be a futile attempt. With dread, I took Mom to her appointment several days later.

It was a miserably hot afternoon and if I ever needed a handicap parking spot for Mom, this was the time. The parking lot didn't agree and I squeezed into a regular parking place about one hundred fifty feet from the store entrance. My car was tightly sandwiched between two pickup trucks, both big and black. There was insufficient room for me to set up Mom's wheelchair next to her car door, so I defaulted to the open asphalt area behind the car. The sliver of space separating my car from the adjacent truck was barely enough to squeeze Mom through. I maneuvered her sideways in slow shuffles to the wheelchair, and we were off to the races. Disgruntled, I wheeled Mom across the broiling pavement and passed the handicap parking area. The figure of an elderly woman, somewhat slumped over, caught my eye. She was slowly making headway from her car while pulling an oxygen tank on wheels. My perspective changed in an instant.

The eye exam was a challenge. I tried to stabilize Mom's shaking head and hold it up while she gazed into the phoropter. This futuristically designed gadget is covered with dials and looks as if it had been hatched in a distant galaxy. It houses an eye chart among other related operational mechanisms. Anyone who has had an eye exam for the purpose of being fitted for eyeglasses has been introduced to the phoropter. Despite my efforts, Mom's uncontrolled head shake all but eliminated her ability to focus. While flipping eye charts back and forth, the doctor asked, "Is your vision better when looking at number one, or two? One, or two? One, or two? Three, or four? Three, or four? Three, or four?" This drill is well recognized to wearers of prescription eyeglasses. Mom hesitated before answering each time and appeared to be guessing. I thought, *We're getting nowhere with this.* It was evident the optometrist was flustered. When he had done everything possible to zero in on the correct prescription, we were escorted to an associate who helped Mom pick out frames.

The glasses were ready in less than a week. We trudged back to the store and the invisible hand of providence guided us into an open handicap parking space. Positive karma was in our court. Mom tried out her new spectacles and exclaimed, "These are wonderful!" When asked if she could see objects in the distance, she said, "Yes." The same answer was given when asked about her close-up vision. I was overjoyed. My elation turned to disappointment a week later when Mom began wearing the old glasses again. She admitted, "I'm sorry to tell you this, but I can see better with the old ones." We had given it our best shot. The new glasses sat in their bright blue case and were never worn again.

Respite at Last

One week prior to Thomas' and my planned trip to Mississippi, I received confirmation Mom's respite care had been approved at Parkside. What a flash of splendid news! Our trip could move forward and Mom would be in her facility "of choice." She was supportive, but dreaded being placed in *any* skilled nursing facility. To mitigate her fear, I arranged for one of Mom's sitters, a competent and compassionate CNA Mom loved, to spend quality time with her while she was at Parkside. I'll refer to this adored health-care professional as Flo, which is a fitting bow to Florence Nightingale.

Thomas, Bella, and I embarked on a one-week getaway to Vicksburg on July 7, 2022. It wasn't Cozumel or Carmel, but it was a pleasant location with Thomas' entertaining family being the major attraction. The almost eleven-hour drive made our destination seem far away. And from a mental standpoint, it was.

The festive events surrounding Thomas' nephew's wedding kept us in an upbeat frame of mind for the most part. With the recent passing of Thomas' beloved mother, there were somber moments. We stayed in her house, which was replete with wall-to-wall reminders. Surely, she would walk through the kitchen at any moment with a pan of stuffed squash or kibbeh in her hands. Her piano, now silent, stood as a tribute to her talents as a pianist and vocalist. She had shared those commonalities with my mother. Though gone, at least in a physical sense, her presence permeated the house. There wasn't much I could do for Thomas except to offer emotional support. Much of the time he needed to be quiet, and I was quiet with him. Simple gestures resonated. A smile, or a hug, or earnestly listening when Thomas needed to talk were my primary ways of extending sympathy. I thought I understood what Thomas was experiencing. I truly didn't. This came later.

Meanwhile, back at the Parkside compound, Flo and Max kept close tabs on Mom, regularly communicating reports. I maintained daily phone contact with Mom and was pleased she was handling her hiatus in stride. Flo visited with Mom several hours each day and occasionally wheeled her across the courtyard to Courtside where Mom used to live. This afforded Mom her own respite, a chance to visit with former neighbors and eat with them in the familiar dining room. To further break the monotony of the sometimes humdrum institutional fare, Flo occasionally brought lunch or dinner items from local restaurants to Mom in her room at Parkside—cuisine Mom typically liked. And Flo stayed to assist Mom while they ate together.

Mom was occupied and engaged for the majority of the time she spent at Parkside as a respite care patient. The entire experience was seamless and Flo was the primary reason. Her services were well worth the investment. I can't say Mom enjoyed her Parkside detour; however, she tolerated it. I considered it a win.

Humpty Dumpty

Since childhood, I wondered who Humpty Dumpty was. He had to be a klutz. His implied balance deficiencies were serious enough to cause a disastrous fall, one most children have heard about. The poor guy's miscues netted irreparably shattered bones and possibly a lifetime in physical therapy. My assessment of Humpty had always been smug when considering my own moments of klutziness. I should have been less judgmental.

Palm trees are ubiquitous in Florida, our yard included. Graceful, feathery fronds are easily rustled by the slightest breeze, giving them an idyllic and inviting presence to landscapes. They're an iconic symbol of Florida, though not trouble free as their appearance might suggest. Palms are messy and need periodic maintenance. Taller palms can easily be trimmed from an aerial work platform, most commonly referred to as a cherry picker. Most homeowners don't have such equipment nor are they willing to pay for professional trimming. I'm in good standing with this crowd. Two options remain for those of us inclined to skip professional attention. The first is to leave the tree alone and the dead fronds will remain an eyesore until they eventually drop—hopefully, not on someone's head. The second, if the tree isn't too tall, is to round up a ladder and a saw, and remove the offending fronds.

Our palms were in the not-too-tall category and two dead fronds were overdue for removal. I planned to saw them off. It was a painless surgical procedure I had employed with mastery for years. When Forrest Gump stated, "Stupid is as stupid does," I didn't get it. On an unforgettable early evening in August, I did. Foolishly, I placed our eight-foot ladder next to the tree and easily scaled the steps until my feet rested six feet from the ground. This was the ideal elevation to exercise my proven skills as an unprofessional arborist. I sawed back and forth on the base of the first frond, expecting a fast excision. The tree didn't cooperate. A slight repositioning of my right foot caused the ladder to begin an unstoppable sideways slide. It fell to the ground in an instant with me, a hijacked passenger. Stupidly, I hadn't fastened any sort of security line. Stupidly, I shouldn't have been on the ladder to begin with. "Stupid is as stupid does," and I became a 73-year-old poster child.

I slammed into the grass at an angle, feet first. The force of the fall caused my entire body to catapult forward, with my legs pinned between two ladder rungs. A split second later, I felt a hard second jolt when my hands impacted the ground. I remained petrified for a few moments, sprawled out in a stunned and confused state. My wits, at least the few I had to begin with, slowly returned. I managed to disengage from the ladder and got up. Thomas wasn't home when the accident occurred, but pulled into the driveway a few minutes afterwards to find me wandering around the yard in a daze. Even though hurt, I had been lucky beyond belief. I had narrowly missed the concrete driveway and a landscape boulder when I assumed the contorted semblance of a swan dive into the grass.

My legs were bruised, bloodied, and, within a half hour, swelling. My right hand suffered much the same fate. When I came inside the house, limping, Mom was horrified at the sight of my soiled shorts, bruised and scraped-up legs, and swollen hand. An inquisition followed. Not wanting to be "taken to the woodshed," I chose to be less than truthful. I told her I had tripped and fallen into the rosebush next to a landscape boulder. She accepted the explanation.

The shock of the mishap lingered for hours while I dealt with painful throbbing in my legs and right hand. It was an agonizing, restless night. In a continual, unrelenting loop, my mind stubbornly replayed the near catastrophe. I couldn't turn it off. The haunting rehash was harder to deal with than the physical injuries. The unnerving realization that I could have been permanently maimed—or even killed—was omnipresent in my thoughts. A scant few inches had made the difference. The next morning, I visited my physician and he sent me to the X-ray place. No fractures were detected, but my psyche was in need of repair.

I was beat up physically and continued to pound myself emotionally. It was difficult to forgive myself for taking such an unnecessary risk. The implications to Mom and Thomas, had I not fallen where I did, were unthinkable. For days I was obsessed with my close brush with disaster. My emotional equilibrium eventually returned. I was deeply grateful for not becoming a real-life Humpty Dumpty. In the meantime, I continued to lick my wounds as they slowly healed. It was a two-month process. It dawned on me that Mom hadn't been the only family member to ignore safety protocols. Human nature!

Another scare came a couple of weeks after the ladder incident. I woke up one morning with a sore throat and runny nose. Usually no cause for alarm, but the definition of *usually* had changed with the unleash of COVID. With a sense of immediacy, I shifted into "crisis management" and began wearing an M95 mask inside the house. If nothing else, donning the mask gave me a smidgeon of confidence my infectious cooties, no matter what they might be, remained in their compound. With religious fervor, I frequently washed and dried my hands, adopting the rituals of a surgeon. In reality, my emergency measures were probably moot. I had likely been spreading an unidentified pestilence around the house for a day or two prior to being transformed into a masked bandit with clean hands.

By late afternoon, my symptoms were becoming increasingly evident as I experienced lethargy and began to sneeze. It was probably a cold, but a shred of doubt kept nagging me. We had recently obtained COVID test kits, and I opened one. The info sheet stated results were highly accurate if the test was conducted while symptoms were present. No problem; I was in full bloom.

The self-administered test was less straightforward than expected, prompting me to read the directions several times before inserting the cotton-tipped "spear" deep into each nostril. I wanted to get it right the first time, lest I end up in the ER with a punctured something. Six steps with detailed instructions were outlined for collection, handling, and testing. Several steps required timing with no wiggle room for error. And I didn't wiggle. One misstep and the test couldn't be trusted. To ensure accuracy, my dependable cell phone stopwatch was designated the official timekeeper.

My nose fully cooperated; the spigots controlling sinus flow were wide open. I had no difficulty saturating the cotton tip with an ample quantity of germ-laced nose secretion, and meticulously followed the instructions leading to the final step. I nervously waited for the result, valid in *exactly* fifteen minutes and not a second sooner. Each minute passed in slow motion. I kept glancing at the plastic-encased test strip. A single pink line appeared within the first minute, which meant the test strip was analyzing my deposit. I couldn't stop myself from stealing cursory peeks, watching for the appearance of a second pink line—the indicator for COVID. When the stopwatch crossed the twelve-minute mark, my eyes became intently fixed on the test strip. I sensed my heart beating faster as the fifteen-minute mark approached with certainty. I took a deep breath when the finish line was reached. The original pink line stood by itself; there wasn't a second pink line. The test was negative.

I continued to adhere to reasonable sanitation practices, including the mask wearing and handwashing. My intent was to keep pathogens to myself if possible. The next day, my symptoms had intensified and I took a second test. It was negative. The week wore on and I slowly recovered from what was likely a cold. Thomas and Mom dodged it. I attributed their escape to my exceptional hygiene. However, what do I know?

Evacuate!

In late September 2022, a tropical peril named Hurricane Ian introduced itself to Florida. We weren't expecting a major wind event in St. Augustine and felt secure, even though our neighborhood was marsh- and water-rimmed. To our surprise, Ian changed course and evacuation orders were issued. A surge of water from the ocean was forecast to course its way through adjacent tributaries and into our marsh. Thomas and I had always evacuated when asked to do so. We weren't second-guessers.

Close friends in Jacksonville offered refuge in their garage apartment, where we had weathered a previous storm. It would have been the perfect solution except for one steep detail. Access to the apartment required climbing twenty-four steps. The logistics of moving Mom and her equipment *anywhere*, particularly with stairs, created a formidable obstacle. Finding lodging in an inland location was our best bet. The headwinds of fate blew in my face, and No VACANCY signs were the rule of the day. Anything within a tolerable drive for Mom was sold out. We had no viable place to go.

Our home was newer, constructed of concrete, and built on higher ground than most houses in the neighborhood. Our house had never flooded and, based on projections, we didn't expect to encounter a problem. Thomas and I took a deep collective breath and made the uncomfortable decision to remain. The next day the winds began to howl.

We watched the salt-water marsh behind the house gradually disappear. Rising floodwater completely covered the grasses, leaving the taller mangroves to preside as wind-tossed watchmen. Relentless fifty- to sixty-mile-per-hour blasts of wind continued to propel the storm surge of water. We expected the worst at the noon high tide. By eleven, our yard had been transformed into a lake. In disbelief, we watched the water overtake the neighborhood, filling the street in front of our house with three feet of water at the apex of high tide. We were grateful our house escaped flooding. Some didn't. Scattered homes in our picturesque but vulnerable borough succumbed to an intrusion of two feet of muddy, bacteria-laden water. Many remained uninhabitable for months.

Hurricane Ian made our street impassable—except for the fish.

To my knowledge, no one in our area was killed or injured. While our brush with nature's fury was miniscule compared to the coastal areas surrounding Fort Myers, I learned a valuable lesson. As I watched the storm's powerful forces swirling around our house perched on an "ant hill," it was evident anyone needing medical assistance might not get it. The streets were impassible for hours. Even though the fire/rescue station was a scant four blocks from our house, it may as well have been a thousand miles. It was an eerie realization.

Burned Out

Through the years, I had read articles about caregiver burnout and remained nonchalant. I conveniently held on to the false assumption that such a plight wouldn't befall me. I hadn't seriously considered that Mom would ever become my responsibility ... surely she would never get *that* decrepit and, if she did, the flu or some mystery illness would promptly take her out. This is what happened to both of her parents in the 1950s and '60s. Poof, they got sick for a week or two and were gone. Mom obviously hadn't followed the same pattern, shattering my prior notions. She had proved modern medicine can slow down life's final voyage even when buffeted by incessant gales.

Dad's protracted illness had shed some light on caregiving; however, the type of caregiving he required wasn't intense. He could bathe and clothe himself, freely walk around without assistance, take care of his bathroom needs, and could feed himself without making a mess or choking. On most days, Dad could be left alone for a few hours at a time. If he was experiencing a "rough patch," Mom remained home. Frequent confinement was her major caregiving hardship. And that's an intimidating foe even as a singular encumbrance.

After nine months of caring for Mom, I hit a brick wall. It was the same week that Hurricane Ian paid us a visit. The nonstop duties of concentrated caregiving had caught up. I was burned out. Months of insufficient sleep worsened when I was slammed with a sudden onset of insomnia. I couldn't sleep even during the few hours usually allotted. The accumulating sleep deficit triggered episodes of depression and agitation that had been tucked away, waiting to resurface. I was unable to think clearly and lost weight. Since I was slender, the weight loss was noticeable. The experience left me with a key takeaway: healthy eating habits and daily exercise, while hugely beneficial, hadn't prevented my burnout.

Insomnia was a hard-to-conquer enemy. The caldron had been simmering for some time and it was stocked with a brew of noxious ingredients. Topping the list were worry, exhaustion, anger, unidentified subliminal triggers, and sleeping in the same bedroom with Mom. She talked in her sleep, frequently coughed, and shifted in bed throughout the night, which rattled the bed rails. She couldn't help it, but the night-after-night constancy was bringing me down.

The work-around was evident ... change my sleeping location. The comfortable living room couch was called into service and became my nighttime haven. It was close to Mom's bedroom though sufficiently distant to shield me from the irritants keeping me awake. The off-duty bicycle air horn was dusted off and commissioned for use when Mom required bathroom assistance. This was usually around one or two in the morning and again before dawn. I anticipated my sleep patterns would normalize. *That* was a pipe dream. Anxiety and a runaway mind—which seemed uncontrollable—stubbornly kept me awake. I felt trapped.

My internal defenses were deteriorating. After lying down on the couch one night around eleven o'clock, irregular heart rhythms began dancing in my chest. My heart was doing cartwheels. All night, the off-and-on phenomenon jarred my attempts to sleep. The same scenario harassed me for the next several nights. Oddly, the irregular rhythms were absent during the day. I had experienced occasional heart palpitations for most of my adult life, but this was frighteningly intense.

Coincidentally, my annual cardiology appointment was scheduled in a few days. I had been diagnosed with a mitral valve prolapse twenty years prior, and yearly checks were routine. The cardiologist met with me and outfitted me with a heart monitor. The three-inch-long, half-inch wide unobtrusive device was affixed to my upper chest for three weeks. Apprehensively, I awaited the results, due in mid-October when the study would be complete. The cardiologist suggested melatonin might help me sleep, and I began taking it prior to bedtime. While not a sleeping pill or sedative, it seemed to help. Within a week, I was sleeping around four to five hours on most nights. It was minimally enough for me to reestablish a fragile coexistence with my emotions.

As if the cardiac scare wasn't enough, I was clobbered with a series of unnerving optical migraines at about the same time. These episodes, lasting around twenty minutes, caused a temporary partial vision loss sometimes accompanied by bizarre side effects that I won't get into. Curiously, headaches didn't accompany the attacks. Medical freakishness wasn't confined to my vision. I began experiencing a condition called pulsatile tinnitus. I could hear my heart beating as if it was a distant drum: *buh-bum, buh-bum, buh-bum.* And the drummer never rested; it was 24/7.

Thomas had a better idea: Drown out the drummer. He ordered a white noise machine for me to use when I was trying to sleep. It worked! To mitigate the effects during the day, I listened to music, or turned up the TV, or turned up the air conditioner fan speed. These bandages were respectably effective but didn't eliminate the problem. After dealing with the outlandish malady for two months, I decided to consult an ear, nose, and throat doctor. Several tests were conducted including a brain scan. The results were clear: I was declared crazy. This revelation had been reached *by me* before consulting the specialist! Though no physical cause could be pinned, the incessant percussionist in my ear was assumed to have an emotional trigger.

My list of troubles was growing. For the first time in my life, I was having intermittent bouts of high blood pressure. This postscript, when added to my concerning collection of symptoms, all pointed to the same invisible yet identifiable opponent—stress. Internal battle lines were being drawn and I found myself in a foxhole. I grappled with myself and searched for a way out. Again, Thomas was there to pull me up.

I took Mom to her 10:15 a.m. eye appointment on Wednesday, October 12, 2022, expecting it to be the usual one-hour visit. The office was crammed with patients, more than I had seen in the past. When checking Mom in, I was advised there would be a longer than usual wait due to COVID-related staffing shortages. Patiently, Mom sat in her wheelchair, bent over with her head hanging almost to her lap, for what seemed an eternity. She was miserable. I attempted to alleviate her discomfort by rubbing her neck and back. She might have realized a modicum of relief, though not nearly enough. Nearly two hours had elapsed before Mom received the quick vision-saving injection.

Before we checked out, the physician informed me Mom owed $20,000 for prior services dating nine months back. I hadn't received a single bill and wasn't aware she owed a cent. I felt sucker punched, although the physician's intent wasn't to deliver a body blow. The number kept bouncing around in my head: *twenty ... thousand ... dollars.* I didn't say a word to Mom about it. It had been a grueling morning.

The inordinately long rigmarole in the doctor's office drained the life out of Mom and she slept for the remainder of the afternoon. While she slept, I spent close to two hours on the phone with two individuals in the physician's billing office. One by one, we reviewed a jumble of rejected insurance claims. The complicated mess could have been avoided had I known to advise the physician's office in December 2021 of Mom's enrollment in hospice. I wasn't aware it mattered. Due to my negligence, claims were incorrectly filed, incorrectly processed, *and incorrectly paid* for nine months. The brakes were slammed and payment was reversed for all claims filed during this period. The finger pointed to no one but me. Nothing was the fault of hospice or the physician's office.

Most individuals enrolled in hospice don't rebound to the point where health care outside of what hospice provides is needed. Mom was unique. The physician's billing office assured me the mix-up would *eventually* get straightened out and for me to sit tight. A $20,000 debt and *eventually* were disturbing bedfellows.

The following morning, Thursday, offered no breaks and was a continuation of my ineptitude. I overslept by twenty minutes. It was the wrong morning to "miss the bus." My miscue prescribed a rushed morning agenda. I all but yanked Mom out of bed, deposited necessary pills down her throat, and hurriedly slung together her breakfast. A visit from Lillian, the hospice aide, was in the Thursday morning lineup and she arrived on schedule. She patiently waited a few minutes for Mom to finish eating her toast, minus the crust, before administering a needed shower. Mom's hair wasn't ignored. It was the recipient of a shampoo, rinse, blow-dry, and a bit of styling.

After all morning preliminaries had been completed, Mom and I were off to daycare, running fifteen minutes later than usual—we had made up five minutes. A tight schedule was now tighter than ever. My oversleeping stunt jeopardized a Jacksonville urology appointment I had in less than an hour. In keeping with the tone established for the day, the Bridge of Lions drawbridge opened seconds before we approached the crest. After logging an eight-minute delay to allow passage of a pokey sailboat (with no apparent appreciation of my time crunch), I dropped Mom off at the facility and sped off. There was a saving grace—light traffic up to Jacksonville. I walked into the office with seconds remaining on the egg timer.

The urologist advised me that recent blood work indicated a potential problem in my prostate. Since Dad's history of prostate cancer put me in a high-risk group, an MRI was scheduled. Late November was the earliest appointment available. My worries shifted into high gear while I traveled back to St. Augustine. It seemed my lineup of infirmities was overflowing. However, there was a reason to celebrate when I arrived … Mom had enjoyed her daycare adventure.

The following Wednesday, the cardiologist's office called and asked me to come in the next morning. The heart monitor test had revealed an irregularity. No details were given and the appointment was set for eleven o'clock. Fearing the worst, I scaled to the top of the emotional precipice where I seemed to reside much of the time. Thomas was there to talk me down. How he continued to tolerate the "circus" existing in our household was beyond my comprehension. He never complained and was supportive to a fault.

Thomas accompanied me to the cardiology appointment. The doctor informed me I had developed an arrythmia, likely caused or exacerbated by stress. My heart was beating too slow at times and there were times when it briefly raced. The fluttering I had been experiencing was caused by multiple palpitations and racing. The condition required close monitoring. I was advised to keep a chart of my blood pressure each day, to note when my heart raced or fluttered, and to come back in three months. The cardiologist suggested a Fitbit watch would be an easy and accurate way for me to keep tabs on my heart rate and sleep patterns. I'm wearing it.

That night, my comfy couch-turned-bed was converted into a think tank during interludes when contemplation thwarted sleep. Insomnia, a heart arrythmia, optical migraines, pulsatile tinnitus, depression, and the possibility of prostate cancer pervaded my thoughts. I felt caught in an avalanche. Was the universe trying to send me a message? I considered Mom could outlive me. If I drove myself into the ground trying to care for her, there would be many losers.

Chapter 11

I Wave the White Flag

Friday morning, October 21, 2022, I woke up and found myself tied in a knot by the summer-weight blanket. It had wrapped around and through my legs like a python, the result of my twisting and turning during the night. It was still fairly dark outside, thanks to the shorter fall days. I relished fall, even with its escort of abbreviated daylight. A tap on my cell phone illuminated the time: 6:55 a.m. Eight hours earlier when I turned in for the night, my *stomach* was in knots. It no longer was.

I wanted to remain swallowed in the couch, but reluctantly rolled out after escaping the entanglement binding my legs. Unraveling the blanket was symbolic. Deep introspection in the immersive night solitude had paved the way for me to unravel the invisible bindings that had me wrapped tight. I came face-to-face with myself and acknowledged what had been *in* my face for months. Waiting for "things to work out" was a sinking ship. Mom could live many months, possibly years. My health—mental and physical—was under assault. Something had to give. At four in the morning, I yielded to the inevitable and concluded my days as Mom's 24/7 caregiver would have to end. In making this concession I found peace. Breaking the news to Mom would likely end hers. A difficult conversation loomed.

Adrenaline was my friend, fueling me through the early morning doldrums. I called Max and he agreed that my decision to seek an alternative solution for Mom's care was essential. As much as I regretted it, the only viable alternative was for us to place Mom in a facility. When the Parkside office opened, I contacted them to check room availability. We had a long-standing relationship with the facility and it was close by—reasons to scout nowhere else. Surprisingly, there were no rooms available. I was informed, "We can place your mother on a wait-list. It could clear next week or it might be two months from now. This is the best we can do." I placed Mom on the list, expecting it to clear in a few days.

Doubt still hounded me. I prayed off and on throughout the day, seeking the right answer. Was I doing the right thing? I let a second day pass and my decision was unchanged. The time for me to broach the subject with Mom had arrived. Being the bearer of unwelcome news made me cringe. It would be a jolt to Mom. After a late breakfast, I took several deep breaths and sat in a chair next to Mom, who was scrunched down in her wheelchair watching *Let's Make a Deal*. I muted the TV and stumbled for words. I began the conversation by enumerating my health concerns. Her eyes widened a bit as she digested the disclosure. She was aware I had been having a few physical problems, but not of their extent. I had conscientiously made a point to shield her.

With a faltering voice, I explained I was no longer in a position to provide the degree of care she required. I reiterated that if my health failed, I would be unable to assist her. I informed her I had been in contact with Parkside and they had placed her on a wait-list for a room. Dead silence ensued. A few seconds passed and I told her a room could become available in a few days or it might be a month or two. There was no reaction. I waited for Mom to gather her thoughts.

She responded: "I suspected more was going on than you had let on. A mother senses these things. I'll do whatever is needed to get you well."

Mom's comments were from the heart. Yet, I was keenly aware of her all-encompassing fears relating to being placed in a skilled nursing facility.

Two nights later while I was getting Mom settled in bed at ten o'clock, her fears took center stage.

Out of the blue, she cried out, "I don't want to go to that place! I don't want to go to that place! I ... don't ... want ... to ... go!"—all while beating her fists toward the ceiling.

Her eruption was a shock. My unemotional mom had tapped into a fuel tank I didn't realize existed. My response was calm and measured.

I emphasized our decision had been gut-wrenching, and assured her she would be visited daily by Max or me. She settled down.

Mom's emotional upheaval was deeply disturbing and swept me with guilt. But it changed nothing. I remained awake much of that night.

God Works in Mysterious Ways

Thomas and I had made plans to travel to Mississippi on November 22. It had been nine months since his mother's death, and he needed to be with family during Thanksgiving. This was understandable and he had my support. Assuredly, Mom would be settled in her room at Parkside well before the twenty-second. A nail-biter was in store.

It took six weeks for the Parkside wait-list to clear. Her move-in date was set for Monday, November 21. This was cutting it close. I packed up Mom's belongings and drove her to the facility right after lunch on the twenty-first. She was quiet, hardly uttering a word. My heart broke for her. After checking Mom in, I was advised to sign paperwork at the nurses station on the second floor, where Mom's room was located.

We proceeded to the second-floor nurses station to handle the paperwork. It was missing. No one downstairs in administration or on the second floor could locate it. The hospice worker had confirmed beforehand that all forms were awaiting her signature as well as mine. While we waited for the forms to turn up, the hospice worker accompanied Mom and me as we searched for Mom's room. We passed a few sorrowful-looking residents in the hallway, either slumped forward in their wheelchairs or, if alert, appearing glazed over. I was aware the floor housed dementia victims, but had assumed a few sane residents would be living in the same area. I saw no one who appeared to be in full command of their faculties. It was my fault for not asking additional questions before placing Mom on the wait-list.

Mom's room wasn't difficult to locate. We entered the bland space, which was worn and devoid of warmth. The blinds were two-thirds closed, with diffused light filtering through. It was depressing. A few moments later a CNA came in. I inquired about Mom's roommate and was told she was one of the glazed-over residents we had passed in the hall. We were advised the lady was a dementia victim and rarely spoke, but screamed out at times during the night.

Following the social worker, Mom and I returned to the nurses station. I requested a different room for Mom—one with someone not inclined to create a nighttime ruckus. There was one available. A second CNA escorted us around the corner and down a long hall to the other room. It was a duplicate of the first one, perhaps worse. The dresser was missing some hardware and the closet had no doors. The roommate was curled up in the fetal position on top of her bed and uncommunicative. The expression on Mom's face was one of dismay. I was aware nursing homes were seldom ideal, but this scenario was much worse than expected.

The hospice social worker wouldn't leave my side. She could sense my bewilderment, even shock. Paperwork for Mom's admission seemed to have fallen into a proverbial crack. The search continued. I considered the snafu could be a providential sign, one that bought additional time for me to make heads or tails of an incomprehensible scenario. The social worker remained with Mom while I escaped the building for some brain-infusing fresh air. I called Thomas. After hearing my description of the conditions at Parkside, he strongly advised: "Bring your mother back home right now. You cannot leave her there. We'll figure something else out." I called Max and he agreed. Mom's belongings were still in the car and our exit would be uncomplicated.

I apologetically informed the hospice worker and the Parkside admissions director I would be taking Mom home. I couldn't leave her where she was the only sane resident. Though the staff had been exceedingly gracious, I imagined they wanted to shoot me. We had been at the facility an hour and a half.

As I wheeled Mom back to the car, the long-suffering hospice worker suggested that I consider investigating a fairly new assisted living facility. She had been informed it catered to individuals who required a higher level of assistance than what's usually offered. Sunny Breezes, as I'll call it, was ten minutes away. Mom was exasperated, exhausted, and wanted to lie down. As soon as we got home, she reclined on the couch and went to sleep. It was 3:45 p.m.

With a renewed ember of hope, I called the facility administrator at Sunny Breezes and described Mom's care needs in detail. After patiently listening to my thorough dissertation, she thought Mom might qualify. I was elated … until the bubble burst. The familiar term, *wait-list only*, was the pin used to burst it.

I called Max again. While we were conversing, it occurred to him a facility of some sort, ten minutes from his house, had opened about a year or two before. I remembered passing it numerous times, but hadn't paid any attention to it or the sign in front. It resembled an oversized white house, nothing memorable. Max couldn't recall the name and hustled to go check it out. Twenty minutes later, he called to tell me the name of the place was Sunny Breezes. I exclaimed, "Sunny Breezes? That's the name of the place I investigated an hour ago! Exactly where are you?" Max assured me he was at the "oversized white house" near his home and it was an assisted living facility. He was with the administrator, Maria, who informed him they were associated with a second location in the area—the one I had previously researched. She showed Max a compact assisted living apartment. It had been vacated hours before. After he described Mom's care needs, Maria suggested Mom might pass their assessment. This was all I needed to hear.

The kitchen clock's digital readout confirmed the time—4:15. Mom was conked out on the couch, recovering from the punishing safari at Parkside. I didn't want to disturb her peaceful repose, but felt we had a clear directive. The possibility that "nirvana" existed and was situated on the horizon sixteen miles up the road seemed unimaginable. Could it be a mirage? Mirage or not, I shifted into high gear and all but dragged Mom off the couch and into the car. She wasn't thrilled to embark on another safari, though was cooperative. We flew up Highway 1 for the thirty-minute trip to Sunny Breezes, arriving five minutes before the office closed.

We were warmly greeted by Maria, who was waiting inside the all-glass front doors. They opened to a spacious, light-filled lobby. A number of residents were watching a large-screen television. A second group was seated on nearby couches, reading or chatting. All appeared happy and well-cared-for. Maria escorted Max, Mom, and me to the unfurnished apartment Max had previewed. It seemed ideal for Mom. The living area and kitchenette were adequate, and a separate bedroom with ample closet space were steps from the bathroom. Most important, Mom liked it … but would she pass the assessment?

The assessment took perhaps two minutes. Maria's cheerful countenance told the story before she uttered a word. Mom passed! Sunny Breezes seemed tailor-made for Mom and was intimate—only sixteen residents.

The clock hands advanced past the five o'clock position and, after a brief consult, Mom's buy-in was effortlessly obtained. We had stumbled into the "promised land," especially after wandering in the desert for much of the afternoon. Maria stayed late to accept initial payment and print a ton of documents for me to take home, review, and sign. The following day, while going through the signed documents with Maria, I learned she lived an hour away, in North Jacksonville, fifteen minutes from Mom's old neighborhood. Our conversation became absorbing when we discovered Maria had a significant connection to Mom—she attended the same church where Mom was a member. The two hadn't met prior to their association at Sunny Breezes.

A New Chapter for Mom Begins

The trip to Mississippi had to be cancelled. Our disappointment was offset by having found an ideal living environment for Mom at Sunny Breezes. She anticipated moving into her apartment in a few days, after minor repairs and cleaning were completed. We needed a few pieces of furniture. An excellent repository—our house—contained a trove of possibilities. Mom's chest of drawers, TV, knickknacks, wall art, and odds and ends were waiting in the wings. Hospice provided the bed. We were short three items: a bedside table, a TV table, and an easy chair. Good fortune graced us. The previous occupant had abandoned a bedside table and an oblong TV table. It was large enough to accommodate Mom's TV, a few knickknacks, and family pictures. By default, the tables were the property of the facility, and Maria loaned the tables to us. All we needed was an easy chair.

Mom, Thomas, and I were treated to an overflowing Thanksgiving dinner with Max and Lois at their house. At their insistence, we didn't have to lift a finger. They provided every morsel and, to top it off, Mom consumed a plateful of food, more than I had seen her eat in eons. Of course, Thomas and I had more than our share. The day was joyful and relaxed, a welcome counter to the fiasco at Parkside earlier in the week.

We moved Mom into Sunny Breezes the next day. After getting her settled, Thomas and I darted to the closest thrift center—St. Vincent de Paul—in search of a comfortable lounge chair. Right off the bat, we stumbled upon a compact, gently used microfiber recliner, light green in color. It would perfectly fit Mom's child-sized stature. Fifty dollars secured it, and Mom was sitting in it twenty minutes later. She was thrilled. With paintings hung on the walls, furniture thoughtfully arranged, and kitchenette stocked with some of Mom's favorite items, the space was transformed into a cozy home.

Thanksgiving week assumed special significance as I reflected on how Mom's placement at Sunny Breezes had transpired. When living arrangements at Parkside unexpectedly collapsed and I had reached the end of my rope, an unimagined door opened. I've concluded the sequence of events that led us to Sunny Breezes was divinely orchestrated. The same week, I received a diagnosis of low-grade, localized prostate cancer. I didn't disclose it to Mom even though my prognosis was excellent. I had many reasons to be grateful.

Within two days of moving in, Mom had met all residents and was assimilating. She began carving out a new chapter in her life, despite her age and physical distractions. Mom had a propensity to draw people in and this never changed. She was loving yet feisty, and an engaging storyteller. Her winsome personality, wit, and sense of humor were undiminished by the years. Mom had an enviable ability to adapt. I wondered if this competence was innate, or if it had been acquired from a century of tempering as she weathered life's storms. I expect it was both.

The attention and care Mom received at Sunny Breezes exceeded expectations. Home-cooked meals, many from scratch, were a bonus. Mom's overall demeanor brightened and she relished being in her own place. Max or I visited her each day and it was apparent Sunny Breezes was an ideal home for Mom. She enjoyed "house" camaraderie and conversations with her mealtime tablemates. By design, the facility nurtured a relaxed, upbeat vibe for the residents, and I conversed with many of them. Max did as well. He and I shared the same impression: Sunny Breezes was exemplary. Neither of us ever heard a negative comment from anyone who lived or worked there. It was locally owned, exceptionally well-managed, and had a courteous and compassionate group of employees.

Hospice seamlessly dovetailed with the staff at Sunny Breezes. Mom was seen weekly by a hospice nurse and a social worker, though not at the same time. Both treated her with utmost professionalism and sensitivity. They seemed to enjoy Mom as much as she enjoyed them. Mom continued to receive showers two or three times a week. Most were administered by hospice personnel, but the aides at Sunny Breezes pitched in when needed, if a hospice staffing shortage occurred. The "machine" was well-oiled.

Mom's 105th birthday in January 2023 didn't escape without being celebrated. Sunny Breezes threw a party, and eighteen friends from Jacksonville arranged a second get-together several days later at the facility. In addition, Thomas and I hosted a low-key family gathering at our home to mark the occasion. Mom wasn't up for a major extravaganza.

Though beneficial, Mom's hearing aids continued to be a never-ending source of frustration. Her right hearing aid came apart during the weekly ritual of inserting a new battery. I took the apparatus to the hearing aid vendor in Jacksonville, and they sent it to the manufacturer for repair. Two weeks later, the repaired hearing aid was returned in like-new condition. I popped the rejuvenated device into her right ear and its functioning twin into her left. Once again, Mom enjoyed stereo amplification—but not for long. The fun was beginning.

Less than a week later, the hearing aid for her left ear was found on the floor, split open into two equal parts resembling a filleted fish. The two parts were tenuously linked together by a tiny tether of wire no thicker than a hair. I sped to Jacksonville, hoping for a miracle. The hearing aid representative offered no assurances, and forwarded the device to the manufacturer. Before I received an update on the critically ill hearing aid, Mom lost the newly repaired one. She remembered pulling it out of her ear after going to bed the night before and placing it on the side table. I turned chairs upside down, stripped her bed, peeled back the mattress from the bed frame, inspected the floor, moved the side table, and scoped out unlikely hiding places. I couldn't find it. Max repeated the process when he visited the next day. He couldn't find it. I assumed it might be in the bowels of the vacuum cleaner. It wasn't.

Mom wasn't a hearing aid enthusiast. This had been confirmed by her frequent complaints and a notable absence of the aids in her ears. When prodded, she always said they helped, but her actions spoke louder than her lips. Max and I concluded purchasing new hearing aids was pointless. We knew Mom would rarely wear them and their fate would be questionable. On second thought, not questionable at all. They would end up missing in action, lost somewhere in a black hole—an expensive one.

Maria, the facility director, was determined to find the hearing aid and, to my confoundment, she did. When Mom thought she had placed the hearing aid on the bedside table, we think it was positioned on the edge and fell off. Somehow it landed in an obscure bed frame crevice *under* the mattress. Maria showed me where she had found it and the location seemed an impossibility. The bed frame and hearing aid were the same color, and this partially explained how it avoided detection. How it managed to end up lodged *under the mattress in a hole* has remained a head-scratcher.

The recovery of Mom's lost hearing aid was a marvel and represented an early Christmas gift. Great news wasn't limited to her ears. The same day, I received a statement from the retinologist's billing office showing Mom's outstanding balance had dropped from $20,000 to $14,000. I called the office and was advised the resubmitted claims were being worked on by Medicare. I continued to *sit tight*, as had been originally suggested, and became less *uptight* with the process. With many situations in life, time will eventually work its magic if a lack of patience isn't allowed to throw interference. (My dad attempted to teach me this when I was an impatient young man.) Within a couple of months, all bills had been paid. Colossal exhale!

Thomas and I occasionally brought Mom home for a change in scenery, and Bella made it her mission to be in the middle of Mom's return. When I last wheeled Mom into the house, our 15-year-old slumbering canine queen came to life. She bounded off the rug and excitedly ran circles around Mom. We were astounded when Bella attempted to jump into Mom's lap, though unsuccessfully. Bella, much like Mom, battled arthritis and had slowed down. She hadn't dared to jump onto *anyone's* lap in several years, which made her memory of Mom and expression of love unforgettable. Mom was overjoyed at the reception and bent down from her wheelchair to pet Bella. I was taken by the moment and managed to get a cell phone video of the last few seconds of the exchange.

Gathering Storm Clouds

We met our Colorado "snowbird" friends, Suzanne and Alana, for dinner on February 11, 2023, at a popular Italian restaurant. It was a joy not to be subjected to time and sitter constraints surrounding Mom's care. However, another cloud dampened the evening. Alana's 90-year-old mother, who was in declining health, had temporarily moved in with them to recover from a debilitating leg injury. Though Alana's mother was otherwise strong and nowhere near the end of life, she required considerable assistance and constant oversight. Her overall upkeep was demanding, exacting, and time-consuming. The weight from worry and the unrelenting nature of caregiving had obviously taken its toll: Alana's puffy eyes, furrowed forehead, and spiraling depression were unmistakable. Unfortunately, Alana had suffered a mild heart attack in Colorado, from the stress of her mother's care.

Alana's story rang familiar, echoing complex and uncomfortable truths about caregiving. Alana and I shared another commonality: she was blessed with a caring and involved partner who was at her side, step-by-step. As of this writing, Alana's mother has greatly improved, requiring much less care. She will be entering an assisted living community and should thrive there.

Mom's cognition and memory were slipping at an escalating pace, becoming conspicuous in February 2023. She was easily confused and got mixed up when discussing details pertaining to familiar events or places. Astoundingly, she had no recollection of spending Thanksgiving Day at Max and Lois' house. A couple of weeks prior, Mom had mentioned how much she enjoyed the occasion.

The phone was another tip-off. Mom blamed her numb hands for being unable to answer the cell phone when it rang, but something else appeared to be going on. While visiting Mom one morning, I called her cell phone, which was in her lap and easily accessible. I wanted to observe her reaction when it rang. She picked it up and stared. I called a second time and instructed her to pick the phone up and open it. She tried but lacked the agility. The next day, I called Mom while Max was visiting her. His observations were the same as mine had been. She didn't seem to know how to answer it.

Concerning indicators became commonplace in late March. Mom had no desire to participate in bingo games with her friends or apply her artistry to coloring book sketches. I walked into her room on many days, to find her sitting in the green lounger with the TV off, her head drooped and eyes closed. Sometimes she was asleep, but not always. Her smile and usual sparkle had been replaced with a heavyhearted, blank look. Operating the TV remote was no longer within her capability, but she wouldn't ask for assistance. Mom told me: "I don't want to bother anyone." Her statement was truthful; Mom never wanted to be "a problem." Nonetheless, my radar was pinging. Mom was rapidly detaching.

In an attempt to jumpstart Mom's memory, I showed her photographs of her beloved house in Jacksonville. The house, our home, had been her joy for nearly sixty years and had been discussed in recent conversations. Mom viewed the imprints and had no reaction. To my shock, she didn't recognize anything about the house—not even her kitchen or the front yard. At that moment the realization hit me: we were losing Mom. I spoke with several residents who said that she had become withdrawn and had lost her chattiness. Her remaining social outlet was community dining. A Sunny Breezes aide continued to take Mom to the dining room for all meals, where she was surrounded by friends, even though she seldom ate anything of substance.

Max had arranged to take Mom to her home church in North Jacksonville on Sunday, April 23. I chose to duck out for inconsequential and selfish personal reasons. It was a decision I will forever regret. Mom hadn't attended a service in her beloved church home in several years, and being able to go back was an event of major significance. When Max walked into her room on Sunday morning, she had no idea why he was there. Mom had no recollection they were going *anywhere*, even though an aide had her "dolled up" and ready for the occasion.

With Max, Mom departed Sunny Breezes and arrived at the church a few minutes early. She didn't recognize the church or the grounds. Once inside, Mom was greeted by many friends. She remembered most; there were a few she should have but didn't. Afterwards, Max drove Mom to her house and pulled over to the curb to afford a clear view. She didn't recognize it. Max pulled off and slowly drove up and down the street, creeping past Mom's house a second time. The result was the same. Sixty years of memories were gone.

Mom had an affinity for hamburgers, and Max picked up a couple on the way back to Sunny Breezes. He planned on the two of them having an enjoyable lunch there. After they settled in the dining room and Max had given Mom a hamburger, she extracted the patty from the bun and placed the patty inside her paper napkin. She attempted to eat the napkin and the patty, clueless of what she was doing. This turned out to be a prelude for a coming event of unthinkable proportions.

A couple of weeks prior to the church excursion, Mom told me something had happened "in her head." She was aware of being confused and said she had lost her ability to think. Mom was perceptive. At the time, I wrote it off, not considering her awareness of a cognitive change was the harbinger of an ill wind on the brink of being unleashed.

There Are No Words ...

The time and date of 12:21 a.m. on Wednesday, April 26, 2023, is imprinted on my cell phone log and in my memory. I was lightly asleep and quickly awoke when my phone rang. I didn't recognize the phone number, other than the local 904 area code on the readout, and held my breath. I answered it. One of the aides from Sunny Breezes was on the line. She advised me Mom had somehow injured her finger, and paramedics would be taking her to Flagler Hospital in St. Augustine. A deep cut and a lot of blood were described. Mom hadn't fallen and her injury was believed to have occurred while she was *in the bed*. This perplexing scenario seemed to be an appropriate script for an Agatha Christie detective novel.

I waited to go to the hospital until the paramedics were en route, about forty-five minutes later. After waiting in the Flagler ER for perhaps twenty minutes, I received a second call from the aide at Sunny Breezes. She informed me Mom had been taken to Baptist South Hospital in Jacksonville because it was closer than Flagler. I hurriedly drove to Baptist South, arriving forty minutes later, at 2:15 a.m., in a frazzled state. I decided not to call Max and wake him up, thinking Mom's finger would get stitched and she'd be returned to Sunny Breezes.

When I walked into Mom's cubicle at the Baptist South ER, I was astounded to find her disoriented and combative. She was hooked up to an IV and her hand was covered in bandages. It was evident Mom's injury was more significant than I had envisioned. She was highly agitated and insisted the bandages needed to be removed. She ordered, "Seth, get these off of my hand and get me out of here. I don't know why they have me here or why I'm wrapped up. There's nothing wrong with my hand."

Shortly after my arrival, the ER physician walked in with a chart in her hand. After introducing herself, she stated, "I've never seen anything quite like this. Do you have any idea how this happened?" I was clueless, and asked the physician when Mom's finger would be stitched. Gingerly, she informed me the injury was severe and stitching wasn't an option … Mom was missing a portion of her left index finger. It was jaggedly severed at the joint, behind the base of the fingernail, and the bone was exposed. There was a high probability of a serious bone infection developing, and an IV drip was dispensing an antibiotic to combat it. The physician was dumbfounded. She wasn't the only one.

Mom was deeply confused and unaware of her injury. It seemed downright bizarre that she wasn't in pain. Could her fingers be *that* numb? Perhaps her mental condition caused her to be oblivious to pain. Mom's aberrant behavior was confounding. She removed the wrappings from her injured finger a number of times and repeatedly attempted to pull the IV out of her right hand. Impossible not to see, I received an unwanted and unobstructed view of her finger; it was a ghastly sight. Mom was given a mild sedative to quell her anxiousness and unsettled behavior.

The sedative's calmative properties weren't fast enough. Mom shocked me with an incomprehensible display of unbridled delirium— she opened her mouth wide and attempted to insert her right index finger. I grabbed her wrist and asked what she was trying to do. She responded, "It's a piece of bacon and I want it." The realization of what had likely happened to Mom's left index finger was mortifying. I called the nurse, and she placed Mom's hands in restraints. They vaguely resembled catcher's mitts, though were white.

Mom was admitted into the hospital from the ER, around five in the morning. I was preoccupied and didn't note the exact time. The ER physician had suggested hand surgery might be a possibility. I couldn't imagine what could be done other than a possible skin graft to close the wound. I called Max at seven o'clock with news so crazy about Mom that no one in their right mind would have believed it.

A hospital physician came into the room and shared his thoughts. He didn't recommend surgery. By this time, Mom was in a deep sleep even though the sedative she had been given was fairly mild. The physician was compassionate yet honest while suggesting the family should consider having Mom transferred to the on-site hospice facility the next day, depending on the outcome of blood work. I was thunderstruck. Mom's vital signs were excellent; however, I couldn't ignore *something* had caused her to unequivocally go mad and, no matter what it was, was foreboding.

Max arrived after breakfast, and we agreed that allowing the hospital to conduct further testing or attempt heroic measures was pointless. We discussed the possibility of Mom being transferred to the hospice floor. I felt it was premature, yet Max was open to the idea. Feeling woozy from middle-of-the-night pandemonium and a lack of sleep, I went home to deprogram and attempt resting. I chalked up two hours of fitful sleep and lay awake another hour or so in deep thought.

When I returned to the hospital around four o'clock, the wheels were in motion. At the suggestion of the hospital physician, a hospice representative had met with Max earlier in the afternoon. She informed him a hospice bed had become available and would likely be filled by someone else if the family waited to make a decision. Wisely, Max had accepted it. Initially, I was startled and upset when he advised me.

After he explained another bed might not be available for some time to come and nothing further could be done for Mom, I understood he had made the right decision. We had expected this day sixteen months prior, yet the reality that Mom was now at the end of her journey was numbing.

Mom wasn't communicative when she was transferred to the hospice facility on the seventh floor. It was a few minutes past six o'clock in the afternoon. Since she had been enrolled in Community Hospice of Northeast Florida well beforehand, the process was seamless. The hospice professionals at Baptist South were caring, understanding, and competent. Mom was in the best of hands. Max and I were, as well; hospice compassion extended to us.

Since Mom was doing well and would remain sedated, I convinced Max it would be better for us to get sleep at home while we still could. Mom was strong and her vitals were all within normal parameters. Sleepless nights assuredly were on the way. We both left around seven that evening.

10:04 a.m., Thursday, April 27, 2023

Early the following morning, Max returned to the hospital to sit with Mom.

I was getting ready to go relieve him when he called and matter-of-factly stated, "Seth, it's over."

I surmised what he was telling me, but initially thought I had missed something. In a state of disbelief, I asked, "What do you mean?"

And he remarked, "Mom's gone. Do you want to come up here?"

I didn't. It would be an hour before I could get there. And for what?

Max recounted Mom's final moments. He said she was sleeping peacefully when her respiration noticeably quickened and her face flushed. Her breathing slowed and, in a few seconds, stopped. Max's son and daughter-in-law had come to visit. Thankfully, they were together to support each other. A half hour prior to Mom's death, her vitals had been checked and there was nothing to suggest her passing was imminent. Mom surprised us all.

I was briefly overwhelmed with guilt for not being with Mom when she passed away. I cried, stopped, and cried again. I couldn't stop thinking, *How could I have let Mom down when she needed me most? If only I had stayed the night in the hospital. If only ... if only ... if only ....*

Once I regained composure, it was clear such thinking was senseless. I could hear Mom saying: *"Okay, that's enough, let's get beyond this."* And I listened. Peace found me.

Mom had dotted the *i*'s and crossed the *t*'s to make a burdensome period in our lives less so; her final wishes were plainly spelled out and prearranged. Details weren't ignored. Through the years, she had informed me: "You make sure to give Scott (the undertaker) a pair of socks to put on my feet since they get cold." Mom always laughed when making the statement, but she wasn't kidding. When I was going through her prepaid funeral and burial documents, I found the same request scribbled on a piece of paper next to a well-drawn smiley face. Without question, Mom meant the note to be funny—and it was—though not enough to stop a brief flow of tears when I saw it. My tears ended with a smile. I complied with Mom's wishes and made sure "comfortable" white socks were placed on her feet.

We opted to have Mom's visitation and funeral service at her church on Tuesday morning, May 2. She had been a member there since 1947. Max and I were brought up in the same church. It was a brilliant day. Cloudless. Slightly breezy. Cool for early May. The weather seemed to be in a celebratory frame. My mindset was initially somber, not in keeping with the stunning morning. Yet, unexplainably, I felt gently nudged and my frame of mind shifted. Gratitude overwhelmed me as I reflected on Mom and the countless blessings she had scattered while on earth. She had been an extraordinary mother and friend. Her life had been jam-packed with fullness. She was blessed with a brilliant mind and infectious personality, which carried her through her entire life. Her love for Dad, Max, and me was undying even though she no longer had breath.

My heart was beating out of my chest when I walked into the church to see Mom before visitation began. She was beautiful, attired in a silvery-green suit she had picked out for the purpose many years before. There was no hint her final two days of life had been tumultuous. Her hair was impeccable. Atypically, there were no specific mentions in her final wishes relating to this most important of all details. I'm sure she knew *that I knew* she would haunt me for the rest of my days if this unspoken directive hadn't been followed. And it was. A friend from high school who was a fantastic beautician for the living—and the deceased—came out of retirement at my request to perform hair and makeup magic on Mom.

I had picked out a Mother's Day card several weeks prior to Mom's passing, wondering if it might be the last one. I had no idea Mom wouldn't live long enough to see it. The words in the card assumed special meaning and were particularly poignant. The preprinted verse succinctly conveyed my sentiments. The card read: "Mom, so often I hear your thoughts in the things I say, and notice your influence in the things I do. I think of you especially when I'm doing something we'd both enjoy and wish that we could share it. It's at times like these when I realize how very much you're a part of me and how grateful I am that you're my mom." I added, "Mama, you are now celebrating your first Mother's Day in heaven with your mother. What a joyous day it must be. Your son forever, Seth." I placed the card in Mom's casket. It was as much for me as for her.

Mom's funeral service was attended by her many friends, young and old, and was conducted according to her wishes. She would have been gratified. I wrote her eulogy and Max proficiently delivered it. Mom's pastor closed with heartfelt remarks. One of his comments profoundly resonated. He said, "A person's obituary is written while they're still living."

I believe Mom's is inscribed in heaven.

"Final" Thoughts

Through the years, friends and acquaintances had told me: "Seth, you have no idea how lucky you are to have a parent to live as long as your mother." Invariably, I would answer *yes*, yet privately admitted there was a huge qualifier, one I didn't feel free to express except to those closest to me. One friend, who was going through a similar situation with her mother at the time, shared parallel sentiments. It was troublesome for me to confess I believed Mom had lived too long. It was cathartic to commiserate with someone who understood my perspective. I loved my mother deeply and losing her was painful. But what does *losing* truly mean? In a sense, losing Mom had been ongoing for a lengthy period. When she was gone, a replacement word to *losing* came to mind—*absent*. She was absent from us, and pain and debilitation were absent from her.

A friend once told me, "The lucky ones are the ones who wake up dead." In other words, they fell asleep and didn't wake up. There's no question the emotional jolt to surviving family is horrific when someone passes away without forewarning. Several years ago, a friend's vibrant and seemingly healthy mother abruptly died at the "young" age of 82. As shocking and inconceivable as her death was to the entire family, they were spared the health-care morass and exorbitant costs that accompany lingering illness and unnerving care requirements. I've come to this conclusion: the no-fuss-no-muss departure is preferable.

Through Mom, I learned firsthand the extreme importance of having a will and making final wishes known. She had those details nailed.

The Latin words *Tempus Fugit* are often boldly stamped on the face of some clocks. The translation is *time flies*. I didn't grasp the personal significance of the phrase until my later years. Now, as an aging septuagenarian (someone in their 70s), I'm keenly aware of its truth, caught in the draft of fleeting time. When I was a kid, an hour's wait sometimes seemed like a day. Now a day seems like an hour, and the months peel off the calendar with such rapidity that another year has escaped before I can barely note its passage.

I've wondered how it might feel to be a mosquito, with a lifespan of a few short weeks. Assuming mosquitos have a perception of time's passage—which I seriously doubt—does their lifespan of a few weeks "seem" much longer to them than it actually is? Is time's passage relative? If so, does it accelerate as we grow older? It seems to me that it does. "The older I get, the faster time flies" is a frequently repeated lyric. Is our sense that time accelerates as we grow older the result of genetic programming? It's an off-the-wall concept for "out there somewhere" individuals like me who occasionally escape to unconventional philosophical pastures.

I was taught the length of our lives is predetermined by God and we can't change it. I can't help but think the number of people who truly believe this is overestimated, based on our appetite for "achieving" longevity. Why do we fill our throats with untold prescription medications, herbals, probiotics, prebiotics, and vitamins, and scrutinize labels, flock to gyms, have frequent doctors' appointments, consent to myriads of tests, and eat organic foods? It's ingrained in our society. And I'm a guilty party, being a subscriber to some of these supposedly life-lengthening pathways. There must be something to it, given how life expectancy has increased with the advent of modern medicine, superior nutrition, and healthy living.

Certainly, death *is* an appointment, yet one with a date that seems to have changed with disease management advances and cures. Remarkable! Like most things in life, there's a flip side. What are the costs—emotional, physical, and financial—of living "too long"? Why do we wrestle with declining medical intercessions in instances when life extension primarily serves to extend misery? Coming to terms with the inevitable is difficult for most of us, even with the belief that a better existence awaits in heaven. A pastor from my childhood once made the following statement, which I never forgot: "Heaven's my home, but I'm not homesick."

We are living in an era when the majority of health-care costs are expended in the last few years of life. This corresponds to the time when quality of life is usually the worst. The "golden years," as they're frequently called, might require a "golden nest egg" to finance the inevitable "rainy day" which usually centers on health-care costs. Today this type of rainy day can equate to a storm. And most Americans don't have umbrellas large enough to weather it. What a quandary!

When I was appreciably younger, I didn't think much about getting old. Surely, I would remain youthful and vigorous. Getting old only happened to someone else. This didn't work out as envisioned. One morning I woke up, took a serious appraisal in the mirror, and realized I had reached a scary destination without buying a ticket.

I'm now pondering my own expiration date, hoping for quality overtime.

REFERENCES AND RESOURCES

The internet references and resources listed in this publication were current at the time of printing, and assisted me as I navigated an unfamiliar maze. I cannot endorse or guarantee the efficacy of any particular reference since information frequently changes without notice.

Home Health Care (Medicare)
https://www.medicare.gov/Pubs/pdf/10969-medicare-and-home-health-care.pdf

Skilled Nursing Care (Medicare)
https://www.medicare.gov/publications/10153-medicare-coverage-of-skilled-nursing-facility-care.pdf

Medicaid Info (American Council on Aging)
https://www.medicaidplanningassistance.org

Taste Buds (*USA Today*)
https://www.usatoday.com/story/life/2016/03/06/smell-taste-loss-aging/81105980/

Long-Term Care Defined (National Institute on Aging)
https://www.nia.nih.gov/health/what-long-term-care

Fall Prevention (CDC)
https://www.cdc.gov/falls/index.html

Subsidized Housing for Seniors
https://www.hud.gov/topics/information_for_senior_citizens

Independent Living
https://www.forbes.com/health/senior-living/independent-living/

Aging in Place
https://www.nia.nih.gov/health/aging-place-growing-older-home

https://www.ruralhealthinfo.org/toolkits/aging/1/overview

Counseling for Caregivers

https://www.medicare.gov/Pubs/pdf/10184-Medicare-and-Your-Mental-Health-Benefits.pdf

https://www.aarp.org/caregiving/life-balance/

https://www.aarp.org/caregiving/local/info-2017/lgbt-resources.html

Continuing Care Retirement Communities

https://www.seniorliving.org/continuing-care-retirement-communities/#cost

https://health.usnews.com/senior-care/caregiving/articles/continuing-care-retirement-communities

Personality Changes

https://www.theatlantic.com/family/archive/2023/07/old-age-personality-brain-changes-psychology/674668/

https://memory.ucsf.edu/caregiving-support/behavior-personality-changes

About the Author

Seth Vicarson is a Florida native whose passions led to occupations in agriculture, aviation, and health insurance education. He is an environmentalist and a proponent for protecting the state's agricultural heritage and challenged wetlands.

He has traveled extensively and relishes opportunities to savor cultures and contemplate philosophies different from his. He considers diversity a multifaceted gift to be embraced, and a portal for personal growth and understanding.

Seth gained invaluable experience when he served as a senior educator for a major health insurer. This platform later doubled as a personal springboard when he became his mother's caregiver. His professional touchpoints with skilled nursing facilities, assisted living communities, and a solid understanding of Medicare assumed enhanced significance when his mother required these services.

As he cared for his mother, Seth diligently took notes while negotiating her ups and downs and eventual entry into hospice. His professional knowledge, extensive personal experience in caregiving, and years of journaling uniquely coalesced. *Beyond Expiration: Surviving a Centenarian Parent* is the result.

Seth and Thomas, his partner of forty years, live in St. Augustine, Florida.

Made in United States
Troutdale, OR
09/14/2024

22808483R00159